W9-AQN-108

Saint Peter's University Library
Withdrawn

To Mother,
Because you are no less
brilliant then thay, I thought you

HONGKEW

might enjoy rubbing sholders with
Amy and others via script. To
be sure, you were born a
century to early, and
so missed knowing
you, but Theyer

POOTUNG

loss is my gain.
In love, in wit, in wisdom
in happiness and in pride of you,
my Mother.

Ts'ao Ch'ang   72 Penang Road
"Mecca"   Shanghai China

Mrs Florence Ayscough

E. W. Dunlap

11×50-012

2
7

FLORENCE AYSCOUGH
&
AMY LOWELL

Correspondence of a Friendship

FLORENCE AYSCOUGH
&
AMY LOWELL

Correspondence of a Friendship

EDITED WITH A PREFACE BY

HARLEY FARNSWORTH MacNAIR

Saint Peter's University Library
Withdrawn

UNIVERSITY OF CHICAGO PRESS
CHICAGO · ILLINOIS

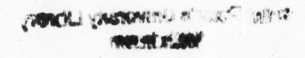

University of Chicago Press · Chicago 37
Agent: Cambridge University Press · London

Copyright 1945 by The University of Chicago. All rights
reserved. Published 1945. Composed and printed by the
University of Chicago Press, Chicago, Illinois, U.S.A.

To

ADA RUSSELL

GREAT FRIEND OF TWO GREAT FRIENDS

"One must go half-way with poets . . . .
keep it somehow still enshrined"

PREFACE

THE LETTERS WHICH CONSTITUTE THE CORE OF THIS VOLUME RECORD, IN part, the almost lifelong friendship of two who became outstanding characters of their generation: Florence Wheelock Ayscough MacNair and Amy Lowell. Both were members of families, English in origin, which have played prominent parts in the history of North America and the Far East from the seventeenth century to the present day.

Florence Wheelock was born in Shanghai, China. Amy Lowell was born in Brookline, Massachusetts. The one began her world travels at the age of three months and resided during periods of varying lengths in Boston, St. Andrews (New Brunswick), Shanghai, London, Vienna, Guernsey, and Chicago. The other, while journeying on occasion in the United States and Europe, spent most of her life in her childhood home, "Sevenels," Brookline. The homes of both served as points of departure for even wider travels in the realms of mind and spirit and constituted meccas for unnumbered explorers, oriental and occidental, in the same realms. Dynamic, charming, warmly affectionate, brilliant, and colorful—wherever they paused on life's highway Florence Ayscough and Amy Lowell drew to themselves those who sought the beauty and all-round goodness of existence on this plane.

Years before our marriage in Guernsey, Channel Islands, I had heard Florence Ayscough lecture in Shanghai on Amy Lowell and read from her poems. On its publication, in 1935, Mrs. Harold Russell sent a copy of S. Foster Damon's *Amy Lowell: A Chronicle with Extracts from Her Correspondence*. This eagerly awaited study formed the foundation, supplemented by my wife's reminiscences and by readings from Miss Lowell's works, of a "seminar" for my mother and myself. I now became fairly intimately acquainted with Amy Lowell—in the spirit and the printed word. That my wife never mentioned the existence of the correspondence, which in later years had centered around the joint preparation by the two friends of their *Fir-Flower Tablets*, and that I found most of it in her files only after her passing, on April 24, 1942, indicates that the idea of publishing it had not occurred to her. Probably both writers would have felt that their letters did not merit circulation. If I am correct in this surmise, I am (I believe) equally correct in my belief that the assumption attributed to them is erroneous. Certainly my mother, to whom I read excerpts from time to time, and Mrs. Russell, Miss Lowell's distinguished and devoted friend and literary executor, agreed with me. To the latter I reiterate my expressions of gratitude for permission to publish the letters and other papers of Miss Lowell's here incorporated, which supplement those of my wife, and which make possible that relatively rare phenomenon in the world of literature—a volume containing the replies of those to whom messages are indited. Too often is curiosity whetted by the publication of letters the replies to which never appear.

In equal degrees, Florence Ayscough and Amy Lowell had the faculty of expressing facets of their scintillating personalities in their correspondence as well as in their respective publications. Not to all scholars and poets is the gift bestowed to express themselves on learned subjects in an epistolary style as fascinating as the writers themselves—and the topics on which they discourse. More than "a little not wrong" was Mr. Nung Chu ("Cultivator of Bamboos") when he observed to the devotee of his country's poetry that her friend, Miss Lowell, wielded a "writing-brush . . . . full of life's movement"—and then added, "But what is the beauty of the peony flower without its green leaves?" In the collaboration entitled *Fir-Flower Tablets* it is impossible to say which collaborator was the peony and which the leaves.

At odd moments, during more than three years, I have derived solace through the reading and editing of these letters—aided often by the counsel and criticism of my friend and student-assistant, James William Christopher. Meticulous though the work was, it was never labor. No work of affection is ever hard—and the near-perfection of the documents made few corrections necessary. Moreover, their vividness of style created an illusion of the presence of the writers within the room. It was, indeed, as if I were overhearing a conversation on the problems and joys of bringing alive into a new world the thoughts and actions—the very life—of an old one.

This is not the place for, nor am I competent to offer, judgment with respect to the significance in the history of American and Chinese literature of the anthology with which these letters mainly deal. Suffice it to say that Amy Lowell's biographer holds that "*Fir-Flowers Tablets* may be looked on as a climax of a literary trend of the times," and in chapter xxii he presents reasons for his declaration.

Regardless, however, of the place in literature occupied by the translations of Chinese poetry mentioned, the value of the letters relating to that work lies in their innate charm as *letters;* in their discussion of literature, Chinese and non-Chinese, and literary criticism; in their portrayal of an abiding friendship (a factor in life more deeply appreciated by Chinese than by Westerners, who, in poetry and fiction, tend to concentrate on the spiritual—and, at times, physical—pleasures of romantic love, which most Chinese literateurs through the ages have considered a topic to be handled with reserve); and, finally, in the light that they throw on the thought-processes of poetic minds, Eastern and Western.

In the chapter mentioned above of his biography, Mr. Damon gives certain of the facts which lie back of Miss Lowell's scornfully humorous "To a Gentleman Who Wanted To See the First Drafts of My Poems in the Interests of Psychological Research into the Workings of the Creative Mind":

> So you want to see my papers, look what I have written down
> 'Twixt an ecstasy and heartbreak, con them over with a frown.
> You would watch my thought's green sprouting ere a single
>   blossom's blown. . . . .
>
> Think you, I could make you see it, all the little diverse strands
> Locked in one short poem? By no means do I find your prying
>   hands
> Pleasure bearing and delightful straying round my lotus lands.
>
> Not a word but joins itself with some adventure I alone
> Could attach consideration to. You'd wrench me flesh from bone,
> Find the heart and count its tappings. At your touch, 'twould
>   turn to stone.
>
> What is I, and what that other? That's your quest. I'll have you
>   know
> Telling it would break it from me, it would melt like travelled
>   snow.
> I will be no weary pathway for another's feet to go. . . . .
>
> Take my answer then, for, flatly, I will not be vivisected.
> Life is more to me than learning. If you clumsily deflected
> My contact with what I know not, could it surely be connected?
>
> Scarcely could you, knowing nothing, swear to me it would be so.
> Therefore unequivocally, brazenly, I tell you "No"!
> To the fame of an avowal, I prefer my domino.
>
> Still I have a word, one moment, stop, before you leave this
>   room.
> Though I shudder thinking of you wand'ring through my beds
>   of bloom,
> You may come with spade and shovel when I'm safely in the
>   tomb.[1]

[1] Amy Lowell, *Ballads for Sale* (Boston, 1927), pp. 3–8.

Interestingly enough, with respect to one important phase of her literary development, Miss Lowell had already completed, in the preceding year (1921), a series of exercises in self-"vivisection," without intention and without awareness. The results are herein embodied sans recourse to "spade and shovel"—or a visit to her tomb. But, as she wished, the "ecstasy and heartbreak" involved constitute no "weary pathway for another's feet to go"—nor are the results, I believe, to be likened to "travelled snow."

In collating the correspondence, I became aware that sections were missing. On my behalf, Dr. M. Llewellyn Raney, then director of the University of Chicago Libraries, kindly inquired of the Harvard University library authorities whether they had, among Miss Lowell's papers, a file of the Ayscough-Lowell correspondence. Miss Carolyn Jakeman, of the Houghton Library, courteously arranged to have copies made of the letters which were missing from my wife's file. To Dr. Raney and to Miss Jakeman I express my sincere gratitude for their aid in making possible the publication of the complete correspondence.

To Mrs. Judith Bond, of the Harriet Monroe Library of Modern Poetry, University of Chicago, for calling my attention to the gift to the University of Chicago by the late Miss Monroe of her correspondence with Miss Lowell, and to Mr. William Stanton Monroe and Mrs. William C. Calhoun, for permission to quote therefrom (in the Appendix), I express, too, my sincere thanks.

Several years ago, Mrs. Albert Dunlap, a prominent American artist in Shanghai, devoted about one hundred hours to the composition of an exquisitely illustrated color map, in the ancient Chinese style, of the way from The Bund in the International Settlement to the Grass Hut (Ts'ao T'ang) at No. 72 Penang Road, her friend's Chinese-style home.[2] This map I wished to have reproduced, not alone for its beauty and interest, but because it would balance the line-drawing map which Miss Lowell had had made to aid literary pilgrims who sought to travel from the wilds of Boston to the less restricted spaces, physical and mental, of Brookline. Since Mrs. Dunlap's original map in soft colors could not be reproduced, she graciously prepared a line-drawing of part of it to serve as end papers of this volume—and also did over a similar type of drawing of mountain scenery which was needed to illustrate one of the letters in which Chinese poetical terms for that type of scenery are discussed in some detail. Without Mrs.

[2] See Florence Ayscough, *A Chinese Mirror: Being Reflections of the Reality behind Appearance* (London, Boston, and New York, 1925), pp. 23–99.

10

Dunlap's assistance, much would be missing of the charm and value of the work done by the University of Chicago Press in attempting, successfully, to make this volume as physically pleasing as are (I hope) its intellectual contents. To Mrs. Dunlap and to the staff of the University of Chicago Press—in particular to Miss Mary D. Alexander and to Mr. John Scoon—I express my sincere thanks.

In conclusion: The Florence Ayscough MacNair Fellowship Fund was established at the University of Chicago, in 1942, for the purpose, eventually, of aiding graduate students in the fields of Chinese literature and history. To this fund will accrue the royalties from the sale of this volume.

HARLEY FARNSWORTH MACNAIR

"THE HOUSE OF THE WU-T'UNG TREES"
CHICAGO, ILLINOIS
September 20, 1945

TABLE OF CONTENTS

REMINISCENCES OF AMY LOWELL

Florence Ayscough to Ada Russell

MY EARLIEST RECOLLECTION OF AMY IS THAT OF A RATHER SQUARE LITTLE girl, with a very fresh color, who came to see me one afternoon when I was recovering from pneumonia. I had been very ill, and my physician, Dr. Charles Putnam, had told his cousin—Amy's mother—about the little girl from China who was just across "the Avenue," as Commonwealth Avenue was always spoken of, and Mrs. Lowell had very kindly sent me cream every day during my convalescence. Then, when I was able to see people, Amy came up to my room.

She was dressed in grey, wearing a rough grey coat—so it seems as I look back through the years. At all events I associate grey with Amy, as I associate blue with E. D., a great friend of mine at that time, who struck up a very intense intimacy with Amy—one of those foredoomed intimacies which punctuated Amy's life until she found her affection satisfied in her friendship with you, Ada dear. She and E. D. were very intimate, and, as they were both a little older than I, they moved in what might be called a "higher sphere"; but they were very good to me, and even after they both came out—which important event took place a few years later—I shared those pleasures which convention permitted. For instance, I used often to go with them both to the Lowell Lectures, and often, if E. D. did not go, I went alone with Amy.

By the time I came out, the crash had come and their friendship lay in scattered fragments which I tried in vain to piece together. Being of a very pacific nature myself, it seemed to me a hundred pities that people should really break with each other, and I did finally induce them to acknowledge each other's existence; but the reconciliation

15

never went further than that. The cause of the split I have forgotten. Hopeless incompatibility was at the root of the trouble. I remember only how hurt Amy was, and how deeply she felt the whole episode. It seemed as if she could not endure such a breaking-up of what was to her a precious relation; and I could not comfort her, although she used to come and pour out her heart to me by the hour. One result of this occurrence was that Amy and I came nearer together, and I saw a great deal more of her than I had done when she was absorbed with E. D.

One of my greatest pleasures was to go out to "Sevenels"[1] and, starting from there, drive for miles through the woods with Amy. As you know, she handled a horse most beautifully, and as we drove we talked—talked about everything imaginable. Her keen common sense and true sense of values often came to the fore. I remember well an occasion when my fancy had been rather taken by a charming youth and I was trying to decide what my course should be. Amy was most definite: "No," she said, "no, my dear, never marry any man *unless you can't help it.*" I cannot imagine better advice.

I am not sure whether the autumn days, when the dry leaves sizzled under the wheels of the buggy, or the spring days, when tiny flowers glimmered in the pale sunshine, remain with me most vividly; at all events, those drives in what was then the open country beyond Brookline are vital memories to me.

At that time I used to go to Dublin every autumn to stay with Mary Hutchinson,[2] and Amy came sometimes to stay with the Cabots and finally took a house. I am not very clear about it all, but I do remember distinctly a picnic we had to Black Top the autumn before I was married [to Francis Ayscough]. Amy was much interested in the prospect of my going to China to live. Later still during that autumn, Mary and I went to stay with her in Brookline, and a great ceremony was indulged in apropos of my engagement. An altar with candles, and Frank's picture in the center, was arranged, and all sorts of jollifications took place; but Amy was not well, and when my wedding actually came off, on December 23, 1898, she was in California.

My wedding present gave her concern. I wanted a very large inkstand, as I knew that correspondence would play an important part in my Far Eastern life, and she had difficulty in finding one which she

[1] The Lowell home at Brookline, Massachusetts: ". . . . it sheltered seven Lowells." See Appendix I; also S. Foster Damon, *Amy Lowell: A Chronicle with Extracts from Her Correspondence* (Boston and New York, 1935), p. 33. For references to Mrs. Russell and Miss Lowell, see *ibid.*, p. 768.

[2] *Ibid.*, p. 756.

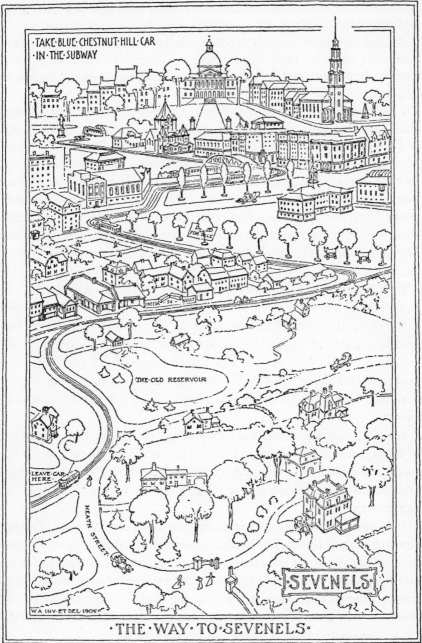

·THE·WAY·TO·SEVENELS·

considered handsome enough. The one which she finally chose was a beauty, but it did not satisfy her so she sent very lovely pepper pots and salt cellars with it.

We did not write to each other regularly, but she *always* sent me a cable on Christmas Day. Never once, during all the years since then, has she forgotten, and, of course, when I came to America I always saw her.

I don't remember when she bought the Dublin house, but I know that I saw her in it once, some years after my marriage, when Frank and I were stopping with Mary Hutchinson, who by that time had become Mary Sumner; and, again, I remember a picnic to Black Top, when I drove with Amy in her buggy. The view from the Dublin house was *wonderful*. Amy was not very well then. The year was about 1905. She and Mary had come to know each other very well. That was a friendship which grew stronger and stronger as time went on, and when Mary died in 1915 it was Amy who sent a cable telling me the news.

In 1910 I spent the summer with my people in St. Andrews [New Brunswick], and Amy came and stopped with us. She thoroughly enjoyed the sailing and delighted in being on the blue bay which lies within a circle of hills. The quaint old town with its grass-grown streets interested her, and she was a most appreciative guest. She had made the changes at "Sevenels" by then and was entertaining a good deal, and I remember a delightful dinner which she gave for me that autumn.

In 1917, you remember, the Compradore embezzled that large sum of money, and I had to come to America to attend to the sale of his pictures for the firm. I wrote Amy telling her about the whole thing, and she instantly cabled asking me to come to her at "Sevenels" to begin with.

It is quite impossible for me to express what an *immense* difference that cable made to me. The matter in hand was certainly difficult, and my heart sank low at the prospect before me, but the thought of Amy and her help was a very "present comfort in time' of trouble." She came to the train to meet me, and as she came toward me down the platform that dark November night, the grimy North Station seemed to be illuminated with a warm and friendly glow.

In the spring of 1918, I was in Chicago and was talking to Carl Sandburg. I remarked that it was difficult to argue with Amy, that

18

she was so quick and definite that she always had the best of it, and he answered:

"Oh! Arguing with Amy is like arguing with a big blue wave."

Do you remember that incident of the theater seats, when you, she, and I went to see Duse in December, 1924? Amy was late; you and I went and took the two inside seats, leaving the aisle seat for her. Presently a woman came and took the seat. You expostulated, saying that the seat was taken. The woman proceeded to argue that she had the ticket, etc., etc., and you said quietly, "But I am very sure that the seat is Miss Lowell's."

"Miss Lowell!!" exclaimed the woman, and she fled like a hare, never to be seen again.

The story of our subsequent intercourse and our work together is told in her files and in more detail in the article which I have written for the *Bookman*.

1925

AMY LOWELL AND THE FAR EAST[1]

Florence Ayscough

IN THE CRITICAL ANALYSIS WHICH IS BOUND TO BE MADE OF AMY LOWELL'S
contribution to literature, it is important that due stress be laid on
her interpretations of the Farthest East—that is, of China and Japan.
The sum total of these interpretations may not be large, but the quality is unique. By virtue of her astounding gift of intuition Amy Lowell
annihilated time and space and seemed to comprehend the thoughts of
men long dead and to visualize the movement of scenes long past, although both thoughts and scenes belonged to civilizations far re-
moved from our own.

I

She visited neither China nor Japan but came in close touch with
Japanese art and legend through her brother Percival Lowell, the
astronomer, who traveled in Japan and Korea during the eighties,
and who found an eager, sympathetic listener in his little sister at
home. Upon one occasion he brought back with him his interpreter,
Mr. Tsunejiro Miyaoka, now a lawyer living in Tokyo, and the
charming Japanese took a great fancy to the intelligent child he found
at "Sevenels." He talked to her at length about his beautiful island
country and told her many of its romantic tales. From those days
Japanese prints and wood carvings became an integral part of Amy
Lowell's entourage, and books on Japan always lay upon her table.

Her first volume of poems, *A Dome of Many-Coloured Glass*, was published in 1912. In it are found two poems on Japanese subjects: "A
Japanese Wood-Carving" and a "Coloured Print by Shokei." Of the
carving (how well I know it!) she writes:

[1] Adapted from the *Bookman*, Vol. LXIII, No. 1 (March, 1926).

20

High up above the open, welcoming door
It hangs, a piece of wood with colours dim.

. . . .

An artist once, with patient, careful knife,
Had fashioned it like to the untamed sea.
Here waves uprear themselves, their tops blown back
By the gay, sunny wind, which whips the blue
And breaks it, into gleams and sparks of light.

. . . .

Hanging above the high, wide open door,
It brings to us in quiet, firelit room,
The freedom of the earth's vast solitudes,
Where heaping, sunny waves tumble and roll,
And seabirds scream in wanton happiness.

The next two volumes—*Sword Blades and Poppy Seeds* (1914) and *Men, Women and Ghosts* (1917)—contain nothing specifically oriental, but the imagery of certain pieces, such as "Off the Turnpike," "Afternoon Rain in State Street," and others, closely resembles the imagery of Far Eastern poems.

At this time Miss Lowell was becoming more and more absorbed in Japanese literature, and, in August, 1917, her great poem on the opening of Japan by Commodore Perry appeared in the *Seven Arts*. The poem, later published in *Can Grande's Castle*, is called "Guns as Keys: and the Great Gate Swings." It is remarkable from both an artistic and a psychological point of view and is especially interesting in connection with present-day developments in the relations of East and West.[1a]

The work is divided into two parts and a postlude. Part I describes the voyage of Commodore Perry's ship, the "Mississippi," and the squadron under his command, from Chesapeake Bay, around the Cape of Good Hope, to the Great Gate of Japan. The passages dealing with the "Mississippi" and her crew are written in polyphonic prose but are interspersed by exquisite vignettes in unrhymed cadence which give pictures of the country the ships are headed toward. These vignettes are positively photographic in their vividness. Of all the many, many descriptions of Japan which I have read, they are far and away the most truthful. In fact, to me they *are* Japan. Nor am I peculiar in this respect. Soon after the poem appeared in the *Seven Arts*, a Japanese wrote to Miss Lowell expressing his wondering admiration of her descriptive power and, in closing, asked how many years she had lived in his country!

[1a] [Doubly so in the year 1945!—H. F. M.]

Saint Peter's University Library
Jersey City, New Jersey 07306

The first vignette reads:

> At Mishima in the Province of Kai,
> Three men are trying to measure a pine tree
> By the length of their outstretched arms.
> Trying to span the bole of a huge pine tree
> By the spread of their lifted arms.
> Attempting to compress its girth
> Within the limit of their extended arms.
> Beyond, Fuji,
> Majestic, inevitable,
> Wreathed over by wisps of cloud.
> The clouds draw about the mountain,
> But there are gaps.
> The men reach about the pine tree,
> But their hands break apart;
> The rough bark escapes their hand-clasps;
> The tree is unencircled.
> Three men are trying to measure the stem of a
>   gigantic pine tree,
> With their arms,
> At Mishima in the Province of Kai.

Whoever has stood on the road above Mishima in the Province of Kai knows that this is a perfect description of the great Tokaido, the Imperial highway lined with pine trees, which runs from Kyoto to Tokyo. And the "tiger rain" of Japan falls just as Miss Lowell describes it in a later passage:

> Beating, snapping, on the cheese-rounds of open
>   umbrellas,
> Licking, tiger-tongued, over the straw mat which
>   a pilgrim wears upon his shoulders.

The account of hara-kiri which closes Part I is blood-curdling in the white heat of its vigor and restraint.

Part II tells of the negotiations between Perry and the astonished, unbelieving, Japanese officials, suddenly confronted with the concrete fact of Western battleships. In her Preface—and Miss Lowell is noted for her prefaces—she states:

I wanted to place in juxtaposition the delicacy and artistic clarity of Japan and the artistic ignorance and gallant self-confidence of America. Of course, each country must be supposed to have the faults of its virtues; if, therefore, I have also opposed Oriental craft to Occidental bluff, I must beg indulgence.

I have tried to give a picture of the two races at a moment when they were brought in contact for the first time. Which of them has gained most by this meeting, it would be difficult to say.

. . . .

22

Just at the edge of moonlight and sunlight—moon setting; sun rising—
they come. Seven warships heeled over and flashing, dashing through heaped
waves, sleeping a moment in hollows, leaping over ridges, sweeping forward
in a strain of canvas and a train of red-black smoke.

"The fire-ships! the fire-ships!"

Slip the bridles of your horses, messengers, and clatter down the Tokaido.
. . . . To Yedo! To Yedo! For Spring is here, and the fire-ships have come!"

Helpless, the Japanese capitulate; to save the violation of Yedo by
the presence of barbarians from over the sea, they suggest a conference
at Yokohama, and the Commodore agrees.

The Americans bring presents. Presents now, to be bought hereafter. Good
will, to head long bills of imports. Occidental mechanisms to push the Orient
into limbo. Fox-moves of interpreters, and Pandora's box with a contents
rated far too low. . . . .

Who thinks of the great Gate! Its portals are pushed so far back that the
shining edges of them can scarcely be observed. The Commodore has never
swerved a moment from his purpose, and the dragon mouths of his guns have
conquered without the need of a single powder horn.

Part II closes with the succinct paragraph:

Ten ships sailing for China on a fair May wind. Ten ships sailing from one
world into another, but never again into the one they left. Two years and a
tip-turn is accomplished. Over the globe and back, Rip Van Winkle ships.
Slip into your docks in Newport, in Norfolk, in Charlestown. You have
blown off the locks of the East, and what is coming will come.

The poem is now quickly ended. In her Preface Miss Lowell says:

The two episodes in the "Postlude" are facts, but they can hardly epito-
mize the whole truth. Still they are striking, occurring as they did in the same
year. I owe the scene of the drowning of the young student in the Kegon waterfall to the paper "Young Japan" by Seichi Naruse, which appeared in the
"Seven Arts" for April, 1917. The inscription on the tree I have copied word
for word from Mr. Naruse's translation, and I wish here to express my thanks
not for his permission (as with a perfect disregard of morals, I never asked
it), but for his beautiful rendering of the original Japanese. I trust that my
appreciation will exonerate my theft.

The Postlude is short and touches upon events fifty years after the
expedition had taken place. It opens with a beautiful, melancholy
picture of a

Deserted ancient moat
About an ancient stronghold,

and closes with the two episodes to which Miss Lowell refers:

1903. JAPAN

The high cliff of the Kegon waterfall, and a young man carving words on the trunk of a tree. He finishes, pauses an instant, and then leaps into the foam-cloud rising from below. But, on the tree-trunk, the newly cut words blaze white and hard as though set with diamonds:

"How mightily and steadily go Heaven and Earth! How infinite the duration of Past and Present! Try to measure this vastness with five feet. A word explains the Truth of the whole Universe—*unknowable*. To cure my agony I have decided to die. Now, as I stand on the crest of this rock, no uneasiness is left in me. For the first time I know that extreme pessimism and extreme optimism are one."

1903. AMERICA

Nocturne—Blue and Silver—Battersea Bridge.
Nocturne—Grey and Silver—Chelsea Embankment.
Variations in Violet and Green.

Pictures in a glass-roofed gallery, and all day long the throng of people is so great that one can scarcely see them, Debits—credits? Flux and flow through a wide gateway. Occident—Orient—after fifty years.

II

The exquisite poems called "Lacquer Prints" which open the volume *Pictures of the Floating World* (1919) are also the result of this period when Miss Lowell lived, as far as her mentality was concerned, in old Japan.

Of these poems she says: "I have made no attempt to observe the syllabic rules which are an integral part of all Japanese poetry. I have endeavoured only to keep the brevity and suggestion of the *hokku*, and to preserve it within its natural sphere."

A LOVER

If I could catch the green lantern of the firefly
I could see to write you a letter.

TO A HUSBAND

Brighter than the fireflies upon the Uji River
Are your words in the dark, Beloved.

These examples, chosen somewhat fortuitously from among the fifty-nine pieces of the group, demonstrate the success which crowned her endeavors. Among her last poems[2] is the beautiful "Anniversary" cast in the *hokku* mold.

[2] *What's O'Clock* (1925), pp. 44–48; see also "Twenty-four Hokku on a Modern Theme," *ibid.*, pp. 37–43.

I cannot leave the Japanese division of Miss Lowell's work, without at least mentioning the very vivid Introduction to the *Diaries of Court Ladies of Old Japan* translated by Annie Shepley Omori and Kochi Doi.

The diaries date from the Heian period of Japanese history, A.D. 794–1186, and, as Miss Lowell says, "it is just because these Diaries reflect the real life of these three ladies that they are important. The world they portray is in most ways quite as advanced as our own, and in some, much more so. . . . . And everywhere, everywhere, there is poetry. A gentleman hands a lady a poem on the end of his fan and she is expected to reply in kind within the instant."

In reading the diaries, Miss Lowell turned back the clock of time and vibrated with the emotion which stirred those charming ladies of long ago. She possessed, in a rare degree, that intuitive gift which she describes so well in her life of Keats (I, 505):

He reflected constantly on his art, and the remarks about poetry scattered through his writings prove him to have possessed—beside, and quite apart from, his genius—a very acute and subtle mind. "The excellence of every art is its intensity" is one of his dictums, and it is absolutely true. Again, he speaks of "that trembling delicate and snail-horn perception of beauty," and if ever man had it, it was he. Once when George Keats had been making some comparison between him and Lord Byron, he answers in a letter: "You speak of Lord Byron and me. There is this great difference between us: he describes what he sees—I describe what I imagine. Mine is the hardest task."

So it was with Amy Lowell. She described what she imagined—and the description rang true.

III

Miss Lowell's approach to Japan sprang from a childish enthusiasm which grew to critical and sympathetic appreciation. Her approach to China and its literature was very different.

The Central Flowery State attracted her, and she loved to read and talk about China. I have lived there for many years, and when I came to America she always plied me with questions, but until the autumn of 1917 she had not studied it seriously. At that time I happened to pay her a long visit and had in my possession some paintings and a number of "Written Pictures"—the latter being examples of that art which the Chinese consider the perfect medium of aesthetic expression. They are, perhaps, the least known, and certainly the least understood, of all Oriental art forms—which is a pity, as these "Hanging-on-the-Wall Poems" are highly characteristic of Chinese idea. A beautiful thought perpetuated in beautiful handwriting, and hung

25

upon the wall, to suggest a mental picture—that is what a *tzŭ hua* amounts to.[3]

Miss Lowell was immensely interested. Her own account of this happening appears in the Preface to *Fir-Flower Tablets* [pp. vi–vii], and I will quote her words: ". . . . among these paintings were a number of examples of the 'Written Pictures.' Of these, she [Mrs. Ayscough] had made some rough translations which she intended to use to illustrate her lectures. She brought them to me with a request that I put them into poetic shape. I was fascinated by the poems, and, as we talked them over, we realized that here was a field in which we should like to work."

It must not be supposed for a moment, however, that Miss Lowell was content to work from my translations alone. By no means. We both realized that it was impossible for her to give an adequate rendering of a poet's thought unless she knew *exactly* the words in which he clothed it. So ideogram by ideogram, line by line, we worked together: I translated and she made careful notes. While so working, Miss Lowell made a discovery which, I believe, will be far-reaching in its result. She found that, frequently, an analysis of an ideogram, rendered by a phrase instead of by a single word, made the meaning of a line far more vivid. The way the discovery came about was this. We were at work upon a poem, and I read aloud the character *Mo:* "It means 'sunset,' " I said, and then added casually, "The character shows the sun disappearing in the long grass at the edge of the horizon."

"How do you mean?" asked Miss Lowell.

"Why, what I say," I replied, and forthwith showed her the character or pictogram in its ancient form, which shows plainly the sun sinking behind tufts of grass on the far-off horizon. She was more enthralled than ever and insisted that I give her a dissertation on the composition of characters, a subject that has always been of intense interest to me, but which I *never thought of applying in translation.*

As I have said elsewhere:

These marvellous collections of brush-strokes which we call Chinese characters are really separate pictographic representations of complete thoughts. Complex characters are not spontaneously composed, but are built up of simple characters, each having its own peculiar meaning and usage; these, when used in combination, each play their part in modifying either the sense or the sound of the complex. Now it must not be thought that these separate en-

[3] For an analysis of the relation between Chinese poetry, painting, and calligraphy see Florence Ayscough, "Poetry, Painting and Calligraphy," in *China*, ed. Harley Farnsworth MacNair ("United Nations Series" [Berkeley: University of California Press, 1946]).

tities make an over-loud noise in the harmony of the whole character. They are each subdued to the total result, the final meaning; but they do produce a qualifying effect upon the word itself.[4]

Although the Chinese have no alphabet, they build up their characters from a set of two hundred and fourteen chosen forms, which are pictograms or ideograms. Occidentals call these forms "the radicals"; but Chinese refer to them as "ideogram mothers," or "origins." One of these "mothers" appears in every written character; and it is in the section headed by its "mother" that a character must be looked up in a Chinese dictionary.

For instance, the pictogram "grain" appears as mother of the word "autumn," composed by adding to it the pictogram "fire," which, in this connection, suggests ripe maturity. Go one step further: add the character "heart" to the combination meaning "autumn" and the resulting word expresses a very special all-consuming grief. Again, a character often used to express the sound of a gale is composed of the wind radical and the figure meaning "to speak." Miss Lowell renders it in the phrase "shouts on the clearness of a gale."[5] The pictogram for "a whirlpool" shows rivers which cross each other, and Miss Lowell's version reads: "the whirled water of meeting streams."[6]

Other examples might be given, but I have said enough to show that the aura of a Chinese character must often be sought in its make-up. In our work, Miss Lowell and I were careful to investigate the ancestry of characters.

The Written Pictures were finished, and, to quote Miss Lowell again: "When she returned to China, it was agreed that we should make a volume of translations from the classic Chinese writers. Such translations were in the line of her usual work, and I was anxious to read the Chinese poets as nearly in the original as it was possible for me to do."[7]

Our correspondence became more and more devoted to the discussion of Chinese poetry, and when I returned from Shanghai to America in May, 1921, we worked together for months, revising the poems rendered when we were half a world apart, and studying the new translations I had brought with me. The result of this collaboration appeared in December as the earlier-mentioned volume, *Fir-Flower Tablets: Poems Translated from the Chinese.*

[4] *Fir-Flower Tablets* (Boston and New York: Houghton Mifflin Co., 1921), Introduction, pp. lxxxvii–lxxxviii.

[5] *Ibid.*, p. 52.

[6] *Ibid.*, p. 132. [7] *Ibid.*, p. vii.

IV

I wish it were possible for the reader to realize how very close to the originals Miss Lowell's renderings are, but this could not be unless the complicated drafts I sent her were published. I often wondered how it was possible for her to decipher them, although they were as simple as I could make them. As she says:

> I had, in fact, four different means of approach to a poem. The Chinese text [in transliteration], for rhyme-scheme and rhythm; the dictionary meanings of the words; the analyses of characters; and, for the fourth, a careful paraphrase by Mrs. Ayscough, to which she added copious notes to acquaint me with all the allusions, historical, mythological, geographical, and technical that she deemed it necessary for me to know.[8]

After Miss Lowell had once read my paraphrase, to get the general drift of a poem, I think she hardly looked at it again but worked directly from the Chinese words themselves.

She found that the analyses of characters, that is, the rendering of an ideogram by a phrase, had to be used sparingly in poetry, because, as she explains in a letter,[9] it is so easy to spoil the cadence. She wrote me:

> I could not get the sun "disappearing in the grass at the horizon" either. Everything I did seemed to spoil the cadence which is particularly good in this poem; so, finally, after struggling and struggling over it, I have determined to leave it as it is, if you are satisfied.

The poem referred to is "The Palace Blossoms," *Fir-Flower Tablets* (p. 155), and the word "sunset" appears at the end of the second line, which is long enough as it is.

Apropos the necessity of having the actual text and all the data I could possibly give her, she declared:

> Now most people do not know this, for they have no idea what it means to translate a Chinese poem. They do not know the combination of qualities necessary to produce anything like the originals. Personally, since doing this work with you, I have become more in love with Chinese poetry than ever. I think it is extraordinarily good and immensely interesting to work with, but it would be no good at all if you did it in free translation; no good at all as an approach to the Oriental mind, that is.

Later, in discussing our collaboration, she said:

> The sinologues do not know enough [about poetry] to make adequate translations, and they do not know enough to get the poets who could; and the poets who have done them best are more concerned in making a name for themselves than in rendering the old Chinese people. . . . . The consequence

[8] *Ibid.*, p. ix.

[9] See letter dated July 24, 1918, for this and the immediately following quotations.

is that you get one of two extremes. You get a scholarly translation which is punk as poetry, or you get a splendid poem which no Chinese ever wrote. . . . .

I think if you do not state this in your prose article, the general reader will wonder why we bother with more Chinese translations when there have been so many. They will not know that we have a reason for doing it which the other people have not. . . . .

To understand the last sentence it must be remembered that, generally speaking, translators of Chinese have avowedly been concerned with making a smooth rendering in the English idiom. They have deliberately rejected the Chinese idiom as being too bizarre and difficult to bring over; and it is certainly very difficult to transfer an idiom from one language to another. Miss Lowell found it so. On June 12, 1919, she wrote:

These things do not go as rapidly as I could wish, partly from press of other work and partly because they are fussy. . . . . I am absolutely in love with this "Li T'ai Po," but Lawks-a-massy, my dear, 'taint easy nohow. However, you shall have it somehow. God knows how.

Another extract in the following month reads: "Therefore, I think it is extremely important not to do any embroidering that the characters do not justify."[10] In August she reported: "I am absolutely drowned in Chinese literature, all I can get in English and French translations, and I am beginning to understand a good many things that I did not understand before."[11]

Miss Lowell's fidelity was amazing. I often said, "This line means so and so," and her invariable reply was, "Yes, but what does it *say?*" And then she would try to render the Chinese idiom, or employ the metaphor used, as nearly as might be in a different language.

It was this absolute sincerity of hers which made her so easy to work with. For many weeks [during the spring of 1921] we studied together each night, and when the pale summer dawn touched the trees towering above "Sevenels," I would leave her to work on alone. She could accomplish the actual rendering far better if left undisturbed. During those weeks we had many discussions, but I cannot recall that in all the weaving-together of our dissimilar work a single hasty, to be regretted, word passed between us.

When the book was finished and I sailed back to China, leaving her to struggle with the final proofs, she sent me a farewell letter, written at midnight in pencil, on the smooth primrose-colored paper which she always used when composing—a letter which I value very highly. A passage reads:

[10] See letter dated July 29, 1919.   [11] See letter dated August 16, 1919.

DEAR FLORENCE,

You have no idea how much I have enjoyed doing this with you. It has brought us so near together. I have learned to know you so much better. . . . . However many books we do, or don't do, lets keep it thus—always.

You have been an angel to me—a monument of patience. I am not easy to work with, I know; I get so excited, and I think only of the work and not at all of anyone's feelings. Forgive me for all my many faults and omissions, and please believe how grateful I am for your wonderful sympathy and understanding.

But we must do other books.

Our different functions were described metaphorically by my Chinese teacher in a characteristic conversation I had with him after he had perused the copy of *Fir-Flower Tablets* which I gave him. Mr. Nung Chu does not speak English, but he can read a little, and I asked him if he enjoyed the book. He replied, "The writing brush of Mme Ai's friend is full of life's movement."

"Ah, yes," I said, "and that, you see, is what Heaven does. Anyone with patience, and your help, could do my part, but hers is a gift from Heaven."

"Not wrong," he assented, "the words of Mme Ai are a little not wrong; but perhaps she has not heard a saying that we have in China? 'What is the beauty of the peony flower without its green leaves?'"

In order to show that I do not lay too high a claim for Miss Lowell's fidelity to the text, I will quote two poems in illustration:

SUNG TO THE TUNE OF "THE UNRIPE HAWTHORN BERRY"[12]

TEXT OF POEM

Line 1	Line 2	Line 3
Spring	Heaven, or the sky	Destroy, broken
Hill	Light in colour, pale	Moon
Mist	Stars	Face
Desire	Scattered, separate	Side
Obscure	Few	Light, illumination

Line 4	Line 5	Line 6
Separation	Words, to speak	Passion, emotion
Tears	Already	Not yet
Bright, clear	Many	Finality
Light of dawn		

Line 7	Line 8	Line 9
Turn	Rise ⎫ = Remem-	Place ⎫ = Everywhere
Head	Accomplish ⎭ ber	Place ⎭
Still	Green	Remind, not forget
Again	Open-worked silk gauze	Sweet-scented
Say, speak	Skirt	Grass

[12] *Fir-Flower Tablets*, p. 121.

30

Miss Lowell's rendering:

Mist is trying to hide the Spring-coloured hills,
The sky is pale, the stars are scattered and few.
The moon is broken and fading, yet there is light on your face,
These are the tears of separation, for now it is bright dawn.

We have said many words,
But our passion is not assuaged.
Turn your head, I have still something to say:
Remember my skirt of green open-work silk,
The sweet-scented grasses everywhere will prevent your forgetting.

THE BATTLE TO THE SOUTH OF THE CITY[13]

TEXT OF POEM

Line 1	Line 2	Line 3
Battle	Fight	Air
Ground	Men	Heavy, thick
How	Like	Sun
Dim	Swarm	Wheel
Yellow-dusk	Ants	Red

Line 4	Line 5	Line 6
Blood	Vulture	Eat
Dyes	Bird	Heavy
{Pêng, a wild chrysan-	Hold in mouth	Fly
{Hao themum	Man	Not
Purple	Flesh	Rise

Line 7	Line 8	Line 9
Yesterday	Today	Flags
Day	Day	Colour
City wall	City wall	Like
Upon	Below	Net
Men	Spirits of the dead	Stars

Line 10	Line 11	Line 12
Drum carried on horse- back	Unworthy One House	All Within
Sound	Husband	Drum carried on horse- back
Killing	And	Sound
Not	Sons	In
Finished		

Miss Lowell's rendering:

How dim the battle-field, as yellow dusk!
The fighting men are like a swarm of ants.
The air is thick, the sun a red wheel.

[13] *Ibid.*, p. 5.

Blood dyes the wild chrysanthemums purple.
Vultures hold the flesh of men in their mouths,
They are heavy with food—they cannot rise to fly.
There were men yesterday on the city wall;
There are ghosts to-day below the city wall.
Colours of flags like a net of stars,
Rolling of horse-carried drums—not yet is the killing ended.
From the house of the Unworthy One—a husband, sons,
All within earshot of the rolling horse-drums.

Having tried so hard to give faithful versions of the poems we translated, we could not but be gratified, at receiving soon after our book appeared the following letter from Mr. Telly H. Koo, a Chinese then living in America. "It is hardly imaginable for an American poetess who does not claim to read and write Chinese to make such a literal and almost exact rendering of some of the greatest Chinese poems. I can still repeat word by word that poem on 'The Perils of a Szechuan Road.' "[14] Mr. Koo then refers to the Chinese scholars who are making translations of English literature for the use of their countrymen and continues: "It is through men like these, and ladies like you, that the exchange of intellect is made possible and that a better mutual appreciation of the East and West can be effected. You are lending immortality to our poets in this part of the world."

Miss Lowell and I had intended to publish a book devoted to the poems of Tu Fu, that grave poet whom the Chinese consider their greatest genius in the realm of poetry. The translation was done before I left China early in 1923. It remained to make the analyses and arrange the poems, so that Miss Lowell could render them. A paragraph in a letter which she wrote me during December, 1922, reads now in the light of a prophecy.

"How is Tu Fu coming along? I hope not too rapidly, for when I finish the Keats book I shall be so exhausted that I shall want quite a long vacation before I attempt anything else."[15]

Summer 1925

[14] See letter dated November 10, 1921; see also *Fir-Flower Tablets*, pp. 6–8.
[15] See letter dated December 7, 1922.

CORRESPONDENCE OF FLORENCE AYSCOUGH
AND AMY LOWELL

RIVERDALE-ON-HUDSON, December 8, 1917

DEAR AMY,

A most successful journey—safely accomplished. Am comfortably installed—a "blizzard" raging outside. I suppose that it is the Halifax storm newly imported. My stay with you has been—delightful. So many things that I want to ask you surge into my mind—"other(?) thoughts overflow," to be quite literal, and I feel that I should like to be sitting in front of the fire with you—my feet resting on "John" —just "yarning."

Mr. [Charles Lang] Freer[1] is too ill to see anyone, so my friend from Detroit writes—has had a stroke, etc. It is too bad.

The surroundings here are most beautiful, and below us in the river lie the interned Dutch ships—their noses painted red, white, and blue. Of course, you will be full of engagements while you are in New York, but I shall hope to have a glimpse of you.[2]

Best love to your dear self, to Ada [Russell],[3] and to the family. I make no attempt to tell you again how much I feel about all you have done and are doing—because I have no words.

Yours,

FLORENCE AYSCOUGH

A letter has just been forwarded from John Sumner in which he says "how delightful Miss Lowell was." It is a nice letter; he also says that being with Mary's friends seems to bring her nearer.

---

[1] See *Who Was Who in America* (Chicago, 1942), p. 425.

[2] See S. Foster Damon, *Amy Lowell: A Chronicle with Extracts from Her Correspondence* (Boston and New York, 1935), p. 437.

[3] Mrs. Harold Russell (*ibid.*, p. 183).

[NEW YORK CITY], December 25, 1917

DEAR AMY AND ADA—

You can imagine how grateful your Xmas word was—thank you both. I wish that you could look in upon my little "Palace"; it is really very cosy and homelike, and I am becoming quite accustomed to a bachelor existence. The old snow storm caused delay—then I got the pictures,[1] but there was more delay . . . . so I have not yet unpacked them all.

The letter opener came this morning and was put to *instant* use. It is a joy; many thanks. I hope that my *tiny* offering will reach you in due course—but, since a letter took ten days to reach Alice Townsend in Long Island, I feel my faith in the post a trifle shaken.

What are you writing? I have read and re-read "Guns as Keys,"[2] which fills me with new wonder at each reading. I am now enjoying *Men, Women and Ghosts*.[3]

How I wish that I could sit down and work hard at *the* book—the name of the river "Wei," in the poem [p. 2, II of "Songs of the Marches"][4] of Li T'ai-po which I gave you at the St. Regis, means rushing-or-roaring as rapids. The name of the poem is: "Song of the Frontier"—literally "Frontier—without Song." All good wishes for the New Year. If *only* it would bring Peace. Love to you both.

As ever,

FLORENCE AYSCOUGH

[NEW YORK], 41 Gramercy Park, February 16, [1918]

DEAR AMY,

Thanks for the note you sent me. The writer was a dear little old lady I conversed with on the train en route from Montreal. . . . .

People seem to be much interested in the written scrolls when I translate them, and express themselves as surprised; they like the sort of chant, too. Am going to have the exhibition of modern paintings at Mrs. Harry Payne Whitney's studio beginning on Wednesday next for ten days. I hope that it may be a success. . . . . Have lectured twice and have had very nice and enthusiastic audiences. Am looking

---

[1] Damon, *op. cit.*, pp. 434–35; see also Introduction.

[2] *Ibid.*, p. 755 (republished in *Can Grande's Castle* [New York, 1918]).

[3] *Ibid.*, *passim*.

[4] The page references within brackets throughout refer to the pages in *Fir-Flower Tablets* (Boston and New York: Houghton Mifflin Co., 1921) on which the Ayscough-Lowell translations appear.

34

forward to seeing you. My love to Ada—was so sorry to hear from Mrs. Carr Cook of the baby's illness.

Much love, yours,

Florence Ayscough

St. Andrews, [New Brunswick, Canada], June 25, 1918

Dearest Amy,

I have gone carefully through the poems which we thought should go to Miss Monroe.[1] It is really a thousand pities that you cannot know how *extremely* good they are! In reading them through I was overcome to find how near the originals they are. You may say that my dry scholarship is again to the fore, but truly, my dear, it is a virtue to be exact—besides being artistic. A few suggestions as follows:

Poem VI [p. 155]. Sunset: the character used means "the sun disappearing in the grass at the horizon"; the towers, or brothels (with which the adjective "green" is used), can be analysed into "a woman imprisoned in the harem." The line reads, literally, "green towers must not close, *wei jui* (the name of a flower which in poetry means a very young girl, a virgin), then a character which is not in any of the dictionaries I have with me, and which the teacher avoided in embarrassment. It is composed of "golden" and "nest." One can imagine the meaning. I think the line had better stand as it is.

Poem VII [p. 156]. Do you think that the Westerner will ever grasp that in the second stanza the passing of two seasons is implied? You know best; of course, Orientals are used to—such allusions. It seems to me that the stanza could be a little clearer.

Poem XI [p. 157]. The word which describes the shadow is composed of "the sun below the trees." The stream is as "small as the silk thread spun by guilty women condemned to forced labour." The rocky ledge (first line) analyses into "stone pedestal." The word for sunset is the same as in poem VI. It reads literally: Stone, stone-pedestal connects clouds, sunset (poem VI) half way up mountain; Green shadow deep obscure (sun below trees) jade fountain flies; Stream (described above) eddies, alone whirls footsteps few; Only promised (taken vows) hill men together pick ferns. (The idea, too, is that they are picking the ferns for food; Buddhists of course eat only vegetable food.)

[1] Harriet Monroe (1860–1936), editor (1912–36) of *Poetry: A Magazine of Verse*. See Appendix II; see also Damon, *op. cit.*, p. 186 and other references to Miss Monroe in the Index.

Poem XII [p. 159]. It is all perfectly delightful and most literal. In the last line an interrogative is used which presupposes, and, indeed, *demands*, a negative answer. Could this be conveyed? The Yellow Emperor does *not* value, because etc.

Poem I [p. 151]. The last line, the "bright busy," etc., is the most literal, but I do *like*, "And the sun which smooths a path on the surface of the sea."

The poems which we chose to go are: I, III, IV, V, VI, VII, X, XI, XII, XV, XX (which is four stanzas), XXI. Numbers taken from the list you gave me.

Yours ever,
FLORENCE AYSCOUGH

ST. ANDREWS, June 25, 1918

DEAREST AMY,

I enclose an effusion which speaks for itself, and which I wrote separately that it might go into the hands of your secretary. This is a personal letter. We are safely installed: Geoffrey [Wheelock][1] seems very well, I am glad to say, and is amenable to a degree. Tommy[2] is huge, amiable, calm and boyish. He is so big that one always expects too much of him, seeing that he is but 14.

The weather is lovely, very cool not to say cold, and it is as beautiful as ever, but, dear me, I do want to go back. I feel a good deal like the lady who sang two thousand years ago: "Who says the Ho is wide? Why, one small reed can bridge it," and so on.

I wish that I could tell you how perfectly delighted I am with the poems. You have caught the spirit wonderfully. What fun it is doing such work. Miss Monroe suggested that they be printed with the author's name and date at the foot in each case, and then, at the end of the whole thing, our names as translator and versifier. I think the way we spoke of the other night is the best, don't you? "Translated by Florence Ayscough, English Version by Amy Lowell." You are an angel to do it and I feel extremely "set up." I will set myself to inditing the little prose part which is to go in the back of the magazine, and then send it to you, to see.

I suppose that Ada's belongings are coming soon. Give everybody my best love.

Yours ever,
FLORENCE AYSCOUGH

---

[1] F. A.'s brother.   [2] Geoffrey's son.

36

FLORENCE AYSCOUGH IN THE DRAWING-ROOM AT ST. ANDREWS

The porcelain jar (*kang*) at the left was a gift from the Empress Dowager, Tzŭ Hsi. Now in the Art Institute, Chicago.

DEAREST FLORENCE:

I was wondering when I should hear from you and was thinking of writing to drum you up, and just now, by this mail, come your two letters. I am perfectly delighted with what you say about the poems, and your root-meanings are so beautiful that I am going to try to incorporate them wherever possible.

I have not been through these remarks of yours with the poems themselves as your letters only arrived about ten minutes ago. I think that we had better call "the towers" in poem VI [p. 155], "green towers," as that is always used to mean brothels. Goncourt used "*maisons vertes*" throughout his volume on Utamaro, and I myself have used it in one or two poems. I think it is quite understood, and, when it is not, it sounds pretty. I am rather sorry not to have that poem exact. We are not a bit afraid of the kind of meaning you represent, nowadays, but I will leave it as it is if you prefer. However, I shall know better when I have gone through the poems and carefully compared your remarks. For a day or two now, I am tangled up with proof, but I shall surely be able to send you the things in about a week.

I had the most amusing experience with Harriet Monroe the other day.[1] She wrote and suggested that we should not write the poems in short lines, and I wrote back and sounded as learned as if I really knew something. I told her what was perfectly true, that to anyone who had studied cadence it must be evident that lines are not determined arbitrarily, but by the very lilt of the cadence itself. I then went on and discoursed about the roots of the [Chinese] characters being the things which give overtones to the poems in the same way that adjectives do with us. I told her that you quite agreed with this idea, and were now busily engaged in searching the roots to their utmost forks. I told her that you and I would get the poems as nearly perfect as we could, and that whatever was sent her would be agreed to by both you and me, and that as the poems were finally sent they would have to remain. It is always well to take a high hand with Harriet.[2] She is of the type that thinks you are really "some punkins" if you appear certain that you know, and I was more than amused at the result, which was a hasty post card saying that she had not meant to dictate, and that she was quite willing to take what we sent, that her remarks were only thrown out "for what they were worth." I felt like replying that "when they were worth nothing, why throw them out at all," but I refrained.

[1] See below, Appendix II.   [2] Damon, *op. cit.*, p. 763.

I also gave her a great song and dance as to your qualifications as a translator. I told her that you were born in China, and that it was, therefore, in some sense your native tongue (Heaven forgive me!), although you had only taken up the serious study of it within the last few years. I lengthened out your years in China until it would appear that you must be a hundred years old to have got so many in, and altogether I explained that in getting you, she was getting the *ne plus ultra* of Chinese knowledge and understanding; it being assumed, of course (though not by me expressed), that in getting me she was finding the best Englisher there was going. Anyhow, judging from the quick return upon herself evidenced by this post card, she is properly impressed with what she will get, as a result.

Do, please, incorporate that root theory of ours in your prose part. It is a brand new idea, and will make Ezra [Pound][1] and the whole caboodle of them sit up, since it will prove that their translations are incorrect, inasmuch as they cannot read the language and are probably trusting to Japanese translators, who have not the feeling for Chinese that you have. I tell you we are a great team, Florence, and ought to do wonderful things. Since reading these root things of yours, I am more and more convinced that my theory is right. That quotation, "sun disappearing in the grass at the horizon" seems to me to prove it absolutely. Of course, I do not mean to say that these exact words appear quickly to the mind of any reader when merely reading the character, but that the knowledge of their own characters (they being presumably learned men) thickens the impression, as it were. You see what I mean—it not only thickens it, it alters and changes it, blurring it over with this or that effect. Oh, I am certain of it; it is a great discovery, and you will admit that your sinologues, not being poets, have not yet found that out, at least if one may judge by the translations they make.

I am awfully glad everything is going so well. I do not wonder that you are a bit homesick. However, I am sure it will end in fame, and one has to go through a lot of loneliness for that. I will send you the poems fixed up with the new things as soon as possible.

Ada joins me in sending much love, and you will be very sorry to hear that the small boy[2] is not at all well, having an acute attack of colitis. I am afraid that this may delay their coming for some time.

Always yours,
AMY

[1] *Ibid.*, p. 767; see also below, Appendix II, for accounts of the acquaintance of Miss Lowell and Mr. Pound.

[2] Mrs. Russell's grandson, Theodore Amussen, Jr., often alluded to hereafter as "Sonny Boy."

DEAREST AMY—

Yours of the 28th came just as I was administering castor oil to my nephew; which operation being completed I wish to send you a hasty line of appreciation. I am thrilled. Of course I laughed hugely over your account of your correspondence with Miss Monroe—If you will thrust greatness upon me!!! Well, I will only try to conceal the extreme shallowness of my knowledge—but I am working, and *I am going to work*. As soon as ever I get back [to Shanghai] I shall tackle the T'ang poets with the best teacher[1] I can get, and then—you shall have some translations. As to your "suggestion" to Miss Monroe that you are the "best Englisher going"—since reading your wonderful version of the French poets (which I am doing now), I am more convinced of it than ever.

The root theory is absolutely sound. You say, "I do not mean to say that the exact words appear quickly to the mind of any reader when merely reading the characters, but that the knowledge of their own characters (they being presumably learned men) thickens the impression as it were," and so on. Now, I think that, to the cultivated Chinese, a glance at the character really does immediately suggest the analysis—as this analysis is a thing that they have studied—and a thing that they know well.

Of course I am longing to get back to a teacher—but am not losing time. I am going faithfully through a primer in eight volumes which was issued not long ago—and which is compiled in order to teach the modern youth of China the "Book Language." A very good sinologue who gave it to me said that did he have to begin his study again he would certainly begin with this primer. As it is compiled for the youthful son of Han there is no translation (thank the Lord there are pictures), so it means a good deal of digging—and I am analysing as I proceed. It ought to help a lot—and I hope to complete the set by the time I return; then I shall be able to read more easily.

In regard to poem VI [p. 155] the difficulty is that I can't be *sure* of that "golden nest" character. The line may just mean that the young girls of the harem, "green towers," must not be shut up in their "golden nest" now that the rain has stopped—or it may mean that they are not to be enjoyed. You see—as I say—the character is not in any of the dictionaries I have.

Again I reiterate—I am thrilled, and most tremendously obliged to

[1] See Florence Ayscough, *Firecracker Land* (New York: Houghton Mifflin Co., 1932), pp. 32–35 and thereafter.

you. I do think that after I get back, and can do some serious work on these lines, I ought to give you something that you can make a great work of—and something that will show what Chinese poetry really is. Do you think that I had better say much about this root idea now? It might start someone else off on the same "tack," and, tho' I don't believe that another such good teacher exists, someone might exploit the idea. And I meant, in the prose bit for *Poetry*, which must of necessity be short, to emphasise the fact that the Chinese treat their poems as "written pictures" and have them in their rooms so that the subtly suggested image may be constantly brought to mind. Would it not be best to stick to this? Merely making a reference to the pictorial form of the characters—and reserve our grand discovery for something more important after the War? I am sure that I can send you something to work on. Please let me know what you think. I will not do anything until I hear.

Had I realised that I was going to write such a large letter I should have used a typewriter. I know that my script is rather "grass"—and the exquisite checked paper from the local druggist does not render it more clear. I am more sorry than I can say to hear about the small boy's colitis. Ada must worry. Give her my love. I hope the news is good.

Yours,

F. W. A.

St. Andrews, July 23, [1918]

Dearest Amy—

I have been "digging," and send you the result. Is it comprehensible in such form? If I send you poems thus, are they lucid? Of course I am banking on your powers of imagination!!

Having obtained a booking on the "Empress," I am starting off on the 8th. Sail from Vancouver August 15, so am now collecting my scattered senses preparatory to starting.

I want to write the prose bit to go with the poems for *Poetry*, but am waiting to hear from you—as to your opinion. Poor Frank [Ayscough] never received my cable saying that I had postponed coming out, and travelled all the way to Yokohama (five days' journey) to meet me. The ship, of course, came in without me—and he had *no* explanation till he reached Shanghai. It was trying—

I have been wondering about Ada's grandson; is he well?

Yours ever,

F. W. A.

I put in the Chinese sounds as you might like to know how it sounds.

Dear Florence:

All your letters have come, and have been duly pondered over, but the last one, that has just arrived, strikes terror to my soul, because to have you leave on the 8th is far sooner than I had bargained for, and I do not see how we are ever going to get through in time. However, I am all ready for you and have been ready for some days, but have lacked the time, owing to this confounded proof, to get my letter written.

The new poem that you sent me looks frightfully obscure, but perhaps I can dig out a meaning later. I do not suppose that you intend it to be done for Harriet Monroe's set anyway, but merely as a kind of test on which to support your future diggings. I will let you know all about the method, and whether I can follow it when I get round to paying serious attention to it, but I shall have to get all the proof off my hands before I do that, since it is not immediately wanted and the other is.

Now here are the results of my re-going-over the poems with your suggestions, and in the first place, here is one of my own. I have never been satisfied with the two lines in the first poem ["An Evening Meeting," p. 151]:[1] "He comes" and "She sings." Those two flat statements of two words each, following directly after one another, are perfectly terrible, I think; and I worked an hour and a half trying to get one of them out, with the result that it seems to me that I cannot get anything that suits me at all. However, I think perhaps this is the best I can do:

> She leans against a screen, arch, coquettish, welcoming his arrival.
> Then suddenly striking the strings of her table-lute
> She sings.

I tried "Flashing upon his entrance," which is rather nice, but I am afraid not at all Oriental. I think, if I were you, I should take "The bright busy movement of the Western sea," rather than "The sun which smooths a path on the surface of the sea." The latter is pretty but not nearly so original, and as the former is the exact translation, I think I should adhere to it, but, of course, here, as always, I will bow to your superior knowledge.

In III [p. 152], I remember how sad you were about that "secret writings." You said that he wanted to proclaim the Emperor's return,

---

[1] This poem and those which follow on pp. 152–64 of *Fir-Flower Tablets* were first published, under the title "Chinese Written Wall Pictures," in *Poetry: A Magazine of Verse*, XIII, No. V (February, 1919), 233–42.

but you see that is exactly what I meant by that line. Originally they were his secret writings, his secret thoughts, his innermost desires, but now that the Spring wind is proclaiming the Emperor's return, he wishes to throw open his heart and give his writings, his acclamations of the Emperor, to the world. Personally, I like that poem just as it is, and if it suits you, we will so leave it.

In poems IV and V you have made no suggestions, so I take it that they may go as they are.

In poem VI [p. 155], I do not know what to do. I guess we shall have to leave out that "golden nest," as we do not know exactly how to put it in. I have tried "green towers" and "green pavilions"; but if I put that in, I shall have to take out the "green water" in the next line, which I do think would be a pity; so I think it would be just as well to leave it as "tower pavilions," and if the world does not understand, that cannot be helped. They would not understand "green houses" either, and that is what the word is usually translated into. I could not get the sun "disappearing in the grass at the horizon" either. Everything I did seemed to spoil the cadence which is particularly good in this poem; so, finally, after struggling and struggling over it, I have determined to leave it as it is, if you are satisfied.

I do not think that there will be any confusion in the reader's mind about the passing of the seasons in number VII [p. 156]. When you have the "Spring wind," in the first stanza, and the "iris splintering the brown earth," in the second, with "again" the head of the stanza, it seems quite obvious that a year has passed. I think that all readers of poetry are familiar with that sort of figure, or rather with that method of indicating the passage of time, and I do not think it is at all necessary to explain farther. In fact, I think that any such explanation would spoil the charm of the poem and take out its Oriental quality. People are getting so familiar now with the Oriental method of expression that I do not think there will be the faintest difficulty.

"X" you also do not criticize, so I suppose it can be left.

But in XI [p. 157] your remarks have caused me to tear my hair out in handfulls. I do like those old women spinning their threads in jail, and how to get them has nearly killed me. Finally, I have decided to do it this way. Here is the poem as I have now got it, and if you do not like it, change it in any way that you like, or we will go back to the original version.

> Clouds brush the rocky ledge.
> In the dark green shadow left by the sunken sun
> A jade fountain flies,

42

And a little stream
Thin as the fine thread spun by sad women
    in prison chambers,
Slides through the grasses
And whirls suddenly upon itself,
Avoiding the sharp edges of the iris-leaves.
Few people pass here.
Only the hermits of the hills come in companies.
To gather the Imperial Fern.

Now one of these lines is very long, and I think that I can probably break it. Also I think that "sorrowful women" would probably be better than "sad women." Perhaps "cold prisons" would be better than "prison chambers," but I do not want so many adjectives if I can help it. Now if you do not like the old women at all, take them out, but as that was in the original poem, and it seemed decidedly picturesque, I thought it would be a good idea to have it.

In XII [p. 159], I do not think that you had better put anything more plainly than it is here. I should leave it with the question mark and let the readers answer it as they choose. Even though a negative is insisted upon by the poet, a negative can be quite easily put in by the mind, and you will spoil the poem if you stick so closely to fact; not to the fact of the translation, you understand, for that you are following now, but to the fact of the fact, if I may so put it. I think that people are thoroughly educated up to the power of suggestion, and I should always leave the Oriental vagueness wherever possible.

You do not criticize XV, so I suppose that is all right, and XX is evidently satisfactory. I have XXI marked down as being one of the ones you were going to put in; but I think that it would be better to leave it out, as it is another of the pictures of the four seasons like XX [p. 161], and I think we have enough, as it is, in this batch, though I see, on referring to your letter, that you also have XXI.

Now what do you propose to do about the prose piece? Are you going to get that done before you leave, as you seem to think? In which case, will you send it to me and have me send all these things to her [Miss Monroe], including your prose piece, or will you do what I think much better, send the whole thing to her yourself, with your letter? I will correct the proofs after you have gone, for she will not have them in for months, if I know her.

My reason for suggesting that you put in the little hint of our discovery about the roots is simply and solely to knock a hole in Ezra Pound's[1] translations; he having got his things entirely from Professor

[1] See below, Appendix II.

43

Fenelosa [*sic*],[1] they were not Chinese in the first place, and Heaven knows how many hands they went through between the original Chinese and Professor Fenelosa's Japanese original. In the second place, Ezra has elaborated on these until, although they are excellent poems, they are not translations of the Chinese poets.

Now most people do not know this, for they have no idea what it means to translate a Chinese poem. They do not know the combination of qualities necessary to produce anything like the originals. Personally, since doing this work with you, I have become more in love with Chinese poetry than ever. I think it is extraordinarily good and immensely interesting to work with, but it would be no good at all if you did it in a free translation; no good at all as an approach to the Oriental mind, that is. Now no one knows better than I how beautiful those poems in Ezra's *Cathay* are, but they are not what he says they are. It would be most impolitic to come out and criticize Ezra in so many words; I do not think that you had better mention him at all. But I do think that a few remarks from you on the extreme difficulty of translating, and this magnificent thing which we have both discovered, would be in order. You might just say that you are merely hinting at it here, and expect to have the theory elaborated (though I do not think that I should call it a theory, but state it as a fact) in a volume of poems which you expect to bring out after the war.

You see, Florence, it is immensely difficult to get such translations done properly, anyway, so I do not think that you need fear competition in the least, even if you give away that root idea. The sinologues do not know enough to make adequate translations, and they do not know enough to get the poets who could; and the poets who have done them are more concerned in making a name for themselves than in rendering the old Chinese people. Now, of course, they could do both, if they were good enough poets, but they are not, and they are not usually in touch with good sinologues. The consequence is that you get one of two extremes. You get a scholarly translation which is punk as poetry, or you get a splendid poem which no Chinese ever wrote. The grand thing of our partnership is that we get both—now isn't that an elegant little nosegay for you and me to carry round?

I think if you do not state this in your prose article, the general reader will wonder why we bother with more Chinese translations when there have been so many. They will not know that we have a reason for doing it which the other people have not, but once you tell them the fact, they will sit up and take notice, and Bang! Whang!

[1] I.e., Ernest Francisco Fenollosa (1853–1908) (see Damon, *op. cit.*, pp. 312, 588).

will go the reputations of those other people who have taken no pains to secure good literal Chinese translations in the first place. Also, I wish that you would say that it is utterly impossible to get the real Chinese effect through a Japanese translation.

I do not know how long an article Miss Monroe said she wanted, but if I were you I would give her about a thousand words. She will not take more, I know; she may not take as much, but I do not think that you can do it justice in under eight hundred to a thousand. I think the thing will be so frightfully important that it ought to appear. Of course you cannot go into it as deeply as you will in the book itself, but I should touch on all the headings if I were you, and so create a desire for the book when it appears.

Of course you must give that idea of "hanging on the wall" [p. xciii], of being a picture, great prominence, as it is extraordinarily important and explains many things. Some time I think I shall adopt it and publish a book of pictures. Anyhow, I am in love with the things, and that's a fact.

Now remember, to make a book successful, you have got to talk about it a lot before it comes out, and the more things you can put into this little article which will make people sit up and take notice, the better chance for us when the book appears. If you could get it done instanter, and send it down to me so that we might have a little correspondence about it before you sail, it would be a good thing.

I do apologize for having been so long in sending you these poems, but the truth is that I have been perfectly swamped with proofs, and I have been a little worried about them, for everything has to be done this month on account of my operation[1] in September, and the book is billed to appear on the 24th of September, and I just simply feel as if I should go crazy half the time.

I am not going to write any more now because I want this to go off on the afternoon mail. I wish you were not going to China.

Sonny Boy is better and they are coming back to-morrow, so I shall lose one of my assistants, and it will be harder than ever to get through, particularly as I am lacking a second secretary for the moment. Oh Hell!

Always yours,

AMY

---

[1] For umbilical hernia; the first of four for a condition which ultimately caused Miss Lowell's death (see Damon, *op. cit.*, pp. 447–66 *et passim*).

Dearest Amy,

Yours of the 24th has just come, and I hasten to answer.

First, as to the new poem: it is only a specimen of "digging," and I hope that it is comprehensible. I enclose a short, bald paraphrase. Would it be better if I always did?

Second, your notes on the poems to go to Miss Monroe: The alteration you suggest in No. I, "She leans against a screen, arch, coquettish, welcoming his arrival, Then suddenly striking the strings of her table-lute, She sings," is an immense improvement. Of course, when you talk of my superior knowledge I cannot help smiling; your judgment is so unerring.

I expect poem VI [p. 151] had better stay as it is. As you say, the cadence is excellent.

As to XI [p. 157], I am simply delighted that you can put in the old women. I did so hope that you could. The whole poem is ever so much better—don't you think so? "Sorrowful" seems to me an improvement on sad, and "cold," too, seems to make the line more poignant; but you know best about the number of adjectives.

No more comments are needed as I am in perfect agreement with all else you say.

Third, as to the prose part: I feel perfectly incapable of saying anything that would "knock a hole" in Ezra Pound's translations. You know I am very diffident of my own powers and [I] know that *you* could say something *so* apt. I hardly know how to suggest it when you are so driven with proof, and when you have only one secretary; but how do you think it would be if you wrote just what you think would be most forcible, and would hit the nail on the head best? People would pay far more attention to you than they would to me. Could you not say that I had shown you the "hanging on the wall" poems (or the "written pictures" [pp. 151 ff.]); that we had talked them over; that you had grasped that here was a new way to translate, etc., etc.? It seems to me that it would be much more effective. Then I can work it out much more thoroughly for the "book," and discourse about the difference between poetic and other styles used in Chinese composition. I enclose a certain amount of data, which you, if you *will* do this, might find useful. Please don't think that I am shirking. If you think that I should do it, will you please telegraph me. I will go right to work so that I can send you something to look at. Please don't think that I am imposing on you; I only want to have the prose part as striking as possible. Of course, if you think that I should send the things to Miss Monroe, I will. But that cannot be decided until you say whether or not you can do the prose bit.

Chinese sayings: "Men of old reckoned it to be the highest excellence in their poetry that the meaning should lie beyond the words, and their readers should have to think it out."

The three canons: lucidity, simplicity, correctness of diction.

"Discard commonplace form; discard commonplace ideas; discard commonplace phrasing; discard commonplace rhymes."

An extract from an article on Chinese poetry, which contains nothing else worth while, reads:

> In the hands of an accomplished writer, the Chinese language is capable of a condensed picturesqueness and vigour such as can be rendered into no foreign language less ideographic in its mode of writing unless by means of wordy paraphrases. Each character in its (often numerous) component parts carries a wealth of imagery to the sense, and a whole series of metaphors are embodied in a single epithet. A language of this kind lends especially to the description of scenery, and the most superficial analysis of Chinese poetry reveals the fact that the productions which are the most applauded in this branch of literature consist simply of elaborate word-painting whose beauty resides rather in the medium of expression than in the author's thought. Hence it happens that when odes, renowned for centuries among Chinese readers, are transposed into the naked languages of Europe, it is found that their charm has vanished, as the petals of a flower are dropped from the insignificant and sober coloured fruit.

I do not know who wrote it; certain of the remarks are true.

Different sorts of characters are used for different sorts of literary composition. There is, for instance, what is known as the Documentary Style, which is quite different from the Poetic Style, though of course some, many, characters are used in all styles. I am quite sure that we are right in feeling that the composition of the character used has much to do with the sense conveyed. Rather a nice character I came across the other day is: *chai*, a study; (place where) one composes oneself to receive the influences from above. A Chinese scholar will often point to a character and say, referring to its composition, "That is a very beautiful character."

In regard to the "written pictures": these the Chinese prefer to painted ones as they consider them more subtle. As my teacher said, when I told him that I was getting to like them more myself, "Why, of course, a painted picture is always the same; these change every time you look at them." The actual writing of the character has a great deal to do with the artistic value of the scroll, but a fine thought is also much appreciated. In regard to the formation of the character the extract (enclosed) from one of Lafcadio Hearn's books is rather good, tho' he does not refer to the actual *composition* of the character, which is its soul.

Fine writing [i.e., calligraphy, e.g., *Fir-Flower Tablets*, pp. 60 and 154—not "purple patches"] is, as I say, the most highly valued art in China; all sorts of cheap reproductions are made of fine specimens in order that they may be available for the humblest home. In Tsingtao, a couple of years ago, the parting gift to me of the greenkeeper of the golf course (a most illiterate peasant), was a little scroll, a reproduction in lovely writing of a line from the Classics. Of course he could not read it himself.

To repeat myself, I don't want to impose on you, and I know that you won't let me, but I do feel that you could present this "discovery" to the world far more strikingly than I could. I can't tell you how excited I am at the whole idea of our collaboration—at the preparing of our "elegant little nosegay" as you call it. Oh dear, I wish China were not so far away. I want to be able to talk to you, and get your help. Hoping so much that you will write that little thing to "make people sit up." (Can't you have discovered me?)

Ever with much love, yours,
FLORENCE AYSCOUGH

[TELEGRAM]

Received at ST. ANDREWS, N.B.   July 27, 1918
Dated   BROOKLINE, MASS.
To   MRS. FRANCIS AYSCOUGH

Awfully sorry cannot write the article myself; not because am busy, but because my relations with Ezra Pound[1] are such that anything I might say in regard to Chinese work would be put down to pique, and, as I am perfectly known not to understand Chinese myself, it would carry absolutely no weight. Even that, however, would not be so much the difficulty as the fact that being a rival of Ezra's, and in some senses his enemy, I cannot directly appear to criticize his work, or, at least if I do, it goes for nothing. If you will write something and send it to me, embodying these excellent things in your letter, I will read it over and suggest what occurs to me, but it must be over your signature, not mine. You can say something about approving my arrangements, if you wish, but you are the important

[1] See below, Appendix II.

person in this, not I. Everything is going finely. I am tickled to death about it, aren't you?

AMY LOWELL

[ST. ANDREWS], July 28, 1918

DEAR AMY,

About 1700 B.C. it was borne in upon a ruler of the state of Shang that the times were very bad, that the king was a degenerate idiot, and that upon him had fallen the duty of raising the standard of rebellion and saving the country. So, "with fear and trembling, feeling as though he stood upon the brink of an abyss"—he undertook the affair and raised a new dynasty. I know just how he felt! Your telegram arrived. I obey—and hope to send you something in a day or two. May I, please, have the two pages from *Poetry*?[1] I want to quote from that critique, and raise the standard of rebellion.

Did I ever tell you that Mr. [John Alden] Carpenter said that he would like to have some of the poems to put to music?

On Sunday I spoke for the local Red Cross on "Painting," etc., and read your version of no. IV, "Manshu" [p. 153]. It was received with great applause. I felt very proud when I said that the English version was by you.

We are going off for the day. I must see that food, etc., is supplied in sufficient quantities for a hungry crew.

Yours,

F. W. A.

ST. ANDREWS, July 30, [1918]

DEAREST AMY,

I wonder if the enclosed is too rough for you to be able to take in? Anyway I thought that I would like you to see it, and I shall warmly welcome any suggestions. You will, I know, be perfectly frank. It is rather difficult to treat such a vast subject in such a very short note, but I hope that it is fairly clear. When it comes back I will work over it some more and insert the quotation from the *Times* which was in the bit of *Poetry* which I sent you; I can't remember it exactly.

Carl Sandburg writes me to-day that he is probably leaving in Au-

---

[1] Apparently A. C. H.'s "Of Puritans, Philistines and Pessimists," XII, No. IV (July, 1918), 228–29.

gust for some part of the Eastern front. That will be an experience for him!

This must go to post as I want it to reach you as soon as possible.

So, with much love, yours as ever,

FLORENCE AYSCOUGH

I am not going to reiterate in every letter how eternally grateful I am to you!! You would be bored to tears.

BROOKLINE, MASS., August 1, 1918

DEAR FLORENCE:—

Your little note has just arrived and I will read it over and write you about it to-morrow. In the meanwhile, I am sending you a rough arrangement of the last poem you sent me. I do not know whether you can make head or tail of it. It is full of alternative readings, and you might mention which you prefer and if you have any suggestions.

I am also returning the *Poetry* pages as you asked me to, but I am carefully preserving your typewritten suggestions because I think that they may be useful to me later on, and you doubtless have the books from which you took them. If, however, you want them sent back, wire me at once. As this letter cannot go off until to-morrow, owing to the necessity of copying my rough draft of the poems, I shall probably be able to send you back your paper.

I do wish you were not going just as we are getting in the thick of this. I was talking to Professor [John Livingston] Lowes[1] about our discovery, and he says that he thinks it is the most interesting thing he has heard of for a long time, and that we have got hold of a remarkable thing there, and I think we have. I do think that it is easier for me when you not only write all the meanings, as you did the first time with the poem, but the paraphrase as well. I need the two things to work from; and when you are sending things from China or anywhere, do it that way, will you, my dear.

No more for the present, and to-morrow I will add a post-script.

Affectionately yours,

AMY LOWELL

P.S. Your paper is bully, but I shall have to write you about it to-morrow.

ST. ANDREWS, August 3, [1918]

DEAR AMY,

Your letter, the rough draft of "Once More Fields and Gardens" [p. 132], and the pages from *Poetry* have just come. Thanks. I hasten to

1 See Damon, *op. cit.*, p. 762.

answer. I like the poem ever and ever so much. It is really wonderful how you catch the Oriental spirit, and how in the *dickens*, you get those characters in a phrase, I don't see; it fills me with admiration.

I send you the "Fields and Gardens" with a few comments. I also enclose the lines from the "Songs of the Marches" [pp. 1–4] which were left out, but which I have found it very difficult to make head or tail of.

You say you are sorry that I am going just as we are getting into this; honestly it is best, as, before we really do more, I want to study properly with this idea in my head. You see I had no thought when I was at work last summer, of doing anything beyond making the scrolls as *clear* as possible, and I feel that even a few months with a good teacher will make a vast difference. What I want to do now is to discover the best method of our being clear to each other. I will send always a paraphrase, a literal analysis, and as many explanatory notes as possible. Do you like the red ink notes?

Who is Professor Lowes, please? I suppose I betray ignorance, but that is a thing that there is no point in trying to disguise, unless one wishes it to intensify in hue.

The more I think of this whole thing, the more excited I am.

Yours ever,
FLORENCE AYSCOUGH

Of course I am impatient to have your comments on the prose bit I sent you.

BROOKLINE, MASS., August 4, 1918[1]

DEAREST FLORENCE:

I owe you a thousand apologies for not having sent this back before. The truth is that I have been quite ridiculously ill. The terrific heat which we had for some days went to my weak spot—my digestion. I could eat nothing without constant distress, and the doctor put me down on two straws a day, supplemented by various doses, and I felt so absolutely rotten and faint that I couldn't even dictate a letter yesterday or the day before.

I am still living on the two straws and the selected pharmacopeia, but I am a little better. But, again, it is Sunday, and I have no secretary, so you will have to wade through this fine, poetic script; in which I do not envy you, for I frequently cannot read it myself.

In the first place, I think this paper completely excellent.[2] I wish

[1] Holograph letter.

[2] See *Poetry*, XIII, No. V (February, 1919), 268–72.

it were longer, because it is so interesting. But I think you were really wise to have it so short, because otherwise (you being away) Harriet might undertake to cut it, out of her head, which would be a calamity.

The only things I should suggest would be a little more stressing of the fact that this overtone business has never been discovered by translators but is well understood by native Chinese *literati:* and a little more emphasis on the fact that no one translating Chinese poems from Japanese transcriptions can hope to come very near the originals. I have put some little footnote suggestions on the text, which you can follow up or not as seems to you good. Remember, this whole idea will be so new to your readers that they will have to have it rather banged into them. Couldn't you elaborate a little where you jump on the [London] *Times* man, and say that what appears as bald statement to one who only takes the final meanings of a character, is most poetically shaded for a person with the knowledge of the roots or modifying overtones? You could say that Chinese is considered so difficult and unlike our sort of languages because so few Occidentals are at once sinologues and poets. That is, men capable of seizing the poetic value of these *nuances*. See! These are merely suggestions, which you will follow or not, as seems to you good. With or without them, the paper is remarkably good. And I am so thankful I couldn't write it, for you have done it so much better than I could. In the first place, my dear, you must see that I don't know enough. It is written awfully well.

I shall have to send fair copies of the poems to Harriet. I think those you have are disfigured by alternatives and alterations. Will you send Harriet your article, and let me send her the poems separately, or will you send the article to me, and let me send her that with the poems? If you do the latter, you must write her a line yourself, giving her your claims to fame—your being born in China, your long residence there, the learned societies to which you belong, those articles for the encyclopedia:[1] etc., etc. Everything that can dazzle her, and make readers sit up and take notice.

I think it was a nasty shame that your husband never got your cable. There seems no excuse for holding such a thing back, or delaying it. If the war continues this way, however, I think that some day we shall return to normal life again. If I hear from you in time, I will wire you to the ship. Oh, I wish you were not going! But you will simply have to come back when the book is ready, for the final touches

[1] *The Encyclopaedia Sinica*, ed. Samuel Couling (Shanghai, 1917).

before it goes to press. Which is, I fear, sure to be "after the war," owing to paper restrictions. But we'll get it out the instant the war is over. I think there should be about 150 poems; we have, I believe, 30. And a good half of the book your prose part with characters broken up into their roots—two or three for illustrations—and a couple (or more) of full-paged plates of some of your best specimens.

I was talking to Professor Lowes about our root discovery the other day, and he nearly burst with enthusiasm at the soundness and general importance of the idea.

Ada sends lots of love. We have our family back again now, and in recovered health, and we both wish you the best of pleasant voyages.

Goodbye for a little moment, dear girl, though I think our correspondence will be a pretty lively one, don't you? Had not I better have your house address, and not merely Scott-Harding?

Lovingly,
AMY

ST. ANDREWS, August 6th, 1918

DEAREST AMY,

Your letter arrived to-day, I am dreadfully distressed that you should have had to write all that yourself, especially when you were feeling seedy. I thought of you in the great heat and wondered how you were; indeed, I do not wonder that you were knocked up by it. Even here it was a little hot, though not for long.

I cannot tell you how pleased I am that you like the paper. I believe you when you tell me that you find it "excellent," as I know that you will speak the truth, and that especially in this affair it is essential that we are perfectly frank with one another. I have made the few alterations which you suggest and enclose it. I would much rather have you send the article with the poems, please; those copies which I have are, as you say, "messed up." I will write her [Miss Monroe], as you suggest, but am not keen about the "claims to fame"; however, I am—as ever—docile. Oh, my dear, I am so excited at the idea of "the book." You are an angel. One thing troubles me—we have not put any titles to the poems. I will think them over on the train and send you some suggestions; my mind does not seem to work to-night.

D.V. I start the day after to-morrow; spend Friday in Montreal. If by any chance you should want to communicate with me there: care, Mrs. George Hooper, 24 Mark St., will find me. Friday night I leave; am due in Vancouver the 14th: care the Canadian Pacific Ocean Services Ltd., will find me. I suppose that it is best not to put on the name

53

of the ship, the Censor might object as no ships are advertised. I will at once advise the company of my arrival and address. Love to you all. I do hope that you are better. Do take care of yourself.

Yours,

FLORENCE AYSCOUGH

CANADIAN PACIFIC RAILROAD, EN ROUTE, August 12, 1918

DEAR AMY,

Thanks so much for the telegram which reached me safely in Montreal. I am thus far, nearly to Medicine Hat, on my journey and trust the ship really pushes off on Thursday. I think that this Siberian expedition[1] may make travel on the Pacific more difficult than ever. I have been thinking over some titles to the poems to-day and, unless you can think of better ones, how do you think these will do?

    I. Waiting [p. 151?].
  III. The Emperor's Return From a Journey to the South [p. 152].
   IV. On Seeing the Portrait of a Lovely Concubine [p. 153].
    V. Calligraphy [p. 154].
   VI. The Palace Blossoms [p. 155].
  VII. Friendship, or, When Will My Friend Return? [p. 156].
X & XI. Put as 1 and 2 under the one title, From the Straw Hut Among the Seven Peaks. (This was the seal used by a well known painter who loved to live among the mountains.) [P. 157.]
  XII. Immortality, or Taoist Alchemy, or On the Classic of the Hills and Sea [p. 159].
   XV. The Scholar's Message, or The Recluse [p. 160].
   XX. The Homesick Magistrate. (Then the four each with its heading, Spring, Summer, Autumn, Winter.) [P. 161.]
  XXI. The Inn on West Lake [p. 164].

I expect that you can think of much better ones, so please put anything you like to them.

I have been writing letters busily the whole way across, catching up with awful arrears. I have not studied a word of Chinese which I had intended to do. I hate to think that soon thousands of miles of sea will lie between us! Will Ada please write and tell me the very moment you have your operation? I shall wait anxiously to hear.

Much love, yours ever very gratefully,

FLORENCE AYSCOUGH

1 See H. B. Morse and H. F. MacNair, *Far Eastern International Relations* (Boston, 1931), chap. xxvii.

DEAREST AMY,

Here I am safely installed in the "House of happiness-which-is-limitless-as-the-country-over-which-the-wild-geese-fly" (all that is expressed in three characters "Hung Fo Chai").[1] Well, I am very happy to be here and find my good man well, which he is. Papa[2] is up in Tsingtao still. I may have to go up to bring him down but I hope not.

An awful thought came over me just as I was nearing here and could do nothing about it: that was, that before there was any talk of the Chinese poem coming out in *Poetry*, I wrote that article on calligraphy and painting for the *Mentor*,[3] and gave them your version as yours, but not as having been in *Poetry* (of course acknowledging it) of the "Emperor's Return From a Journey to the South" [p. 152]. The whole subject was dismissed from my mind, and I didn't think of that article again. If it comes out before the poems appear in *Poetry*, will Miss Monroe be annoyed? It ought to have *Poetry*'s name appear with it in some way, ought it not? I don't know when it will come out. October or January, he said. If you think anything should be done about it, perhaps Miss Moran could write to Mr. Moffat, Editor, the *Mentor*, 114 East 16 St., New York. I am so sorry that I should have been so stupid, but my mind was so exercised over Geoffrey and his affairs that I found it hard to concentrate on anything, and the thing never occurred to me till one rather rough day on the Pacific. . . . .

I have been . . . . seedy since I got here; however, I am recovered now and ready to go ahead with life generally. Have begun with my teacher; am not sure that he will do; if not, must get another. Have not yet had time to see people I can trust about it.

Waley's book [*A Hundred and Seventy Chinese Poems*] is here. It must be in U.S. It is good. I shall avoid poems already done by him. His version of our "Return to Fields and Gardens" is on page 77, called "Returning to the Fields."

This is not a proper letter; will write again soon. I wanted to tell you about the *Mentor*. Am thinking so much about you and your operation. I wish I knew when it was to come off. Ada will let me know at once how you are—please.

Much love, as ever, yours,

FLORENCE AYSCOUGH

---

[1] See *Firecracker Land*, pp. 30–32. [2] Thomas Reed Wheelock.

[3] See "Chinese Painting," by Mrs. Francis Ayscough, *Mentor*, Vol. VI, No. 20, Serial No. 168 (December 2, 1918).

DEAR FLORENCE:—

I sent you my new book [*Can Grande's Castle*][1] yesterday. You know all the poems in it except "The Bronze Horses,"[2] and I am very curious to know how you will like them.

I have not yet re-fixed that last poem you sent me, for the very simple reason that I have had my operation and am only slowly recovering. I have been down-stairs for a couple of hours, but that is all I can yet stand out of my bed. And when I suggest working the doctor looks at me with scorn. I meant to send you an arranged copy with this letter, but as the time for arranging it seems to become ever more remote, I think that I will write you a little line now. I really believe that in a couple of weeks I shall be all well again, but apparently operations take a longer time to get over than I had supposed, although they tell me that I am a model patient and have healed up with remarkable celerity.

I sent our combined efforts to Harriet Monroe, and received from her the following pleasant remarks: "I have given the Chinese things a very swift once-over, and they seem to me beautiful. I congratulate you both."

I forgot entirely to make arrangements with you as to the payment which we shall receive. I think that the best way would be to divide it into thirds. I will send you two-thirds and keep a third myself. Certainly your work was two-thirds as hard as mine [*sic*], if not more. If this suits you, let me know.

I had a letter from [John Gould] Fletcher[3] the other day from London, and he says that Ezra has already had to come out publicly and admit that he attributed one of his translations to the wrong poet, following a blunder by Fenelosa.

Those Chinese poems that we liked—the quotations from which appeared in the *Transcript*—it turns out are by Arthur Waley,[4] called *A Hundred and Seventy Chinese Poems*. They are published by Constable & Company, and I have sent for a copy. I think that you can probably get them more easily in Shanghai than by sending directly to England, but at any rate, that is the book. Judging from the specimens we saw, his translations are very charming, but I doubt extremely whether he has done any of the researching which will make our book (!) so indispensable. Harriet has not told me when she ex-

---

[1] See Damon, *op. cit.*, p. 749.
[2] *Ibid.*, p. 748.
[3] *Ibid.*, p. 753.
[4] *Ibid.*, p. 772.

pects to publish our poems, but I suppose that they will come along in the course of the Winter.

It seems so funny to have you drop out of existence, as of course you did when you sailed. I suppose that sometime I shall receive a note telling me of your voyage and sending me some poems to work on. What a frightful time it takes to hear from China!

The war news is so good, however, that I really think that some day the nasty thing may be over. I confess to a sad regret that I cannot pull one trigger before it is over. To make up, I am trying to pull lots of triggers of *Phantasms*,[1] and get the book out before the war ends. My diatribes are so violent that they surely cannot be post mortem.

We are having a terrible time here with an epidemic called Spanish influenza. There seems to be a general opinion that the germs were let loose by the Germans. At any rate, all the theatres and churches are closed. Even funerals are restricted in numbers. Ada is acting like the very devil, refusing to stay entirely out of town, refusing to promise not to enter shops, altogether courting the disease. I call it suicidal mania. I, being in bed, have no temptations. Heaven knows what I should do if I were up; but of course I am not afraid for myself, merely for her. The terrible thing is that it turns into pneumonia, but in the better classes it seems to be seldom fatal. Bessie Perkins, and Alison Hill, and my sister Bessie, and my brother, have all had it, but have recovered after a few days' illness; but the mortality in the camps and in the poorer portions of the community has been great. All of which proves, I think, that cleanliness is the great desideratum.

Do write and tell me everything, and send me a nice batch of poems which I can work at in my off moments; and, above all, be sure and tell me what you think of "The Bronze Horses."

If the war does end, why of course we can be published any time. Just now, they have restricted the output of all publishing houses. I do not know whether I am ever going to be able to publish another book or not. I suppose my whole future, until the war is over, depends on how this book sells, as doubtless Mr. Brett will not be desirous of according me any of the small quantity of paper he has, if he can use it to better advantage elsewhere. Mr. Marsh tells me that the advance sale of the book is quite good for the times, but he has given me no figures, and as the first advertisement only goes in to-morrow, of course we have had no reviews as yet. I sent you an advance copy.

Ada sends much love and hopes that you had a pleasant and un-

[1] *Ibid.*, p. 767.

eventful voyage, and I trust that you found your husband and your father well and are now working sixteen hours a day at Chinese translations. I miss you awfully. Why on earth did you have to marry in China? However, if you had not, I suppose we should not have had any Chinese poems—so there you are.

If the war ends soon I suppose you will have to come right back and sell the rest of those pictures[1]—an added reason for desiring the war to end. Till next time.

Affectionately yours,

AMY

[SHANGHAI], December 22, 1918

DEAREST AMY,

I was perfectly delighted to receive *Can Grande's Castle* the other day, and have enjoyed it more than I can say. "Sea-Blue and Blood-Red" I had not read, you know, and found it thrilling. The "Bronze Horses," if you remember, you read to me—when it made a tremendously vivid impression which was only enhanced by a reading. What strides you have made—compare any of these four works with your early poems and one realizes how far you are going. Of course your workmanship is always exquisite.

There is quite a large organization here called "The American Women's Club"; on January 7, I am going to speak before it on—yourself. I wish that you were here to read your poems for them, but as you are not I am going to try. I will write and let you know *which* I choose. At present I am torn—as I should like to read nearly all. Of course, "Guns as Keys" is too long, if one reads anything else as well. I have read it to various people in its entirety and they have always found it thrilling—which it is. Well, I am puzzled but shall evolve something out of it all. I know that they will be interested, but I feel myself inadequate.

Your letter of October 4 took forever en route; the American censor is evidently very thorough and keeps things for ages. In regard to the payment for the Chinese things, I think that 1/2 and 1/2 would be a much better arrangement. Without you where should I have been? And then, too, look at the difference in the sort of book we did. I only delved; you had to give of your brain power.

I don't know what you will say to me when I tell you that I have been drawn into a vortex of work that has obliged me to put poetry

[1] A supposition contrary to fact: the pictures form part of The Florence Ayscough and Harley Farnsworth MacNair collection in the Art Institute, Chicago.

58

quite aside for the moment. For the first time the necessities of the War have come to us in the Far East. I mean: before this everything that was done was—(Dec. 28. At that point I was interrupted, and have not had a moment—and I haven't one now. But it is mail day and I must close this, so, while the amah combs my hair, I proceed), of course, useful—but not of vital necessity as, if the Far East didn't help, other people did. Now, the door to the front is only three days' sail away, and the needs of Siberia are simply *awful*. In a small community like this there are only a certain number of people who work, and they have to do double duty. It is especially the organizing of work that is needed, and that happens to be my talent—so I am working about 24 hours a day. I feel rather like John the Baptist, anyway, as it is difficult to interest people in the Czechs, and there is a great prejudice against Russia generally, so it is exhausting.

I began working hard with my teacher, but had to stop as it was overwhelming. I am longing to begin again. . . . .

I must go. Much, much love. I am thankful that you are well over your operation—my best love to Ada. There is one poem partly done which I hope to send you before very long, but I know that "driblets" are no use. I can't tell you how I long to be at the work—but this other must be done.

Yours,

FLORENCE AYSCOUGH

BROOKLINE, MASS., 11 February, 1919

DEAR FLORENCE:

I am delighted to know that you like *Can Grande*. I did not know that you had not read "Sea-Blue and Blood-Red"; I thought you had. I wish that I could have heard you talk about me before the [Shanghai] American Women's Club on January 7th; I know that it would have been interesting for me to hear.

Our poems have come out in this month's *Poetry*,[1] and I am sending you two copies. Harriet paid me fifty dollars for the poems and ten dollars for your prose article. I am, therefore, sending you a forty-dollar draft, your own ten dollars and thirty dollars for your share of the poems, keeping twenty dollars myself. This is not exactly the two-thirds I wrote you about, but that splits up into such small dollars and cents that it seemed hardly worth dividing closer.

I am sorry that you have not had time to do any more about the

---

[1] XIII, No. V (February, 1919), 233–42; see also below, Appendix II.

poems, for I think, now that the war is over, there is a splendid chance for them in book form. I did not send you the translation I made of the last one you sent me because you told me you did not want anything that was in Arthur Waley's book, and, as that was in his book, I supposed that it was better to just can it. When I receive anything from you, I will start work on it right away.

Of course I do regret your spending so much time on good works,[1] for someone else can do good works, and you were made for something bigger; but I suppose that is just the artist in me who cares next to nothing for anything but art.

I have been terribly ill with the influenza, which is annoying for I got over my operation beautifully and felt better than I had for ten years, but I have had the "flu" for seven weeks and am only just getting round again, and the worst of it was that I had to give up four lectures.

I do not mind having your poems in driblets at all; I can get them off to you quickly that way, so send them along whenever you have anything.

I heard the other day from my quondam French teacher, Mlle. Chéron, and she said that you had read some of these poems to a friend of hers last Summer in Saint Andrews, and she was thrilled over them. I think the book will be very useful, and liked very much, when we get it out.

Harriet left out your sentence about the originals of these things being exhibited in Cincinnati.[2] I blew her up about it and put it back in the proof, but she said that nothing could be done about it because it took her over on to another page and upset her make-up. That is the worst of these editors; I believe they would cut any masterpiece to bits for the sake of their make-up.

Well, my dear, this is a frightfully dull letter, but when one has passed seven weeks in bed with a trained nurse to hold one's hand and a Bolsheviki digestion—for my "flu" having gone through the regular gamut of colds and coughs and temperatures seems to have settled there—one has very little to say. I think, however, that the trees are beginning to thin, and that some day I shall be out of the woods. . . . .

Ever so much love from us both,

AMY

---

[1] *Inter alia* acting as factotum to her friend, Lady de Sausmarez, president of the Shanghai branch of the British Women's Association, in war and other work, in part connected with the Allied expedition to Siberia.

[2] See below, Appendix II.

DEAREST AMY,

Poetry [with the "Chinese Written Wall Pictures"][1] has just arrived and I am very delighted. Don't you think that it is nice? I was rather interested in the review by John Gould Fletcher[2] to see that he had singled out from among Waley's poems, for special admiration, that one ["Returning to the Fields"] which we began to work at (Waley, [*A Hundred and Seventy Chinese Poems*], p. 77). I thought it one of the ones in which Waley had had the least success, but, when I saw that he had done it, felt that perhaps we had better leave it alone. However, as Mr. Fletcher has chosen it, don't you think that it would be rather interesting to show what *can* be done with the poem? Show how much finer it is if one uses the "overtones" idea? Mr. Fletcher again labours the idea of each "word being sheer commonplace," which is really so absurd, but which seems to obsess the Western critics.

Well, in case you think that it may be amusing to counterattack with the poem, I have worked over it with Chinese and with Dr. John Darroch, of the Religious Tract Society, a very fine sinologue and a most delightful man (if you do counterattack, please acknowledge him), and send you the result of my labours which involve some corrections. Oh, dear me, how I wish we could talk!! Dr. Darroch is much interested in our "root idea" and quite agrees with its possibilities. The formation of the character is his special hobby. In case it may interest you, I enclose the first instalment of a paper by him on the character; will send the rest when it appears. He has also found what sounds like a very promising teacher whom I may be able to get, and I am going to try to settle down to work again.

The last six weeks have been *dreadful*. Papa, having had repeated heart seizures, has been lying at death's door. He is in the hospital, and as the hospital lies nearly six miles away and as I have been there twice—sometimes three times—a day, my life has been spent on the road. . . . . I have lost count of how many times during the last five weeks I have been called. . . . . Then, of course, Science steps in, oxygen is pumped into his lungs, camphor is injected, strychnine is given, and he is *made* to live—only to have another attack. It seems rather a mistaken kindness.

Well, during this time, Frank has asserted his authority and a great many of the public things I have been doing have been taken from

[1] Vol. XIII, No. V (February, 1919).　　[2] *Ibid.*, pp. 273–78.

my hands. I don't see how I can take them on again; so I hope to commence my Chinese again.

I am spreading your fame far and wide. Your poems are being read on every side and are much enjoyed. I will not gossip on longer but will proceed to write out the result of my investigations.

Very best love to Ada and to yourself, my dear. I am very, very, grateful to you.

Yours,

FLORENCE AYSCOUGH

SHANGHAI, CHINA, April 25, 1919

DEAREST AMY,

Many thanks for yours of February 11, which arrived only a few days ago; the mails are—awful. Also for the cheque. Of course it is not on the two-thirds basis, and you are absurdly generous about it, but I accept your generosity in the spirit it is given. Thanks so much, dear. It is, indeed, distressing that you have had influenza, and I am most awfully sorry. It seems to be the most trying thing to get over. Do hope that by now you are yourself again, and, as you say, "out of the woods."

As far as my personal situation is concerned since I last wrote . . . . [conditions] have changed as follows: Papa is still in the Nursing Home, but the doctor stopped my going more than once a day. I have, therefore, begun Chinese lessons again. Papa is better, in so far as things have adjusted themselves to each other, and so he goes along; on a perfectly artificial basis of course.

Now to turn to . . . . the poems. The *China Press*, a paper here, was much interested and published them all, as well as the prose article, on two consecutive Sundays; then last week they published the enclosed "argument." I don't send the others as they were simply taken bodily from *Poetry* and not reviewed. They have, however, roused a good deal of interest, and I have had several of the sinologues arguing. (In re-reading my letter of March 14, I see that I have said nearly all this before.) . . . .

I had rather a funny time with my teacher, who is supposed to be a very fine scholar, over one of the characters in the *fu* of "The [Terraced Road of the] Two-Edged Sword Pavilion" [p. 52]. [1] Line 5, Character 8, *Yu*, "wind in a gale." The characters for "sun" and "to speak" are almost indistinguishable when written or printed in the modern form, and this *Yu* is composed of "wind" and *either* "sun" or "speak." I

[1] "Pavilion" should be "Mountains." See, below, letter of F. W. A. under date of September 14, 1919.

asked the teacher which the second was. He replied "sun." "Well," I said, "I don't think it is; I think it is 'speak'; it is the voice of the wind the man who made the character was thinking of." Not at all; he wouldn't have it. After arguing for some time, I said "Well, please look it up in the *Shuo Wen*."—It *was* to speak!! Teacher crest-fallen; F.W.A. triumphant. *Fu*'s really are like polyphonic prose; it is quite amusing. I enclose a list of the sounds in Chinese, as you may like to read over the characters and hear how they sound. The rhymes are not always very distinct.

Besides the *fu*, I send four Soldier Songs; the other two of the six do not seem worth translating. I am now at work on a *tzŭ*, which is a song with a well known tune. In the Soldiers' Songs, the "Snapping Willows" [p. 134] is a song, and if the tune alone were heard it would be as well known to a Chinese as, say, "Annie Laurie" to us. This *tzŭ* is rather nice. I hope to send it by the "Empress" on May 10, the best mail there is. I am trying to make them as clear as possible for you; if you can suggest anything that would help, please do.

I was much interested to see that the *Literary Digest* reprinted a number of the poems from *Poetry*.

I hope that you are attacking with "Return to Fields and Gardens." Shall wait anxiously for the result of your polishing of it.

Much love to you and to Ada.

Yours ever,

FLORENCE AYSCOUGH

[SHANGHAI, CHINA], May 10, 1919

DEAREST AMY,

Herewith a Song by Li T'ai-po. It is very different from the other things I have sent. I hope you will like it. Of course you cannot use any form which would be like the original; but if you could, in this case, use a definite form which would be the same for the three verses, the effect would be more like that of the original than would a *vers libres* rendering. Your poem "The Road to the Mountain" appeared in the *China Press* this morning, taken from the *Tribune*. Some of the figures are most lovely, but, taking it all together, I don't care for it as I do for some others.

Things with me are about the same. Papa is taken out in a motor occasionally. I expect to move him to Wei-Hai-Wei[1] on June 13. Am

[1] See *The Autobiography of a Chinese Dog, Edited by His Missuss (Florence Ayscough) with Writing-Brush Sketches by Lucille Douglass* (Boston and New York, 1926), pp. 8–11:

"The coast-line of China is not especially jagged as coast-lines go, but between the thirty-sixth and thirty-eighth parallels of latitude, the Promontory of Shantung thrusts its bold outline trying to get the very good teacher, of whom I have spoken, to go too, and, if I manage that, shall be able to do a lot of work.

There is only just time for this to catch the post.

Ever much love,
Yours,
Florence Ayscough

Shanghai, China, May 23, 1919

Dearest Amy,

I send herewith three lyrics, and have a long narrative poem almost ready for you . . . . hope to get it off some time next week.

---

into the depths. At this point the water of the Yellow Sea is no longer coloured by sediment from the Great River, but sparkles in the clear atmosphere, larkspur blue. Flat-bottomed coast steamers move in a very strange manner as they round the point and passengers are as a rule extremely glad to reach the deep-cut bay which stretches to the South and East of Wei-Hai-Wei—Outpost of Defence by-the-Awe-Inspiring Sea. High hills encircle it West and North, so the little walled city lies in a veritable sun-trap, and even cold winter days are tempered, while Summer heat is mitigated by the South-west monsoon, which sweeps across the water, cooler here than it is South of the Promontory.

"Even so, it was fairly hot and during the sun-high hours of day, we were apt to stay indoors. I had a delightful shallow round basket which Amah called my official residence; and I cannot imagine that in the wide world more comfortable baskets can exist than those found in the 'Outpost of Defence.' They are pretty, too, in their weave, and Missuss always covered mine with a square of deep purple raw silk, most becoming, in colour, to me. Staying indoors was therefore no hardship; I simply curled up and dozed. While I dozed, Missuss studied with Mr. Cultivator-of-Bamboos, whom she called '*hsien shêng*, 'prior-born'—a term my country-people apply to fathers, elder brothers, or people who instruct them. As a rule he and she translated Chinese poetry together, and many letters travelled back and forth between Missuss and a person to whom she seemed very devoted. Mr. Cultivator-of-Bamboos always referred to this person as Love-Poetry-Mother's Friend. I learned that her surname was 'Lowell' and her name 'Amy.' It seemed that she rendered into English un-rhymed cadence the translations which Missuss made, and she was always asking questions about Chinese poetry and its composition. She wanted, for instance, to know exactly what the form called *fu* was like, because she thought it resembled 'polyphonic prose,' a medium she used herself. So Missuss wrote her what a Chinese writer had to say on the subject:

" 'There is no hard-and-fast pattern for "tones" in a *fu*, but words must flow naturally from the lips in a smooth and musical manner. A *fu* must be like a good road on which there are no rough places or inequalities. Phrases may be long or short; phrases may be many or few; but the rhymes in each group must be of the same "tone"—that is, either *p'ing*, level, or *tsê*, oblique; and each rhyme can only be used once.'

"We Chinese cite six laws which govern *fu:* they shall possess: 'firstly, variegated colour, generously laid on; secondly, a display of scholarly ornament; thirdly, perfection of literary style; fourthly, they must set forth aims, desires, and ambitions; fifthly, a *fu* must stir and exalt the emotions; and sixthly, it shall induce passion.'

"A great master of *fu* was the one-eyed Emperor Yüan, of the Liang Dynasty, who lived A.D., 508–554. He was doubtless a very learned man, as he possessed one hundred and forty thousand ancient books. He loved them so much that when he realized that his enemies were about to kill him, he set his library on fire and burnt them every one. Personally, I felt but very little sympathy with him. He is supposed to have expressed a hope that no earthenware *dogs* should be placed in his grave—saying, in a supercilious manner, '*Dogs* will not be able to guard my grave,' a man of but little imagination indeed. He seemed, however, to understand birds better than he did dogs if one can judge by the Mandarin Duck *fu* which Missuss sent her Friend."

Since I wrote I have had to make a flying trip up the coast, but am now back. Having made all arrangements for the summer for Papa's comfort, I came back one fine evening, to find the whole thing upset, as the doctor, under whose care he was to be, had been invalided home!! Knowing that one cannot do things satisfactorily by writing, I put my tooth brush in my bag and started off, on a couple of hours' notice, to Wei-Hai-Wei, a forty-eight hours' journey. Was able to settle matters. Of course there was no ship back, so I had to wait, and was away, in all, a week; most inconvenient!!

In another three weeks we are off up there for the summer. So far I have not succeeded in finding the teacher [Mr. Nung Chu, i.e., "Cultivator-of-Bamboos"] that I want; he is adrift somewhere in the country. But if I can't get him I shall take someone, and shall hope to have some good things to send you. Oh, dear me, I wish I knew more!! I read *so* slowly, and the whole thing is so dreadfully difficult that I can't pick and choose the way I should like. I have to depend too much on the teacher, and he, of course, often has the conventional Chinese point of view. Conventional views are *always* wrong.

Much love, yours always,

F. W. A.

What are you writing now? I am sure that your fertile brain is not at rest. The acting editor of the *China Press* here, a very clever young man, is much stirred by "Guns as Keys." He said that he thought he would write something about it and send it to you. I said I was sure that you would be interested. . . . .

SHANGHAI, CHINA, June 9, 1919

DEAREST AMY,

Herewith the Narrative Poem of which I wrote. I *wonder* whether you will be able to make head or tail of it. As I say, at the end of Analysis Pt. II, I will send the two poems referred to as soon as they are ready.

We are off to Wei-Hai-Wei, D.V., in a day or two, and I have my hands full. I have got the promising teacher of whom I wrote, so shall hope to do a lot.

Will write at length from there.

Yours ever,

FLORENCE AYSCOUGH

DEAR FLORENCE:

I have a lot of letters to answer, and I feel very guilty not to have sent this enclosed thing to you before; but the "flu" left me very weak and I had a lot of things to do, and, with one thing and another, they got put off. I did not answer Mr. Waley's strictures in *Poetry*[1] because I did not feel competent to answer him, but I think you could do it beautifully and I wish you would. It does not make any difference how many months after it appeared the answer gets in.

In the meanwhile, I have been working on "Once More Fields and Gardens" [p. 132], with your suggestions, and I send you the result. The alternatives I have written over the other lines, and you will easily be able to decipher them. You can see the changes from the old copy which you have. Please send it back to me marked with what you prefer; or, if there is anything wrong, what you want changed. I really think that if we go on now we ought to have a book pretty soon, and I think we ought to get one out within a year. It will be very good I am sure, and very much liked.

There has been a great deal of favourable comment about the eight poems we printed in *Poetry*.[2] They were reprinted in the *Literary Digest*, and one or two of them in various other papers. Why on earth did the *China Press* take "The Road to the Mountain" to reprint? That seems a singular poem to have chosen. I quite agree with you that it is not one of my best poems.

I am awfully sorry to hear that your father is so ill. The anxiety for you is terrible, and I realize perfectly your feeling about the horror of keeping a person alive when all real life is ended for him. Personally, I do not approve of it at all.

You will be going to Wei-Hai [-Wei] very soon, but I suppose that anything sent to Shanghai will always reach you. I will send you the new translations shortly. These things do not go as rapidly as I could wish, partly from press of other work and partly because they are fussy. So far as the "Li T'ai Po" thing is concerned, I will do my best to use some definite form, but I do not know. I will see how it goes. It is an awfully nice poem. I think we have beaten Waley all to smash on "Once More Fields and Gardens," which gives me some pleasure. I am absolutely in love with this "Li T'ai Po," but Lawks-a-massy, my dear, 'taint easy nohow. However, you shall have it somehow. God knows how.

[1] XIV, No. I (April, 1919), 55–56.   [2] XIII, No. V (February, 1919), 233–42.

I will send this off without writing any more, because it ought to go. Ada would send her love, but she is in Salt Lake City for two months, alas!

AMY LOWELL

WEI-HAI-WEI, July 8, 1919

DEAREST AMY,

We have been here for three weeks and more. My teacher [Mr. Nung], the one I wanted, came a little over a fortnight ago. He is a most interesting person, and I am enjoying studying with him very much. There is only one trouble—that is that he is *so* interesting, and has so many things to tell me, that I don't do as much definite work as I mean to. He is absolutely full of stories and tales of all sorts and kinds. He has had a most romantic story, and uses an assumed name. I have not time to-day to write it all out, but it is very strange. He is extremely well educated and knows his "books" down to the ground.

I have had some difficulty in making him understand what I am driving at, in the dissection of the character, but think that I have succeeded in knocking it into his head at last. You see it is hard to make a Chinese realize how very bald our translations are.

He is most keen about the intelligence of women, and is quite determined, I think, to make me see how much Chinese women have done and written. I said that Europeans were apt to think that Chinese ladies were not often considered as their husbands' companions or equals, and he is bound, I think, to convince me that this is a wrong opinion. Nearly every day he brings me a poem which is connected with some old story. It is fascinating, but there is a good deal of sameness in the stories, which are of harem favorites, deserted wives *et al.*, the sort of story that belongs to a state of society when thousands of women are kept in "captivity," as it were, on the chance of their giving pleasure to one man. I wish that you were here to consult with; I would like your opinion of some of them. They have not been published, that is, the poems have not. Some of the stories connected with them I knew. Do you think that a small portion of *The Book* could be devoted to them—the little poems with the stories?

The ones I send to-day, which are connected with Li Tai-po's poem of "The White Heads,"[1] are fairly representative, though some are longer and better—more important.

The teacher has a great scorn for very artificial poems, and those

[1] In connection with this see Cho Wēn-chün's "Song of Snow-White Heads," pp. 50–51, in Arthur Waley, *A Hundred and Seventy Chinese Poems* (London, 1918).

that are studied. He likes those by women because they come straight from the heart, and, to his understanding, carry conviction of real tragedy with them. I wish that you could hear him read them and explain them. He is most dramatic, vivid, and full of imagination; quite different from any teacher I have had anything to do with. Of course, when they are translated and when they have to be explained to the last degree, they must lose their spontaneity.

Sometimes, too, I feel that I am very stupid. If only you were here you would know what he is driving at. Of course, we have only been working together for such a little while that we do not understand each other's point of view as well as we shall do. He is now at work writing out one of the "Odes" in the original characters. It takes *forever*, as he has to hunt up the characters in a book which has no arrangement that can be dignified by such a name. He has been days over this one Ode, so, unless I find that the result is very illuminating, I shall not have him write out many. I expect it will be, though. The ancient characters are *fascinating*.

I must reply to Waley's criticism in *Poetry*, April. If you remember, those two lines which he criticizes worried me to death. The teacher says there is no ground for Waley to assert that T'ao Ch'ien was a *Taoist*, in contradistinction to a *Confucianist;* that, indeed, as he lived at home with his wife and had five sons, he cannot be said to have "dwelt with Huang [the Yellow Emperor] and Lao [Lao Tzu]"— which is a saying the Chinese have, meaning that a man leaves all his family ties to go to live in the hills as a "hill man." I will send you a corrected translation of the last two lines, and a little reply. This must go to post now; I do not want to delay it. I wish a letter might come from you. It seems years since I heard. Papa is much the same; things are running smoothly. Much love, yours ever,

FLORENCE AYSCOUGH

WEI-HAI-WEI, July 26, 1919

DEAREST AMY,

Herewith two little poems which I think make a nice contrast. I am becoming more discouraged than ever; it seems so utterly *impossible* to render, or rather to make clear to you, all that the poems contain. I wish you could hear (and understand) my teacher. Every character, every phrase, means a whole history to him, but when I try to write down what he says it seems to me that I fail utterly. He makes all those past days very vivid. I seem to be living, for a good part of the day, in a world of palace intrigue, deserted ladies, etc., *et al*. It is very fascinating. For the first time, I feel that I am making pretty good progress with the language—though, at intervals, I am more and more sure that I am really a "congenital idiot." It is so easy to forget.

We are at work still on the Ode of which I wrote last time; the pulling of the character to pieces is evidently *all important* in those older poems. I think that you will like it; but it is hard, and the hunting up of the ancient forms is very slow work.

Papa is about the same; goes out every afternoon, and is, mercifully, very cheerful. The nurses seem very nice.

Much love, my dear; I wish that I might hear from you. It seems at least a century since a letter came.

Yours ever,
F. W. A.

WEI-HAI-WEI, July 28, 1919

DEAR AMY,

Yours of June 12 reached me yesterday with the "Once More Fields and Gardens" [p. 132]. I enclose a copy with the readings I prefer, with one or two notes which are the result of discussing it with Mr. Nung, my present teacher. It is almost impossible to make the Chinese understand what we are driving at; while the ordinary sinologue thinks we are *mad*.

I am more convinced than ever that we are right, but I am also rather discouraged at the *impossibility* of conveying to a Western reader all that a Chinese poem conveys to a Chinese. Apart from the makeup of the character—which . . . . does not, literally, analyze itself to a reader of to-day—there is so much allusion suggested by the lines that one feels hopeless. To hear Mr. Nung tell one all that a poem means is enough to drive one to despair. Even if I wrote it all down we would not be justified in giving it as translation—as it is, most of it, not contained in the words written, but in the ideas suggested. A Chinese reading this poem would know (partly because he knows it anyway) that T'ao Ch'ien [pp. 132, 192, 215] had been in official life, had hated it, and had come back to the natural life of the fields.

I am so glad to have heard from you. It is most exciting. I wonder to which Li T'ai-po thing you refer. The "Songs of the Marches" [pp. 1–4] and the "Pavilion of the Two-Edged Sword" [p. 52] went on April 25.[1] I expect you mean the latter, especially as you refer to "form."

It is hot as the dickens. As I sit here the perspiration pours down

[1] See note on "Pavilion" to the letter of April 25, above, p. 62.

my person—forgive details. We have none of the luxuries of civilization such as electric fans.

Much love to both you and Ada, who is, I hope, back with you.

Yours ever,

FLORENCE AYSCOUGH

BROOKLINE, MASS., 29 July, 1919

DEAR FLORENCE:

In the first place let me humbly apologize for not having sent you this letter before. I trust that it does not contain anything of importance. How I came to lose it and leave it in the bottom of my wire basket for three months, I cannot see. Now I can only wipe the floor up with myself and beg you to forgive me. I will try not to let it ever happen again.

I am perfectly delighted with these poems that you have sent me of Li T'ai Po's. "The Lonely Wife" [p. 10] especially I think most beautiful, and I am sending you various versions to read and decide which you like best. As a matter of fact, there is one trouble, to my mind, in all these versions, and that is that I think perhaps rhythmically they are not particularly interesting. I could not follow your suggestions of having all the stanzas the same, and keep to the original, and I think it far more important to keep to the original than to give the rhythm. Looking back over my older translations, I see that I was much less exact then than I am now, but since reading Mr. Waley's criticisms of the one poem he knew in *Poetry*,[1] I fear that we shall have all the sinologues about our ears if we do not stick carefully to the original. Therefore, I think it is extremely important not to do any embroidering that the characters do not justify. This rather upsets my ideas, because it becomes necessary to sacrifice rhythm and appearance for exactness; but still, even as they are, these versions are attractive I think, and I wish you would go over them carefully and tell me just where you think they can be improved.

It is not very easy doing the thing so far away from you. I constantly want to refer to you and ask you little questions which are difficult to put into print; but perhaps you can get from these various versions something of the idea that a number of questions would give you. I have marked them preferred and alternative versions, but, as a matter of fact, even the preferred versions have various alternatives in them which will require going carefully over with your knowledge of the original to determine which of all the versions is the best.

[1] XIV, No. I (April, 1919), 55-56.

I have not received any answer to the new versions of "Return to Fields and Gardens" which I sent you on June 12th. I do not suppose there is yet time, and I am very sorry that I kept it so long. At this rate we shall be through in fifteen years, but I do think that the moment is ripe, and somebody will get ahead of us if we do not hurry. I will try to be quicker in returning the things to you in future. I am getting tremendously interested in Chinese things and am working up a Chinese story for myself to use in a new book I am writing in poetry, a sort of series of semi-legends, semi-folk tales, of different countries, and I have now the right to take everything out of the Harvard Library, and I am perfectly steeped in Chinese literature. I am quite as excited about it as you are.

Ferris Greenslet[1] said, the other day, that he would like to bring out the book; and, if the Macmillans do not take it, we shall at least have the best thing possible, a publisher who has invited himself to print the book. If you could get them to me a little more quickly I think it would be a good idea. I wonder whether that letter of mine was lost; I notice you always send duplicates. I think that I shall register these manuscripts in order to insure their reaching you.

I think that the new version of the "Songs of the Marches" [pp. 1–4] is extremely interesting, and I think that it makes a much better poem this way. It is practically done, but I do not wish to keep these others any longer while I tinker with it. The "White Heads" I am very doubtful about. It is immensely difficult to do, rather involved, and so full of native symbolism that I think it would require an enormous number of foot-notes, and I am really loath to attempt it. These long narrative poems are awfully difficult, and I do think that it would be better for us to stick to lyric poems and not try these long narrative poems at present. I think the lyric poems are more human and will be more understood, and if we make a success of these we can always go on to narrative poems in another volume. I am amused at the story, since it happens that I came across somewhere (I cannot remember where, possibly in Waley[2] and possibly elsewhere) the tale of the White Heads, and wrote out of my head a possible poem written by the first wife to her husband before he had absolutely gone off; in fact I do not think I knew that he did desert her entirely until after it was written. For amusement I will send it to you.

Now do these up quickly and send them back to me, and send me a lot more. I think we ought to have at least 150 for the book, and I

[1] Of Houghton Mifflin Company (see Damon, *op. cit.*, p. 755).

[2] See *A Hundred and Seventy Chinese Poems*, pp. 50–51.

think we have now exactly 30. There is one thing of which I am absolutely convinced, and that is that before the book appears in print you will have to come over here, for I dare not put it through the press with all the little questions that will come up if you are not here to settle them.

I am terribly sorry to hear this very sad news of your father, and only hope that the Summer will overcome your prognostications. It must be very trying for you as well as for him. I agree with you in thinking that it is a doubtful kindness to keep people alive after their interest in life has gone.

I will not write a longer letter now for I am anxious to have this go as soon as possible. Ada joins me in much love, and I am

Always lovingly,

AMY

[Holograph postscript:] I wish we could talk. I am perfectly *thrilled* over the work, and cannot get too much of it. But, oh, how I wish you were here! My Dear. I know so terribly little.

WEI-HAI-WEI, August 1, 1919

DEAREST AMY,

Not another poem for you to-day, I only want to say that I find that I have misunderstood one of the characters "T'ing." There are two of identical sound and tone. They differ in this way:

T'ing = a pavilion, kiosk, summer-house in the garden or on the hills—in fact all varieties of little pleasure houses.

T'ing = A *Courtyard;* the space between the *entrance* gate and the door of the house, or an inner court-yard, between two of the buildings. At the foot I draw a sort of ground plan of a Chinese house. This sort of a T'ing has no roof, and things are planted in it.

"Return to Fields and Gardens": Waley [*A Hundred and Seventy Chinese Poems*, (9), p. 78, l. 5] has: "At gate and courtyard—no murmur of the World's dust."

We have: "There is no dust in my summer-house,
There is no clatter beyond its clear windows."

The literal is: Hu   Door of house (not *outer* gate)
T'*ing* Courtyard
W'*u* Without
Chen Dust
T*sa* Clatter

"Courtyard in front of my house is without dust or clatter."

So both Waley and we are wrong. I am so sorry to have been such a dunce about it; but, truly, you cannot imagine how hard it is, especially when one's teacher speaks no English—so cannot see whether what one has written is correct or not.

In the poems of the Courtesans [pp. 145–56], No. 4, that of "Ch'in, the 'Fire-Bird with Plumage White as Jade,' Longs for Her Lover" [p. 146], Line 2, Character 2, T'ing. I have given you the same meaning "pavilion in a court-yard" (which of course I thought it was); it really is an *inner* court, where pepper trees grow. These trees are very plentiful in Shansi, and, as the scent is much liked, they are often planted in courts.

Forgive me. I can't remember giving it to you wrong otherwise, but will have a look. This must go to post. I do not want to delay as you may be sending "Return to Fields and Gardens" to *Poetry*.

Yours ever,

FLORENCE AYSCOUGH

WEI-HAI-WEI, August 9, 1919

DEAREST AMY,

I had the enclosed nearly done; so, as they have just come and told me that a ship is going, I have finished it up, and send it to you. I have a long letter of Chao Fei-yen's [the "Flying Swallow," pp. 184, 217–18] also. Am not sure whether it is worth a lot of work. Will send you a paraphrase so you can see, but cannot get that done to-day. I do like this one, don't you? Why [Herbert A.] Giles should speak of "friendship" in his version, I cannot imagine. *All* the allusions are to the love between Pan Chieh-yü and the Emperor [pp. 142, 217], which was of the most intense nature. To a Chinese this poem is full of feeling.

I have no time to write a letter so will say adieu. I wish I had six pairs of hands. It takes such a time to make the things even partially intelligible (?) to you that I get way behind. I have a whole portfolio full of poems half ready to depart.

Yours ever,

FLORENCE AYSCOUGH

Dearest Amy,

In *Poetry* for July, which has just reached me, there is a series of poems by a girl of eight. I wondered if it would be of any interest to send a poem by a small Chinese girl of seven written between A.D. 600–700, during the period when the Chinese throne was usurped by that most remarkable person, the Empress Wu[1] [Hou], upon whose example the late Empress Dowager [Tzŭ Hsi] is supposed to have fashioned herself. For twenty-one years she [Empress Wu] reigned supreme, everyone being in terror of her. I enclose a short memo. Hearing of the little Miss Hui who was celebrated for her poems, she ordered that the little girl should come to court.

Wu Hou was extraordinarily conceited, and, even in her old age, demanded homage of all sorts as though she were still beautiful.

You can see from the memo whether or not you like the things. It struck me that they might be apt.

Yours ever,
Florence Ayscough

Brookline, Mass., 16 August, 1919

Dear Florence:

I have so many things to write about that I hardly know where to begin. I am enclosing a revised version of the "Songs of the Marches" [pp. 1–4], which I think is ever so much better than Giles's version. The more I read Giles the more of an ass I think he was; or, rather, he did not have the feeling for the Chinese in the least, although he had lived in China so long. His translations give one not the slightest idea of the place. I speak as one who knows, for I have just finished *Strange Stories from a Chinese Studio* and also his *History of Chinese Literature*.[2] I think these "Songs of the Marches" go very well now, and I would not worry about notes. There will have to be some notes about all of these poems probably, for instance, explaining the significance of that portrait of P'iou Yao [i.e., Ho P'iao Yao, p. 2] in the Lin Pavilion. Please like my humorous touch in that! I do not think that short notes of this kind matter in the least.

It seems to me that I should pretty soon be getting an answer to my "Fields and Gardens" version; then we ought to go along swimmingly. But I am a little discouraged about the last things you sent. I do

---

[1] See *Fir-Flower Tablets*, p. 181, n. 23: "There was only one Empress, whose *title* [editor's italics] was *Hou*, and, if the wife of the preceding monarch were still alive, she was called *T'ai Hou*, or Greater Empress."

[2] See also H. A. Giles, *Chinese Poetry in English Verse* (London, 1898).

AMY LOWELL

A portrait presented to Florence Ayscough. Now in the Harriet Monroe Library of Modern Poetry at the University of Chicago.

not think they are possible or worth while, one or the other, with the exception of the one written by Wên Chün to Ssŭ-ma Hsiang Ju which Waley[1] did. That I think is good, but the others, and the tales, I do not think are appropriate. They would require too much annotation and I do not think we had better have any prose whatever in this book. If we are successful, we can go on to prose books later on.

Now here is the way it appears to me. The great poets of the T'ang Dynasty, particularly Li T'ai Po, are without doubt among the finest poets that the world has ever had. I am perfectly willing to shriek Li T'ai Po's fame to the winds of Heaven. He seems to me to rank second to none in any country in lyric poetry, and it seems to me as though Tu Fu were equally fine, and a number of these T'ang poets, as I keep coming across them, are remarkable. But, as a rule, the later people are not so good, not nearly so good; and as to those ladies' poetry which your teacher is attached to, they simply are not worth anything. I think that your teacher [Mr. Nung] is perhaps not the best you could have found for this particular purpose, for, from what you say of him, he appears to me to be a rather blasé person who is doing what so many blasé scholars are doing, trying to find something fine aside from the accepted paths, which attitude confers—or those kinds of people think it will confer—a sort of fame on the finder. So little is known of these Chinese poets that we had best stick to the beaten paths.

The best translation of all is Waley's, and he hardly gives anything of Li T'ai Po and, personally, considering how greatly you improve upon all of Waley's translations, I do not think it matters if we duplicate some of the things that he has used. The French translations are, on the whole, better than the English, but even they have not the peculiar flavour of the originals. Therefore, it comes down to the fact that any one who wants to know anything about Chinese poetry must read Waley or nothing, for in no other way can one get anything at all. Now that is exactly where our position comes in. We are to give other things from those Waley has given, and do those in which we duplicate his choice better than he has done them. We are to keep the Chinese flavour, but it is absolutely imperative that we pick out the best Chinese things to translate and do not spend our time wandering down bypaths, no matter how inveigling the bypaths may be. I think also that we cannot, in this book, go in for narrative things. They are too long and too complicated; and I do not see anything to stop us

[1] *Op. cit.*, pp. 50–51; see also H. A. Giles, *A Chinese Biographical Dictionary* (London and Shanghai, 1898), No. 1753, pp. 668–69.

from going on translating other books later, if this is successful and we feel inclined to do so. But, in this book, we must stick pretty closely to the best lyric poetry that China has produced, and do not let your teacher keep you away from the main track or we shall never be finished. I think you are so much interested in the whole subject that it is very difficult for you to keep single-minded along the line, but if this book is to be done at all before everybody else does it—for Chinese poetry is much in people's minds at present, largely owing to Waley—we must work hard and work quickly.

All those lyrics which I sent back a couple of weeks ago, by Li T'ai Po, are splendid. Now I do not say that we should stick entirely to Li T'ai Po. I should stick to the old classical masters in lyric poetry for they are exceedingly new and beautiful to the Western mind, and do not take anything second best, no matter how intriguing to the native taste. We cannot afford anything second best in this book at all.

I will do the Waley thing and send it to you in a little while. I do not think it worth while to do the others, because I do not think they amount to anything. The lady who sends word to her husband and then jumps off the parapet may convey something to the Chinese, but it conveys nothing to me any more than it did to you, and I think it is a complete waste of time to do anything with it whatever.

From what you tell me, I do not think that this teacher is as good for our purposes as the other was. My experience is that teachers are of three kinds: the best kind is the real genius, he does not usually teach for money and he is seldom found anywhere, so I think he may be discounted for our particular purpose; the second is the perfectly commonplace conventional man who allows himself to be turned over like a dictionary, and one can get out of him just what one would get out of a dictionary; he does not stand between one and the masterpieces; the worst kind is the would-be clever man with ideas of his own, who is too smart to follow the beaten track and not smart enough to know that the world's opinion is always right in the long run, he is constantly obtruding his personality and interpretations between his pupils and the books they are studying. From what you say of this new man, I think him exactly of this type; and from the things which you are doing with him, I know him to be that kind. Stick to the classics, Florence, and get back to your old teacher as soon as you can. Then, indeed, we can get ahead. Your new man may be absorbingly interesting, but he is holding up the book awfully, and I am getting so thrilled that I want to work at it and work hard.

76

I do not think we had better attempt any of the odes in this volume. They are too long and to me not as interesting. It is the lyrics and the human lyrics to which we want to cling, and the lyrics of the best poets that China has produced. Never mind if they have been done before fifty times; they have never been done well except by Waley, and that is all that need concern us.

By the way, I have been reading a most fascinating Chinese novel of the 16th Century. It is called *Yü Chiao Li* and is translated by Rémusat. I can imagine that in the original it must be extremely charming. Even in the translation, with most of the local colour taken out, it is very beautiful. Get hold of it in the original. We might possibly do it in English when we have finished our book of poems, but for God's sake, don't go off on it now.[1] Let's stick to our lyrics until we have translated two hundred of them. If your teacher objects to these remarks of mine, put it down to Occidental taste, but remain firm.

I am absolutely drowned in Chinese literature, all I can get in English and French translations, and I am beginning to understand a good many things that I did not understand before. For instance, your "tiger tallies" [p. 3] in the "Songs of the Marches" took the place of our wrist numbers. They were for the purposes of identification on return from the war, and, although nobody says so, I presume that when a friend died you took his talley home to his wife to prove that he really was buried up there in the desert of Gobi. What happened if the edges of his talley wore down so that it no longer fitted its other half does not appear.

By the way, the *lan* does seem to be an orchid; at least it is given as an "epidendral orchid" in the dictionary; namely, an orchid which grows on a tree (I thought they all did that). I am going to try and look for it in a botany and see if there is any other definition given. You can keep my "spear orchid" if you want to. It does not much matter. I doubt whether the word has an exact English equivalent. That is the worst of a good deal of this fauna and flora. There is nothing to match it.

As to your Phoenix, [i.e., Feng Huang, p. liii], the creature is entirely mythical. It is as much like a phoenix as it is like a pheasant, although it was probably originally taken from the silver pheasant. I think the usual translation as "phoenix" is as good as "firebird" as it had nothing whatever to do with fire in Chinese mythology. One cannot call it "pheasant" very well, and I rather think we had better stick to "phoenix" as it has begun to have a significance used that way.

[1] See Amy Lowell to Florence Ayscough, below, January 9, 1922.

77

Now, dear Florence, I must stop, for I want this to carry the "Songs of the Marches" to you at once. Be firm with your teacher, hold him strongly between your finger and thumb, and keep him to the classics. Never mind his chivalrous affection for the ladies. The ladies—and I hate to have to say so—are seldom worth bothering with; and do impress him with the fact that what is an old story to him is as new to us as though it were just written.

I do trust that your father is feeling better this Summer. Ada joins me in lots of love. In haste,

Affectionately,

AMY

P.S. You will notice that I have changed that bow shadow of the moon. I was a perfect fool about it before. Of course what it means is that the sickle shaped moon looked like the bright shadow of a bow. That there can be no such thing as a bright shadow does not matter in the least as it is a charming image. I think this whole version of the "Songs of the Marches" is a thousand times better than our first version, and I think you will agree with me here that the "Preferred Version" is far better than the "Alternative Versions." Lord, but I am excited over it!

[Holograph:] This is a weird looking letter, but my secretary left for her vacation tonight, and I think the anticipation of coming pleasure was a little too much for her. At any rate, she has left me this, and as it is now 2:30 a.m. there is nobody here to correct it. Of course I may be wrong about the teacher, but I do want the crackerjack Masters. A. L. I have left no room to speak of personal matters. . . . . What an odd world this is! I wish you were here; it takes such ages to get answers.

WEI-HAI-WEI, August 21, 1919

DEAREST AMY,

Herewith three little "Songs of the Courtesans" [pp. 145–46] which, as the teacher explains them, are rather fascinating. I don't quite see how you are going to manage them as "translation," but perhaps you can make paraphrases of them. The literal translation, to one who did not understand the allusions, would be bald—would it not? Whereas a paraphrase would be quite nice. Well, I must leave it all to you.

Yours ever,

F. W. A.

78

DEAREST AMY,

How I wish you were here to talk matters over. I am rather tossed up in my mind about these old songs that I am sending you. I mean as to whether you think it better to have these or whether you think that it would be better to stick to the more well known poetry? That, of course, is always there in the collections; these things are quite impossible to get at will. I mean, they are from all sorts of books and collections. My teacher happens to have them in his head and considers them very beautiful. I can get them from him and could not have them otherwise. They are the sorts of things that have not been translated, and give one very vivid pictures of the old Chinese life at Court, etc. In studying them I have gained an immense amount—but I want to know what you think of them.

I am doing some Li T'ai-po at the same time and will send you a couple of his poems next. One is my version of one which appears in [L. Cranmer-Byng's] *A Lute of Jade*—very different. One trouble with these love songs is that they take so much explanation in the way of a story, as it were. Perhaps if we had one part of the book devoted to them it would be nice? It would most certainly be new. I have just been struggling with a most passionate one. Got into very deep water —will send it to you when it is ready. It is *fearfully* difficult. I really did feel discouraged sometimes.

I will go on as I am doing for the present, sending you as much variety as possible. But, please let me know your opinion in regard to this matter, for the future. As I say, in the meanwhile, I am acquiring a great deal of knowledge that I could not have in other ways. It is strange; men do not write love poems, as a rule. I asked if Li T'ai-po had done so, and the teacher said "No." In that *tzǔ* to a deserted wife which I sent you, the words are supposed to be from a woman. He wrote many poems to a famous courtesan, Hsieh T'ao [p. xcv], but they are all as if written to a man. The more I read your rendering of "[Once More] Fields and Gardens" [p. 132], the more I like it. I am longing for the next to come.[1]

Yours ever,

FLORENCE AYSCOUGH

[1] For an analysis of the two poems of correspondence between Ch'in Chia and his wife, Hsü Shu, which were not included in *Fir-Flower Tablets*, see below, Appendix VII, p. 281.

DEAREST AMY,

You can imagine how absolutely *delighted* I was to receive to-day that glorious packet of really beautiful poems. As there is a ship going to-morrow, I set myself at once to peruse the "Lonely Wife" [p. 10] and enclose the result of my cogitation.

The time consumed in communicating is appalling. Just think— your letter, written July 29, reached me September 8! If your secretaries could keep an eye on when the "Empress" mails close (see *Transcript*), a good deal of time could be saved. They must be marked *per "Empress"* as the U.S. Post Office never sends them by Canada if it can help itself!! Another thing, please ask your secretaries to use thicker envelopes, linen-lined if the packet is large. The one that came to-day was hardly hanging together; in fact, I don't see how it arrived at all. The reason of duplicates is that if the ship goes to the bottom, a copy of the work is en route. Duplicates are better than registration, which in itself causes slight delay, and does not prevent shipwreck.

I am so perfectly delighted that you are keen; if only you could hear this teacher you would be keener than ever. He is a find and is as interested as possible. Since having him I am perfectly convinced that the character can and should be analyzed. I am having an interesting time arguing about it. Sir James Stewart Lockhart, [H.B.M.'s] Commissioner [of Wei-Hai-Wei] here, is a sinologue. I do not know how good he is, but his knowledge of the Classics is deep. Of course he will not *hear* of the possibility of doing such a thing. I had a long talk with him a few nights ago, and send you a copy of the letter I wrote him afterwards.[1] I also send a copy of the letter I wrote a Consular man [Mr. —later Sir—Herbert Phillips], who is here, with whom I had another discussion. In the latter letter I try to make clear the difference between his work and ours.

We are going to be slated, in any case, by the conservative sinologues, if we analyse one character or twenty, and I am quite ready to take the responsibility for this. You see, the method is absolutely new. In their eyes we could *never* be justified. (You say that we must be careful that we do not analyze characters unless we are justified.) The whole of the study—translation—of Chinese so far has ignored this point of origins. The sinologues declare that the ordinary Chinese scholar probably does not know the origins himself. I think they are

[1] See below, pp. 87–88.

largely mistaken in this; it is a matter of degree. That a highly educated man with a taste for poetry *does* realize the force of the origin, I *know*.

I wonder if my letter to Mr. Phillips will be intelligible to you. You see, [Chinese] being a monosyllabic language, the characters have come to be used in connection, and certain phrases have come to mean certain, definite, perfectly arbitrary things. Now, I do not for a moment suggest that in such cases one could *possibly* analyze the character. But *that* is not the poetic style: you remember I have said, again and again, that the style used varies with the use it is put to. Certain combinations—phrases of numerous characters—which are being added to every day, have become stereotyped; but these are not, except in a very limited sense—that is of two or, possibly, three characters—used *at all* in poetry. If I talk politics with the teacher, I have to turn continually to a dictionary called *New Terms and Expressions*. There are several such. If I am translating poetry, I never touch it. The business of Consular men is to keep in touch with this constantly changing language—the Japanese are helping to alter it—and not to bother about anything except the meaning of the characters *in combination*. A man just returned from the front told me that in the years he has been away the language has changed so much that he does not know where he is. He has had to come down here, have a teacher, and study six hours a day to try to get back to where he was before the War—not only in proficiency but in actual fact. It would do him no good whatever to use our method.

With poetry it is another story. Doubtless certain characters have come to be used in certain manners; there are ever so many "clichés" —as they are quite fresh to us, and very beautiful, there is no reason they should not be used—but the poet who originally used the character, in this certain sense, thought of its origin in choosing it. Of this *I am sure*. In any case, I am quite ready to stand by it—and the ratings will concern me, not you.

As I point out to Sir James, it is a question of *method*—not theory. The sinologues say, "You have no right to look at the origin of the character, to find your modification of meaning." Very well—that may be; it has not been done before, but the meaning I give will not be a theoretical one; it will come from the ancient form. No one can argue *that*. It is really a far more sure ground than the "meanings" one. For instance, in criticising us, Waley has come a far worse cropper than we did. Sir James absolutely *snorted* at his saying T'ao Ch'ien [pp. 132, 192, 215] was a Taoist!!—and utterly condemned his trans-

81

lation of the last two lines. Waley's poems [*A Hundred and Seventy Chinese Poems*] which I have compared with the originals show a certain lack of realisation. I do not think he can ever have been in the East.

But the last thing I want to do is to "throw bricks"—it is the *curse* of sinology. Waley has produced far and away the best translations so far—and I shall not waste my time in searching for, and pointing out, his "howlers"—as Sir James calls them. However, I will cite one or two to you: the "migrant bird" in the T'ao Ch'ien poem [No. 9, p. 77, l. 5]; his criticism of our translation; . . . . "The Autumn Wind" [pp. 48–49, l. 5]. Here he speaks of a "Floating-pagoda boat"—anything more utterly and entirely ridiculous cannot be imagined. A pagoda is a sacred edifice, of many stories, erected as an "act of faith"; a *lou chuan*, which is what the text reads, is simply a boat with a sort of house on it. When I told my teacher that he had translated *lou chuan* a "pagoda-boat," he—the teacher—nearly fainted.

I am sure you will agree when I say that I think it would be shocking waste of time to search out all the things one can criticise in Waley's book. He has protected himself by publishing no Chinese text. It means a fearful fag to look up all those poems in the originals. As they are really very lovely, and *very* Chinese in spirit, I don't see why one should—especially as one would rather not translate them over again. In the *Bulletin of the School of Oriental Languages*, he publishes a Po Chu-i poem in which he says a very absurd thing—so absurd that I felt obliged to obtain the original and compare it—but, as I say, do not, I pray, let us go in for brick-throwing. Let us calmly adopt our method (which, I reiterate, the sinologues will none of them look upon as justified) and stick to it. I don't suppose any of the men who do "practical work" know what on earth the origins are of the characters they are using.

The sinologues may disapprove our *method*, but they can have nothing to say in regard to accuracy of rendering. They may say: "The poet *never* had that in his mind when he used the character." We can say: "*How* can you prove it? *That* is the meaning of the character; it means *that* to an educated man now. *How* do you know that the poet didn't choose it because it carried the very shade of meaning he was searching for?" Why did poets, until the poetic language became more or less stultified—it has just occurred to me that in later years the clichés may have begun to pall, as with us—choose with such care certain characters? Why did they often alter even the wood blocks when the poems were ready to print? Because: in the body of the char-

82

acter they found their "overtone." Nobody has even attempted to give the force of the character, but I assure you the Chinese feel it.

Funnily enough, Sir James himself, after we had been arguing ardently for over two hours, gave me an awfully good peg on which to hang my argument. I said, "What character do you use for your name, Sir James?" He replied, "Lo—the prancing horse Lo" [i.e., in preference to some other of several "Lo" characters with less auspicious, or agreeable, meanings]. I said nothing!! The Chinese have a nice saying: "If it cannot be done, the only thing is—to stop."

Our idea is so foreign to their traditional method that it is hopeless to think for one moment that the sinologues (with the exception, possibly, of Mr. Hopkins) will entertain it for a moment. Nevertheless, I feel perfectly calm about it. We will produce poems that are far more beautiful, and that give the Chinese spirit far more faithfully than do any of these others. Believe me, we *will*. Chinese poetry is magnificent. Shall we be the people to reveal it?

If only you could come out for a bit. Why can't you come this winter? Nothing *I* can say will give you the spirit of China. If you could only *see* it, then you could visualise so much better the "camel-backed" bridges, etc. I can't offer to put you up, as, with Papa and two nurses in the house, there is not a corner available, but I can make some not too impossible arrangement. We could do so much. One of my great difficulties is that of choice. If you were here to help, it would be so much simpler. It takes just as long to translate a poem that cannot be rendered, as one that can. I feel so confused: I can see the beauties in the original, but sometimes I cannot make up my mind whether or not I had better even *try* to make it comprehensible. You have often spoken of coming to the East: why not come now? I feel that you, Mr. Nung, and I could do—great things.

As far as the method is concerned we must either stick to it and make the most of it, or give it up. We damn ourselves just as much in the eyes of the sinologues by rendering "whirled water of meeting streams" [p. 132] as if we forced upon them the most utter "piffle." If you want to stick to the accepted meaning, you must just say "pool," "expanse of water," or something equally far from the real character.

The character *su* in the Pan Chieh-yü denunciation of the theory that she had been talking to the demons about the Emperor [p. 142], is one of the best examples. *Su*, the character in common use (Giles, 2nd edition, No. 10,357) means: To tell; to inform; to state; to lay a plaint; to accuse. It is composed of words, and a figure which means a repeated attack with a staff. *Su* (Giles, 10,365), used by Pan Chieh-yü, is composed of the heart, and a figure which is the moon refusing to receive the light of the sun. This figure, *shuo*, is used for the first day of the month when there is no moon visible and means northern—which is a synonym of darkness. The meaning of the *su* used by Pan is something very, very secret, kept in the darkness of her heart. Giles simply says "same as 10,357." In the rare cases that it is used in despatches, and such things, it probably has the same meaning as 10,357. *But it is not at all the same, really,* and when I told the teacher what Giles said, he simply shrugged his shoulders. I think that if you had a look at Giles, you would understand what I mean in what I am going to say below about phrases. Of course it would be at Harvard. John Lodge has one in the Art Museum. Be sure you look at the 2nd edition.

Our position, stated briefly, is this:

We have the Chinese characters which are divided into six categories. See Giles 7,276. 1. Pictorial. 2. Indicative or self-explaining. 3. Suggestive compounds (these give ideas). 4. Deflected. 5. Adoptive. 6. Phonetic. For our purpose we think principally of Nos. 1 and 3.

In translating, the dictionary-makers have adopted the nearest English *equivalents* that they can find. I use the plural as the sense of the character varies in the combination in which it is used. If you look at the lists of phrases given, you will see what I mean.

It is the *shades* of meaning of these phrases used in different combinations which the sinologues argue about so heatedly. They quote the Classics at each other endlessly.

These phrases: this method of translation does not concern us—the poet can't use phrases, except in quite a limited sense. He is restricted to a definite number of characters for each line and cannot waste a single one. He must use his pigments very carefully.

Now, we argue that Western readers should be shown a picture painted as nearly as possible with the same pigments that the Chinese poet has used. It is absurd for the Sins (I must abbreviate) to say that the Chinese don't realize at all—when they, in their art, their literature, and, really, in their everyday life are perpetually playing with the elements of which the characters are composed. I have a poem now which I don't think I can manage as so many of the allusions are a play on words using half the girl's name; this half means to pluck.

Mind you, the *method* of application that we are using is what the Sins won't admit. It seems to me they are going to find themselves in rather a difficult place: if they admit anything, they ought to admit the whole. *Tan* is the moment of sunrise; as you see, the sun is appearing over the horizon.—I think even a Sin would admit that.—Well, if you can find an exquisite phrase that will bring this picture vividly to the Western reader's eye, should you not do so? Our word "sunrise" connotes the red glow before, the light afterwards: the whole business. *Tan* really means the *moment* of rising. After that comes *Tsao*, the sun is the height of a helmeted man; it is now used in a loose manner for "early." After that comes *Jih*, sun, i.e., day. In talking of day one generally says *pai jih*, "white sun"; the poet contents himself with *jih*—that is, as a rule. It is less wasteful.

The teacher himself reminded me to be sure to use *chih*, to arrive (a bird dropping to earth), when talking to Sir James. I said to him, the teacher: "In reading, do you see it?" He replied, "Of course—although now I don't pay any attention to it. It is like this, the first time your little dog[1] came into the room, I looked to see what was coming; now he comes and goes continually. I know what it is and pay no attention. So it is with a character; at first, I carefully analyse it; then—afterwards—it is there." Can you find a better simile for subconscious? Even I, with my slight knowledge, see the characters I know pull themselves apart before me.

I propose that we give as many concrete examples as possible in a sort of index. For instance: *Yuan*, a whirlpool; (analysis) water, and a figure of meeting streams. [Miss Lowell's rendering: "the whirled water of meeting streams."] Then, we should have one plate of one of the odes written in the ancient character, that people may see how pictorial it is. I want the poets, and the people who love beautiful things, to say, "Now, for the first time, we can see how beautiful Chinese poetry is!!" As for the Sins, I don't exactly see what they can say. If they admit the "sunrise" for instance (and I know they won't—though I don't see how they can help it), then the rest must follow.

Of course, we must not let the analyses interfere with the sense, in any possible way—it must only make the whole thing more *vivid*. In future it might be a help if I mark the characters which I think it important to analyse—and I will make the analyses more clear. . . . .

When it comes to classical allusion—that is the very devil. As the poet can't use passages and phrases, he makes these allusions in a

---

[1] I.e., Yo Fei (see *The Autobiography of a Chinese Dog*).

character or two, and it is impossible for anyone not a classical scholar to realise. That is the reason it is so important to have a highly educated Chinese to help one. This classical allusion happens more in the highly artificial, very "scholarly" poems. It could not be in a thing like a *tzŭ;* and we will, if you please, avoid these. Sir James helped me there inasmuch as he pointed out an allusion which had been missed in the last line of "The Emperor Returns" [p. 152]. I don't blame myself as I make no pretensions to being a classical scholar, but I simply can't imagine how Dr. Darroch's writer, whose advice was asked, missed it. It must be altered, and will be an improvement. But I won't stop now to explain.

I send you, though I really hesitate to do so, the last [Vol. L (1919)] *Journal of the North China Branch, Royal Asiatic Society,* with the page [228] turned down where the critique of our work appears. It is so *hopeless.* Evan Morgan, who wrote it, is, I suppose, quite one of the best Sins of the day; his knowledge of poetry is, however, non-existent. When he argues about rhyme, it is so asinine!! Unless one could write in five or seven monosyllables, one could not give the same effect as the Chinese: Cat, dog, pig and hen. Each is friend of men!! Isn't that handsome! Can't you please write a poem, several lines of monosyllables, either five or seven words to the line, each alternate line to rhyme? It would be a jolly good example of what a faithful rendering of Chinese technique would be.

Oh, if only it were possible for you to come out!!! We might produce something very fine.

I agree that I must try to be in the U.S. when the book goes through the Press. But we are losing so much time now; and even if I were not tied as I am it would do no good for me to come; besides, if you could *see* things it would be such a help. I think you would be not *too* uncomfortable, but of course travelling is not comfortable—there is no gainsaying that.

I am so thankful that you are still keen; when things didn't come I began to feel that perhaps something else had filled your mind to the exclusion of this.

It is strange to feel as calm and as confident as I do about flying in the face of all the accepted ideas, but I *do;* I *know* we are right. I promise you I will not give you an incorrect analysis, and working with this man is utterly different to working with anyone else, as far as meaning is concerned. He has an extraordinary way of explaining. It seems to me that whenever we can add to the vividness by dissecting a character we *ought to do it*. That is the picture which is there for the Chinese to see, if he knows enough. Unless we give it to him, how can the European, be he never so learned, see it?

Very excitedly and ever affectionately,

FLORENCE AYSCOUGH

I have just read my letter to the teacher. He says be sure to point out about *Chou* (see "The Lonely Wife" [p. 10]). One has only to glance at it to see the meaning. An autumn heart!! What is that? Is not autumn the saddest of seasons: no flowers, all the leaves falling off the trees, everything dying. What could be sadder? Why, in autumn everyone feels very sad. Autumn, is as I tell you, "grain and fire": ripe grain burnt, dry and lifeless, as if in fire.

F. W. A.

[Enclosure]

WEI-HAI-WEI, September 7, 1919

DEAR SIR JAMES,

Herewith the T'ao Ch'ien Poem, and the unfinished draft. The Commentary says that the 30 in the fourth line should be transposed to read 13. This holds with what one knows of T'ao Ch'ien's official life for which it gives chapter and verse.

It is very nice of you to be interested, and, as you are, I hope that you won't mind if—at the risk of boring you—I supplement some of the things I said last night.

Method.—In leaving, you said that you did not agree with my "theory." If you do not mind, may we please change the word *theory?* That suggests that an uncertainty exists. If I said that because I thought the character resembled two sheaves of ripe grain held in people's hands, I intended to analyse it in translation, I should call that a theory. As there is no argument on this point (it *is* a picture of the sheaves), and as there is no gainsaying the fact that the origin of the Chinese language is ideographic, it does not seem to me correct to say that you do not agree with my theory. What you disagree with is my *method* (and, mind you, I do not expect for one 100th part of a second that you will agree)—that is, my use of the ideographic form in order to convey to the Western reader, some of the marvellous vividness of Chinese poetry.

Translation.—In the making of English dictionaries in general use (with the exception of Baller's), the composition of the character has been largely ignored. In K'ang Hsi many of the original forms are given, so if the Chinese student chooses he can quite easily and quickly realize an origin—which is not the case with the European student. Very few Europeans have bothered much about the structure of the character, and those who have, like Chalmers, Chalfant, Couling, and Hopkins, have confined themselves largely to research work. I think I am right, therefore, in stating that, for practical purposes in translation, the origin of the character has largely been ignored.

Chinese Poetry.—The outstanding features of Chinese poetry are its astound-

87

ing vividness, and its infinite suggestion. Four lines containing a handful of characters bring before one's mind, with an amazing intensity, unforgettable scenes, or wring one's heart with poignant emotion. How is this result accomplished? By simile, of course, and, *very largely*, by the choice of character. (I entirely agree with Waley who, in the most excellent preface to his *170 Chinese Poems*, remarks that Classical allusion is the vice of Chinese poetry.)

Translations of Chinese Poetry.—What should be the aim of the translator? I think it should be to render as *vividly*, as *faithfully*, and as *beautifully* as possible the thoughts of the author. You entirely agree with me that a poet should render the poem. If, some day, a poet with a knowledge of Chinese appears—why—it will be magnificent; so far this has not occurred. Waley seems to me the nearest approach. What I am trying to do is to provide Miss Lowell with the pigments which will enable her to paint, as nearly as possible, the pictures painted by the Chinese poets that Western readers may see them. Why should that reader not have the benefit of the shades of meaning brought before the Chinese reader? . . . .

You argue that if one character is analysed, all should be. Of course they all can be reduced to their elements, but in many cases (especially in the names of birds, beasts and flowers) the phonetic has a purely phonetic function. One must use one's common sense, and I am fully aware that there are many pitfalls on the road I have chosen to explore. I am willing to risk a good many bruises, however, to obtain beautiful phrases such as Miss Lowell's "whirled water of meeting streams," "calm with the leisure of moonlight through an open door," etc. (which are absolutely literal), and such lovely bits as "From the Straw Hut among the Seven Peaks" (those two little poems in *Poetry* which I lent you), which are like some of your lovely paintings.

My attitude can, indeed, be explained in one sentence: I do not claim that all characters can be analyzed to advantage, but I consider that those which can be, especially in translating poetry, *should* be.

You must be exhausted. I will spare you more. Please don't think that I am asking you to approve my method, or to agree with me. I only (as you are so kindly interested) wanted to express a few thoughts that came to me after you had left, and have therefore written this very lengthy letter.

I do not see Mr. Nung on Sundays, so cannot ask him about the jade until tomorrow.

Yours ever sincerely,
FLORENCE AYSCOUGH

DEAREST AMY,

I am involved in controversy—and send you a copy of a letter which I wrote this morning. These Chinese scholars are most *difficult*. Sir James Stewart-Lockhart is a well known sinologue; how *good* he is I do not know. That he is absolutely without a poetic instinct I do know.

Yours,
F. W. A.

WEI-HAI[-WEI], September 12, [1919]

DEAR AMY,

I find that I left off the last line of the "Lonely Wife" [p. 10]. It was careless, but I was working against time to catch the ship, and, as it was perfectly splendid and didn't need any alteration, I suppose I felt that I had reached the end of what I needed to do. It was not until I was re-reading it that I noticed it. No time for more to-day.

Yours ever,

F. W. A.

WEI-HAI-WEI, September 14, 1919

DEAR AMY,

Please read this letter before looking at the enclosed poems. I want to give you an instance to show you (if you are in need of such a demonstration) what an extremely difficult thing we have undertaken to do—viz, to show the West how beautiful Chinese poetry really is.

First, let me speak to you of my teachers.

When the Compradore's[1] scrolls fell into my hands, I was working with a teacher from the Chamber of Commerce Language School; he at once frankly said that he knew nothing about such work as translating scrolls and would not undertake it. The man I did the work with was found through the chief "Writer" at the [British] Consulate, who is a highly educated man. He—the man, Hsieh by name— was not at all interesting to work with; for one reason he himself was so bored. However, we worried through, and I had a good deal of outside help. When I returned to Shanghai last September, I began again a search for a teacher, not wanting Hsieh. None of the Sins I asked was able to recommend anyone. I did get a man for a month or two; he was not much use. Then the Siberian [war] work came up and I was obliged to stop for the time being. When I wished to begin work again in March, after having tried, unsuccessfully, to find the right man from all the Sins I know, I went to the [Tung Wen Kwan] Translation Office run by [Charles] Budd, feeling that, although his English poems[2] were very bad, he must have had a scholar who knew poetry to get them out of the Chinese. In a day or two he sent me a man called Tang who was evidently a very learned person. We began to work. He was infinitely better than any of the previous ones had been. One day he remarked that he knew Evan Morgan (who, as I

[1] See *Firecracker Land Pictures of the Chinese World for Younger Readers* [of All Ages] (New York, 1932), pp. 100, 102.

[2] *A Few Famous Chinese Poems* (Shanghai, 1911).

have told you, is one of the leading Sins of the day), so I asked Mr. Morgan about Tang. He replied, "Oh, a very fine scholar, very fine indeed, a *real* scholar." I felt quite happy; I knew that *he* often asked Tang's advice—and so had no qualms myself; indeed, I think Tang is a very fine scholar, real "old school." I worked with him till I came up here, doing the "White Heads,"[1] the "Lonely Wife" [p. 10] the "Two-Edged Sword," [p. 52], etc., with him.

When I had asked Dr. Darroch (a well known scholar) about a teacher, he had said, "There is one man only [Mr. Nung Chu] whom I know, who would do what you want, and he, I think, would be just the person. He lives in Nanking, not Shanghai, and may not be available now, I will try to find him." In the course of time he found him and he is the man who is here now with me, and, as I have told you, work with him is an entirely different proposition to what it has ever been before.

I have been so lengthy as I have wanted you to realize that I have done my best to get a suitable teacher *all along*—and that it is an *extremely difficult thing to do*. Even good scholars do not, of necessity, know poetry, any more than good writers with us can write poetry. Now, I am coming to the point of my story.

The other day your packet of "renderings" came. I handed Mr. Nung the Chinese text that afternoon, when he left me, that he might be prepared the next morning. We began; did the "Lonely Wife" [p. 10] with comments as I have sent you.—I then took up "The Pavilion of the Two-Edged Sword" [p. 52] and began to translate to him your rendering.—He looked very much puzzled. When I reached the third line, he said, "But there is no gate, the 'Chien Men' is the name of the Mountains.

"Well," I replied, "is the Pavilion (i.e., *Ko*, then, as I thought, a Pavilion) up among the peaks?"

"The *Ko*," he answered, "does not mean here a Pavilion; it means a road."

"Road?" I said, "*Good heavens!*" and hurriedly turned up Giles, No. 6037, which gives no hint of such a meaning. "But what do you mean?" I asked. My teacher drew me a picture of the whole thing, and I hastily sketched him the picture which I sent you. I shall never forget his face. He got up and went over to the table on which the *Tzu Yuan* stands (this is the encyclopaedia which gives "The Origins of Expressions") and turned up the several references which I send you. Although you have a vivid imagination, I do not think it is

[1] Waley, *op. cit.*, pp. 50–51.

possible for you to realize the utter dismay I felt. It was as though all the breath had been knocked out of my body—not so much from the point of view of the poem, as it is not difficult to alter and will be one hundred per cent better, when it is read with the real meaning—no, what made me feel so flabbergasted (it is the only word strong enough) was the thought of *you*. Of how you would feel, in thinking that such a terrible misreading could possibly occur, of how your faith might quite easily be shaken, of how you might feel "I cannot trust her"!! I cannot blame myself; there was no *possible* way of my knowing that this very special road was called *Ko*. The usual name is *Chan Tao*. As you see, Giles gives no hint of its being used *ever* as a "road." How to excuse Tang—is difficult. The commentary, which I distinctly remember his reading, does not point out that the Chien Ko is a road because, as Mr. Nung says, "The Commentaries do not tell people the things they *should* know." My only theory is that though Tang is a fine scholar, he has not made a special study of poetry and can, therefore, miss points—not that one can call this exactly "a point."

Well, I have now given you chapter and verse for *Ko*, and also enclose you a picture of the sort of mountain scenery that is so often described in Chinese poems, with a sort of little dictionary accompanying it. I wish it were larger. I can buy nothing here and have taken this out of a book I had. I hope that it may be a help. I am not going to waste space and energy in saying "I am sorry"; it would be so futile. You must know that I am utterly disgusted. I don't know what the expression of my face must have been, but, after we had thrashed the thing out, Mr. Nung said, and he took up the edge of his coat, pulling it tight, as an illustration: "People's minds are like cloth; if you stretch them too tight they—crack, or rip, you must relax"—he let the bit of cloth fall together—"I will tell you an amusing story."

RETURN TO FIELDS AND GARDENS [P. 132]:

There is one line in our rendering that worries me. It is:

"Elm Trees, from which little boats are fashioned."

In my own opinion, charming as the line is, we are *not* justified in using it. I feel sure that "the little boat" part of the character has a purely phonetic function, and that we are not adding in any way to the vividness of the poem by using it. I have always been uncertain about it, and, the more I think of it, the more I study, the more sure I feel that my doubts were reasonable. You see, the names of plants, trees, birds, beasts, etc., have been arrived at thus: the plant, tree,

91

bird or beast has originally been called by a certain sound; the man who wished to write down the name of the plant, etc., chose a character of a certain sound and joined it to the "grass," "tree," "bird," or one of the "beast" radicals. Sometimes it seems as though they had been influenced in their choice of character by something except sound, but as a rule not. (I enclose some examples which I hope may be comprehensible to you.) Now, I am unable to discover that elm trees have any real connection with boats—the phrase certainly does not serve to intensify T'ao Ch'ien's picture of his country home. In my opinion it should not be used. Mr. Nung shrugs his shoulders and says: "I consider it is to be avoided. There is no use in opening a door through which people can enter to attack you." Strangely enough Mr. Morgan was inclined to admit it, and that was the reason I left it in, in sending the poem back to you. Upon mature consideration, however, I feel that it should not be used. After all, the method is ours, and we must use it as we consider logically. I remember that I, perhaps rashly, said that you might publish "Return to Fields," etc., without sending it back. I hope you, in your wisdom, have held your hand, especially as I made the assinine mistake about *T'ing.*

Oh, Lord! It is a difficult task. The other day I said, despairingly and rather fiercely, to Mr. Nung: "You don't *know* how difficult it is to translate the——!" He answered, rather sadly, and very gently: "We have been working together every day, and you think I do not *know?*"

I enclose a note *re* "Ch'in Ch'ia,"[1] for your private edification. Other people's mistakes are helpful. I still stick to my idea, however that there is no point in "brick-throwing." Let someone else point out our superiority. I hope that your friend, Mr. Lowes, will write something illuminating. When you get a chance you can tell him of these "howlers"—if you think it wise.

The scene, mountain scene, which I am sending you, will, I think, be helpful in future. When I want to tell you what a thing is, I will refer to a number.

Yours ever, with much love,

F. W. A.

I just want to add that in the nice name which you are going to make for Hsien Yang, I think it would be best to call it the Capital, or City of —— what-ever-you-decide-upon. It had better not be too long, and we had better always use it. Then, perhaps, Hsien Yang will come to mean that to people in the future. Someone once christened the

[1] *Ibid.*, p. 53.

MOUNTAIN SCENERY OF THE TYPE OFTEN ALLUDED TO BY
CHINESE POETS

KEY TO PICTURE OF MOUNTAIN SCENERY IN CHINA

1. *Tien* = The topmost peak of a mt.
2. *Wei* = Approaching the peak, very high, not level
3. *P'u* = A water-fall.
   Fei Ch'uan = Flying Water
   P'u Pu = Cloth cascade—that is, water like a strip of cloth. These three all mean water-fall, cascade
4. *Feng* = Peaks
5. *Hsuan Yai* = Over-hanging precipice
6. *Luan* = Peaks which are lower than *Feng* and sharper
7. *Ch'uan* = Spring. Of course, one can't see in the picture where the spring really is.
8. *Shan Lin* = Forests on the mountains
9. *Shan Shih* = Temples on the mountains
10. *Yai* = A Cliff, both its flat top and its side
11. *Chan Tao* = The road, highway, or throughfare on the side of a cliff
    Ko = The road, highway, etc., up which you see the travellers are going
12. *Shan Ting* = A pavilion in the hills
13. *Tien* = An inn; also a collection of houses and little shops where things can be bought
    Ko Yo = Inn, hotel.
14. *Lien* = A flag, or sign, which shows that wine is sold; you can see one is flying from the *Tien*
15. *Lan* = Mountain mist or vapour which makes the bottom of the far off peaks indistinct.
16. *Kang* = High level ground on a hill, or, rather, among hills
17. *Chia* = The steep side of a hill; Mr. Nung describes it as the *thigh* of the hill, the part that a *Chan Tao* or *Ko* would be built against
18. *Lu Ko* = Travellers, who are on a long journey
    Cheng Jen = Travellers
19. *Chi* = To ride (a horse, a mule, a donkey)
20. *Ling* = A pass in a mountain range. Mr. Nung wanted me to be careful to warn you not to think that the bottom of the picture is level ground. The picture is painted from a point high among the hills, so one looks down to a pass.
21. *Che* = Cart; this one is being pushed by a man.
22. *Sun*
    Lan Yu } = A carrying chair, made of bamboo for use in the mountains
23. *Chien* = Water in a ravine
24. *Ku* = Gully between hills
25. *Ho* = Pool at the foot of a water-fall

I hope and feel that this key . . . . will be a help to you. The type of scenery is that principally described in Chinese poetry, and painted in their pictures. From the descriptions of people who have been to Szechuan, neither poetry nor pictures are at all exaggerated. The roads, *Chan Tao* or *Ko*, exist and are used to-day. The idea of them is to make a short cut, a throughfare through the hills. I wonder what nice name you will make for them.

Feng, "phoenix," which worries me so, and it has stuck. Our "Crested Love Pheasant" is much nicer and truer. In Williams' dictionary he gives for the *Feng* the following: "the type of this bird seems to have been the argus pheasant, which has been gradually embellished and exaggerated." See in the *Journal of the North China Branch, Royal Asiatic Society* which I sent you last week, page 26, a description of this bird. I think that the whole article we shall find useful. Let us always call the *Feng* the "Crested Love Pheasant."

F. W. A.

WEI-HAI-WEI, September 26, 1919

DEAREST AMY,

I have no time for more than a line. It has been a week of perpetual upsets. Papa has had "attack" after "attack." We have decided to try to move him back to Shanghai on a boat which calls in here to fetch mules for India. She is a liner and, so, larger than the coasters. She has a doctor on board which helps with the responsibility. . . . .

I send you two Li T'ai-po's. There will, I fear, be an hiatus now for a bit.

Yours in haste, boxes, nurses, tips, bills, etc., etc., etc.

F. W. A.

[SHANGHAI], October 3, 1919

DEAREST AMY,

We are just back from Wei-Hai[-Wei]—chaos reigns in the [Wild Goose Happiness] house[1] with building operations [for the invalid and the nurses], which are not finished, we having returned sooner than we intended. Papa and his nurses are at Geoffrey's. How he goes on living is a mystery—he was miserable all the voyage down, and had a bad attack this morning. As you can imagine, life is fairly complicated. All one can do is to live from day to day. I hope I shan't "jack up"; thought I was going to last night; the strain is more trying than I can possibly describe. There is nothing to be done.

I found yours of August 16, and was especially glad to have it, as it answered various questions that I was going to ask; so we have saved a lot of time. I won't stop to ask them but will simply say that I have come to exactly the same conclusion you have—that the best thing to do is to stick to Li T'ai-po—and possibly Tu Fu. I have a lot of the

[1] I.e., *Hung Fo Zah. Hung* "means primarily wild goose. Because the wild goose is the bird of limitless spaces, it means limitless or great. Thereupon . . . . the name of our home became 'Wild Goose Happiness House' " (see *Firecracker Land*, pp. 30–32).

former's in hand. I am glad you tell me that you think we had better not go in for narrative now. In fact, since your letter came, I feel quite definite. I am glad, too, that you say you do not think it matters if we do things that have been done before; it is quite true that most of the translations are—parodies. If I could read Chinese sufficiently easily to take up a volume of Li T'ai-po's, for instance, and run things through, in order to make my choice, it would help—but I can't. If, also, the translators would use the proper titles, it would help. But they don't, as a rule. If one reads in translation something that seems quite charming, it is extremely difficult to find it, unless it happens to be very well known to the man one is working with, and one can make him remember it from the very poor translation before one. I don't suppose it is possible for any one to imagine how awfully difficult the whole thing is. Sometimes I want to tear my hair!! But I do love it. You are quite right—I am so interested in the whole subject that it is hard for me to keep single-minded—but I will do so.

In regard to the teacher;[1] you are wrong. This one is not a bit blasé —far from it. He is as keen as possible. And, now that I have managed to make him see what we are driving at, I think he will do what we want. I fancy that after you receive my reply to the "Pavilion of the Two-edged Sword" [p. 52], you will not want me to have the Old Thing back!! One thing I could not induce the Old Thing to do was to consult the *Tzu Yuan*, which is an extremely good book of reference, published lately. He, being of the most rigid, old type, scorned it—because it was modern. Thank heaven, Nung will turn to it whenever there is any doubt about anything. It is most useful. As soon as he returns from Nanking (if he can be induced to come down for the winter; it is still uncertain), I will ask him about the "tiger tallies." I very much doubt if they were given to all the troops. Where did you get your reference?

The "lan" [p. lvii] does not grow on trees; the best come from mountains in Fukien. It is grown in pots. I always have some, and always go to an exhibition or two of them during the year. There are many varieties. I believe that there is an autumn variety, and will try to see if that differs from the usual one. The usual one is that referred to as a rule in poetry; it has the most *exquisite* scent, so subtle and refined. I like your "spear orchid." As you say, there is no equivalent in English.

The *Feng* [p. 21, see also pp. 10, 180, 188, and liii–lv]: I like your "silver-crested love pheasant" immensely. You are quite right in say-

1 *Ibid.*, pp. 32–35 *et passim.*

95

ing that the *feng* has no connection with "fire." But, you see, in the *tzŭ* of "The Lonely Wife" [p. 10], the poet is not referring to the *feng* (when I translated "a bird connected with fire" line 1, stanza 2) but to the *luan* [p. lv], quite another affair. My Giles is not unpacked, so I cannot give you the number of the character. I will next time as you can then see how often it is used in phrases referring to marriage, etc.

Luan and *Feng* are embroidered on wedding quilts [p. 10] etc. The *Feng* and the *Huang*, its mate, are not used in quite the same way, though they do refer to "seeking a mate."

The "Songs of the Marches" [pp. 1-4] read really beautifully. I have not had time to compare them with the original, and shall not return them until I have been able to go through them with Mr. Nung.

I have learned a very great deal this summer, and shall be able to work more quickly and definitely now. I quite realize the need of haste—but, Amy, do you know how devilishly hard it is? Oh lord, if only I had a greater command of Chinese!! I sometimes feel that nobody in the world knows as little as I do!

This shall now be closed as an "Empress" mail goes to-day. I will try to prepare an enclosure—but if it is not there it will be because I shall have been called away to see the steam heating man—and the man who is to make an alteration in the drawing-room. I have already, to-day, had the architect and the electrician—and the others are coming.

The mails are so *very* bad because there have been quarantine regulations on account of cholera. All mails are transhipped in Japan—to be dealt with as the Japanese think best. It causes appalling delay. . . . .

Love to both your dear self and Ada.

Yours,

FLORENCE AYSCOUGH

SHANGHAI, October 15, 1919

DEAREST AMY,

I had translated this poem ["Hearing the Early Oriole," p. 119] of Po Chu-i's as I wanted to see if it were possible that a Chinese poet made such a mistake in Natural History as to say that an oriole sat on a roof. As you do not think it matters if we have some poems already done by other people, I have finished it up, done the analysis, and send it to you. I think that by analysing the dawn and dusk you can make the poem much better; to say nothing of some of the other characters.

Absolute chaos still reigns in the house, and the smell of paint is enough to turn one upside down. I hope that another week will see it through, but when I contemplate the amount of energy I have got to expend in getting the "hospital" running—my heart fails. . . . .

Yours ever,

F. W. A.

[SHANGHAI], November 22, 1919

DEAREST AMY,

Your book [*Pictures of the Floating World* (New York, 1919)] has just arrived, and I am delighted to have it. There are ever so many things in it that I have not seen before, and there has not yet been time for me to take it in a bit completely. The Lacquer Prints are— *remarkable;* you seem to have caught the atmosphere of Japan (that unpopular little kingdom) absolutely.

The Chinoiseries I do not care for. They do not "connote" China. That is, several of them do not. For instance: in "Reflections"— "tinkling pagodas" are never in gardens; they are sacred edifices and are near temples or tombs. Both "Falling Snow" and "Hoar-Frost," are charming, but "Gold-Leaf Screen" does not suggest anything Chinese to start with. Those "gold" screens are essentially Japanese. Chinese screens are of many varieties, such as wood, lacquer, wood set with semi-precious stones, and marbles. In old pictures one sees pictures of screens that may have been of paper covered with gold-leaf and painted; but, as far as I can remember, there are no relics of such things now-a-days. So, when one thinks of a paper screen one thinks of either a Japanese or a Korean one. Your description sounds like the picture of *Korean* screens, which are just like that. I shall be very much interested to know if you have ever seen a Chinese paper screen covered with gold-leaf.

"The Poet's Wife" [p. 30], does not really "connote" the story of Cho Wên-chün at all. It was not the love poems he[1] had written to her which he sold, and which made his fortune, but wonderful *fu* [*Fir-Flower Tablets*, pp. lxiii, lxv–lxvi], praising the Emperor, etc. As a matter of fact, love poems from men to women are *very* rare in Chinese poetry; that song Ssŭ-ma Hsiang-ju sang to his lute, when he first

---

[1] Ssŭ-ma Hsiang-ju, who died 117 B.C. (see H. A. Giles, *Biographical Dictionary*, No. 1753).

came to Wên-chün's father's house, comes as near it as anything I have seen. I have asked Mr. Nung to find some, but they don't seem to exist, that is as a usual thing. As far as the wine is concerned, Cho Wên-chün was the person who suggested that they should keep a wine shop, just outside her father's house. She was herself a "bartender" and helped, until the father, to save his face, gave the couple enough to go to Court with.

Moreover, I am quite sure that we (that is Westerners) have all much misunderstood the Chinese use of wine. To use it as a stimulant, they considered, and do consider, quite the right thing to do, and desirable. Poets and painters, many of them, did their best work under these circumstances. Li T'ai-po did sometimes become *Ta Tsui*, and *Lan Tsui* ("great drunk," and "rotten drunk") which, of course, *is* undesirable—but not a tithe as much as he is credited with doing. As a matter of fact, it seems to me, from what I read and find out now, that our Temperance Union, blue-ribbon ideas have come into the thing far too much. Your "Poet's Wife" could have been written by a Western woman, never by a Chinese.

"Spring Longing" is very nice, and "Li T'ai-po" very interesting with some lovely lines, but I am sorry to have him perpetuated as an *everlasting* drunkard, which he was not, and which all the Westerners, who have written about him, make him out to be.

I am writing thus frankly as I feel that you would want me to do, especially as we are working together. Just say if you would rather I did not!! and I will desist.

I have begun regular work again. Mr. Nung is here, having brought back from Nanking a large choice of poems by Li T'ai-po, Tu Fu, and others. These we are now working through. I send a few to-day, and also return the "Songs of the Marches," with which I am much delighted. You will be disappointed that there are some alterations to be made especially in No. 3, but it is that "Old Thing" again. I wish it didn't take such an age to analyse the poems; the work piles up in front of me. Twelve are now in my portfolio translated and ready to be typed. A large pile of untranslated ones sits in another drawer.

The "Nursing Home" runs along smoothly. Papa just drifts on—he is practically bed-ridden.

Much love—and a thousand thanks for the book.

Yours ever,

FLORENCE AYSCOUGH

98

DEAREST AMY,

I am beginning rather to worry, as to whether or not you are ill. It is three whole months since I have had a word from you. I do hope you are fit, and that soon a letter will come.

I have been pegging away, and am glad to say that I have now got some help with typing. You see, the analyses are not the sort of work that I can give to an ordinary typist, and, of course, unless the typists had a knowledge of Chinese they would be no use whatever. The person I have is a very interesting woman who came out six years ago as a missionary, revolted (she must have been a sore trial to the missionaries among whom she lived), married, and came to Shanghai not so long ago. Her husband is in a big educational book-shop here. She is much interested and as keen as possible, so I am very much pleased to have her. She is inexperienced in this sort of thing but will improve, and is very quick. Her knowledge of Chinese—that is the colloquial—is much greater than mine, so she is a great help. In March she and her husband go to U.S.A. for a year's leave—possibly for good. It has occurred to me that she might be a help at your end, if she absolutely understands the method on which we are working.

I send you to-day, besides the eight poems, very rough biographies of Li T'ai-po and Tu Fu. I scribbled them down as my teacher read them out and have not spent time in putting them into shape; but thought that they might be of interest to you. There is no doubt that the Chinese think Tu Fu was a greater poet than Li T'ai-po. He is far, *far* more difficult to translate; I wonder how you will find him to "render." I mean by-and-by to make a regular study of his poems.[1] But if you think that, for the present, we had better stick to Li T'ai-po we will do so. I think there is no question as to the versatility of the two men. Tu Fu is a master of every style, while Li-po confines himself much more to the lyrical. Tu Fu's poems are supposed to give one an epitome of the whole of China's history. He was a great patriot, and a most uncompromising person—while Li-po is most lovable. Don't you think so? Do you think that short biographies should appear in the book?

I was much pleased to hear from Miss Monroe of our Honorable Mention. The note came on a day when I had been especially harassed, so was doubly welcome.

[1] For the results of this study see *Tu Fu: The Autobiography of a Chinese Poet, A.D. 712–770* . . . . *Arranged from His Poems and Translated by Florence Ayscough*, Vol. I: *A.D. 712–759* (London, Boston, and New York, 1929), and Vol. II: *Travels of a Chinese Poet, Tu Fu, Guest of Rivers and Lakes, A.D. 759–770* (London, Boston, and New York, 1934).

Since I last wrote I have had time to read your *Pictures of the Floating World*. My dear, it is most beautiful. It must have had a great reception. Are you not pleased? A thousand congratulations. . . . .

Further trials in the domestic line. Geoffrey after a sharp "go" of influenza and pleurisy, has gone to hospital with para-typhoid!! After months of waiting . . . . everything was straightened out and he was to go on the ship that takes this letter to Canada to be married to Lois Grimmer. Did you see her when you were in St. Andrews? The telegram saying that all was well came at nine a.m. and at noon he retired to the hospital. Is it not hard lines?

I hope you will not be annoyed: I have given a letter of introduction to a Russian pianist—Mirovitch—who is going to U.S.A. He plays very beautifully and will, I hope, have the success he deserves. I think you will like him.

How Papa continues to live—I do not know; one feels that every day must be his last.

Much love, my dear.

Yours ever,

FLORENCE AYSCOUGH

[SHANGHAI], January 4, 1920

DEAR AMY,

Your ever welcome Christmas cable, nine days en route, was very reassuring, as I really had begun to feel that you must be ill or that something must have happened. Now I know that, at any rate, you are well enough to think of your friends—that is a great thing. You have no idea how I depend on that word from you at Xmas. I do wish, however, that letters would come. The mails are beyond any description; the delay is far, far worse than it was during the war!

The ship that is to take this [S.S. "Ecuador"] is as slow as a top, but there is nothing fast until the twenty-fourth, so this poem of Tu Fu's had better start off on its travels. The duplicate will go in the next boat.

I shall hope to get off a good batch on the twenty-fourth. It makes such a tremendous difference having someone to type for me.

Papa is sinking; it seems to me very fast. The doctor said yesterday that he did not see how he could live more than a week or so. It is really cruelty, now, to go in to see him as it is almost impossible for him to talk; he just lies and dozes. All I hope is that he may slip off in his

100

sleep, and be spared any more of those distressing attacks, which are so painful for everyone concerned.

Much love.

Yours ever,
FLORENCE AYSCOUGH

[SHANGHAI], January 24, 1920

DEAR AMY,

There seems to be hardly a moment to write to you, so I shall have to be telegraphic! I send a budget of new poems and also a duplicate of the "Grass House."

You will not be surprised to hear that Papa died on the fifth of this month. I can feel nothing but thankfulness that he is released—the last months have been dreadful. He was spared any more of those awful attacks, and died very quietly on a Monday evening. He had not recognized me since noon of the day before.

Geoffrey goes on the ship that takes this to Canada to be married to Lois Grimmer in St. John. She is a fine creature and I hope to goodness that he will have some happiness with her after all his misery. He has been in hospital since practically December 1st with a perfect series of illnesses—influenza and pleurisy, then para-typhoid, then a bad tonsil. He goes from the hospital to the ship to-day.

Naturally, I have had what might be described as a "picnic" as I have had to do everything with lawyers etc. By strenuous efforts I have managed to get the Will proved, and all papers ready, so I got G. his "exemplification" yesterday afternoon. Having it will make things much simpler at the other end.

I wish I could hear from you. I can't help feeling that something has gone astray—perhaps dropped out of its cover; the last packet which came (Oct. 1st) was *very* dilapidated. One would think, however, that the cover in any case would have turned up! I really wish you would telegraph whether you are alive or not. My love to Ada.

I keep on wondering whether or not I make things clear? If you have any suggestions, I wish you would make them.

Yours ever,
FLORENCE AYSCOUGH

BROOKLINE, MASS., 24 January, 1920

DEAREST FLORENCE:

I have not written to you for so long because I had such a number of poems of yours to do that I wanted to wait until I could send you a reasonable batch and because I have been so fearfully busy with my own things. And now I am to have an operation next week.[1] This is especially annoying as I have not been so well in years as I am this Winter. After my operation last year I had the flu, and it seems as if in coughing I must have coughed through a badly healed inner stitch or something of that sort. At any rate, the whole thing is to do over again and seems much worse than it did last year, and the knowledge that this was hanging over me and that I had a certain number of things that I had to get through first has made me very much rushed.

Now I have a lot of poems to send you which I have been working very hard to get done before my operation, and the eight you sent me, which arrived yesterday morning enclosed in your letter of December 28th, will have to wait for a couple of months or so until I am round again. I am sorry that it goes so slowly, but that cannot be helped, because you know it is not my only work and I cannot give all the time to it that I should wish.

I read in the paper of your father's death. My dear, I am just as sorry as I can be, although I know that, ill as he was, it was far the best thing that could happen for you and for him. But, in spite of all the worry and anxiety it was to have him suffering, I know that, now the separation has really come, you will go back in mind to the days when he was well, and the sense of loss will be very acute. I wish I were somewhere near you and could do anything for you, but that I know is impossible. However, you must realize that our old affection and friendship, which has stood the test of so many years, is never more active than now, and I send you my heartiest sympathy and my warmest love. . . . .

Your news about Geoffrey is both good and bad. I am delighted to know that he is to be happily married at last. I did not meet Lois Grimmer. I hope she is going to be a real comfort to him; he has had such a hard life. And I do trust that he is all well by now and able to come over and marry her.

I shall be very glad to do anything I can for your Russian pianist [Mirovitch]. He has not turned up yet.

I am sending you eighteen poems with this letter, which I think should give you consideration for some time to come. I will begin first by commenting on the ones I have done over.

THE TWO-EDGED SWORD MOUNTAINS [P. 52]:

It certainly was a facer that your Pavilion of the Two-Edged Sword was not a pavilion but a road. However, I have gone over the poem

[1] See Damon, *op. cit.*, chap. xx.

and changed it as it seemed to me best. Your teacher undoubtedly knows a great deal of Chinese, but he does not know anything about poetry. The suggestion that the sun would look dark because the man felt sad is perfectly foolish. It is what is known in literary technique as the "pathetic fallacy," and is considered one of the very worst things to do in literature. The reason I had my water flowing "brightly" was because of the breaking up of the character which had the sun coming through trees, meaning East of course, but seeming to me to make it possible to say that the water was flowing brightly. The juxtaposition of the bright water and his own sorrow made the sense of the line, in my version. But I am quite willing to leave out the "brightly."

It is also very amusing to have Mr. Nung explaining the use of suggestion to me. Evidently the Americans with whom he has come in contact do not understand suggestion, but he need not bother to do that with me since I am quite capable (I think from his expositions more capable than he is) of understanding his native poetry.

As to your suggestion that we translate the name of the town of Ch'in, I do not believe in translating the names of any of the towns. It does not go well in English, and, by keeping the Chinese name in the title of a place or province or things of that sort, we keep the Chinese flavor.

I cannot give the "surface" or "skin" of the water as "lines" as Mr. Nung suggests, because the only translation in English would be "ripples," and that is not half so pleasant a word as "surface" in this sense. Your and Mr. Nung's criticisms are a little difficult for me to follow as they are not the criticisms of poets, and I am sorry to say that, owing to Mr. Nung's influence, you are falling into the pedantic method of looking at these things and are departing from our original intentions. I notice that when I do split up a character, which I do occasionally, Mr. Nung almost always makes me take out the word which was the result of the split. This is, of course, what most scholars would do, but it is entirely against the spirit of our work as we originally planned it. You, not being literary by profession, and not having a long training in having your own ideas and keeping them, are a little prone to take the ideas of the people you are with, and if that person happens to be a pedant and scholar, you naturally take that attitude. Try to get away from Mr. Nung when you are not with him and look at the thing from your own unaided mind, and in sending me translations try to send me the original word of the Chinese in English and not Mr. Nung's translation, because I notice that the old translations sent me with your old teacher were ¦very much more imaginative and helped my imagination to function much better than the translations you have sent me since you have been working with him, since the words you now use are conventional and not literal, and the conventional word simply stops all thought in me, whereas the literal starts it working. In other words, if they say "skin" [p. 164] of the water, do not translate it as "surface," translate it as "skin," and so on. I can get something out of that, because it is in these very words that the Chinese excel and beat us English. I should probably not think of the Chinese expression alone, whereas, if you say "skin" I know you mean "surface." This is merely an illustration.

You misunderstand, I think, my function in our collaboration, for you constantly refer me to Giles's book in the Harvard Library, and now you suggest that your missionary lady would be a help to me. It is quite impossible for any Chinese words, or any knowledge of them, to help me in the least. I cannot acquire a sufficient knowledge to make it of the slightest value to me to look these things up in the dictionary or to talk to any one about them. That is your function. I like the sound of them as you put them down; the way you send them is perfect. But as to going behind your translation and trying to find out whether I agree with your meaning by hunting up Giles or discussing it with a person who speaks Chinese, that would not only be impertinent in me but futile, since it would simply be substituting one authority for another, yours for Giles or your missionary or whoever it might be. I consider that it is for you to give me the translations, and for me to put them in English from your material, but emphatically not for me to do anything whatever with the original Chinese, because, if you will pause to consider a moment, you will see that it would be perfectly ridiculous for me to attempt anything of the sort. If you give me the literal translations as literally as possible and all the splits up that you like (and I do agree with you that the splitting has to be done very charily so as not to lose the original flavor, and it is for that reason that I disapprove of translating the names of places except on special occasions when they add to the poetry) I will be the judge of the poetical effect, and you of the correctness of the translations. That is my idea of our mutual functions. All you can get out of Mr. Nung in the matter of historical and philological or folk lore sources is very important, but it is very important that you get away from his *translation* before you send it to me, and immensely important that you do not consider his remarks on the translations from the point of view of poetry in the least in the world. There is

104

one poem here where I think he has entirely misunderstood Li T'ai Po's meaning. Your opinion of the result passing through his brain cannot fail to be wrong, since I can tell that his feeling for poetry is almost nil, what he has being a student's knowledge of it, and of course when you put it into a foreign tongue, it is more worthless on the literary side; on the literal side it is, of course, of the utmost value. But when he starts to explain the poets, that I think is quite unnecessary, except in matters of folk lore or historical allusion. Of course I do not need explanations personally; whether you need them or not I do not know. (I am speaking now of the suggestion in a poem, not of the allusions aforesaid.) Could I read them in the original Chinese, I should prefer my own intuition of what the poets were trying to say to that of any one else who was not a trained poet. It is a poet's business to get just the things that Mr. Nung constantly expects me to miss. I hope this does not sound as if I did not appreciate his very real value. It is only that you are losing your eye for literature a little in your desire for accuracy. It is the poet's business to reproduce the effect in a translation; he must, of course, be as accurate as possible, but the effect is the real accuracy—the perfume of a poem, as I said in my French translations. Without that, no matter how literal the translation, the poem is by no means rendered. There is a long spiel about our different functions with which I am sure you will agree. The next one of the repetitions is:

THE SONG OF THE MARCHES [PP. 1–4]:

Here I have made the changes you desire in almost every instance. In the first part, I have put "Playing 'The Snapping of Willows' " because I cannot put "playing" and "snapping" in such close conjunction as one immediately after the other on account of the sound. I cannot remember the book in which I read that all the soldiers had tiger tallies, but I certainly did read it in some account of China, and it makes much better poetry as I originally had it; but I have changed it to the singular as you desire.

There is not the slightest reason for going into the details as to why the frontier moon cast the shadow of bows upon the ground. It means the same in English—that they were on the march—as it did in Li T'ai Po's original Chinese. What I have got is sufficient as it stands, and conveys the impression accurately to one with a poetical attitude of mind; any more would, I think, be a mistake.

Personally, I greatly prefer "The Heavenly soldiers" to "the soldiers of the Heavenly One"; it gives the feeling of being exotic, of coming from another country, much better than "The soldiers of the Heavenly One" does. I do not think that translations should read as though they were originals. I think they should retain, as far as possible, the quaintness and difference of the language in which they were written, and, to my mind, "The Heavenly soldiers" does this much better than the alternative.

To come back for a moment to the first section. Your comment on the fact that the trees have no colour. That was not what you originally gave me. Your rendering was: Spring

Colour

Not

Done, finished

Soon[1]

which would mean that the trees were not yet in full leaf, but that they must have begun to bud. You added after "done, finished" "sense of completed." I think, therefore, that my translation is exact as it now stands. It is impossible for me to translate "P'iou Yao" and keep the cadence, and it is obvious that this is a name. What the name means I think we need not bother with for Western readers. All these things can be explained in notes, but we must not ruin the original poems by trying to put in things that were not there, but were understood by Chinese readers. If we try to interpolate all the meanings in the poem itself, we have ruined the poem, which would be foolish.

Once more you have forbidden my split up. I put "Attack with spears and battle cries" in the third section, because in your rendering "fight" you said "one who attacks with yells and a stick." I am perfectly willing to leave it out, but you see what happens when I follow our principle. I do think, as I go along, that the less we amplify on the originals the better. Sometimes it can be done with great effect; sometimes, I think, it cannot, and probably it is better to leave that out, but that is why I put it in. The rest of the poem, I think, needs no comment.

ONCE MORE FIELDS AND GARDENS [p. 132]:

This is the third of the corrected ones. It would be perfectly ridiculous to say that the fish in the garden pool was once a wild fish. Of course it was a wild fish; nobody could ever suppose it to be otherwise, considering the context. You must not be so literal. The "but" in the last line of the first stanza can be put in if you prefer; I do not think

---

[1] Not "soon" but "seen"—corrected by F. A. on receipt of the letter.

it necessary and should rather have it left out. I think "caged" bird is much better than your suggestion of "netted," and should prefer to leave it. The effect of the distant village being seen through the branches of the trees is quite charming, although of course it is not given in the original. I have left various alternatives at the bottom of that stanza from which you can choose.

You do worry over that cock, don't you? As a matter of fact, I have often seen hens and cocks in trees myself, and I do not understand why you have not. However, I think by putting in "clipped mulberry" we have got all the effect that is necessary. In fact, I like the new way better than the old, and I hope you will be willing to let it stand.

NIGHT THOUGHTS [P. 74]:

This is most amusing, for in it I am sure that Mr. Nung has gone completely wrong. His description of the poem made me shriek, because any human being who had any poetical feeling could have got everything he said without his intervention, with the exception of the thing where I think he is wrong; namely, I do not think that the poet thought that the moonlight on the floor was frost. I think that, seeing the moonlight on the floor, cold as the night was, it made him sure that outside there was frost on the ground. I am quite sure of it, both from your literal translation and from the way a poet's mind would work. That Mr. Nung does not see it, is another evidence of his lack of poetical comprehension. Poetical comprehension is not common; if it were, poets would not be such rare persons. When you think of all the people there are, and how few of them are poets, you will agree with me that it is not an attribute of every one. I have given you the alternative version with his reading, but I know that it is wrong, and if you are wise you will take my say-so in this instance rather than his.[1]

I want to give an example of what I mean. Some years ago my friends, the Aldingtons,[2] undertook to translate a little series of poems from the Latin and Greek which they called "The Poets' Translation Series." They said in beginning that they were going to take no notice of the various readings of the scholars, but were going to translate the poems as seemed wise to them as poets. The result was a complete success, so complete that Professor Mackail wrote an article in the *Times* commending H. D.'s[3] "Choruses from Iphigenia in Aulis" for

[1] But note letter of A. L. to F. A., February 16, 1922.

[2] See Damon, *op. cit.*, p. 745.   [3] *Ibid.*, pp. 751–52.

107

their beauty and accuracy. Believe the poets, Florence, and let the pedants go hang.

AUTUMN RIVER SONG [P. 67]:

Here I have given you two titles, and also two readings. It has a nice cadence.

A LETTER OF THANKS FOR PRECIOUS PEARLS BESTOWED BY ONE ABOVE [P. 143]:

This has two versions which you can choose. All of these poems are beautiful, I think.

PARTING FROM YANG, A HILL MAN WHO IS RETURNING TO THE HIGH MOUNTAIN [P. 73]:

Here I have given you some alternatives on one page. There seems to be no doubt about the reading. His friend naturally becomes an Immortal after his year of probation in the mountains. Mr. Nung seems to think that is difficult of understanding. Mr. Nung is amusing, however.

HEARING THE EARLY ORIOLE [P. 119]:

I am indifferent as to which of the two versions you choose. I think they are both better than Waley's.

THE POET IS DETAINED IN A NANKING WINE-SHOP ON THE EVE OF STARTING ON A JOURNEY [P. 20]:

I have changed this according to your new reading. Perhaps it is a little clumsy as it is, but it seems the best I can do to get all the meaning.

PARROT ISLAND [P. 61]:

I much prefer the new reading of this poem, which I always thought was the proper one. In fact, I hardly need any notes on these poems if I have the literal translation and your original one. I can get very much nearer the real thought if I can get as close to the Chinese as possible.

VISITING THE TAOIST PRIEST [P. 68]:

This has no alternatives. It is the best that I can do.

SONGS OF THE COURTESANS [P. 145]:

I am very much in love with the "Songs of the Courtesans." The "Song of the Ten Requests" has no alternatives; nor has "Ai Ai Thinks of the Man She Loves." This is also true of the lady who was a common willow and which, I think, is the most beautiful of all. The

"Fire-bird" has an alternative in the second line so you must choose. If you have "Ai Ai Thinks of the Man She Loves" in the second poem, you cannot use the words again in the fourth poem. In one case it must be "Her Lover" to make a difference.

DANCING [P. 144]:

This is a charming little thing. I have tried to give it a special rhythm in order to give the effect of the dancing. I trust you will like it.

The Li T'ai Po "Drinking Song" [p. 58] is very difficult. I am still working over it to get it somewhere near what I want. Whether I shall ever succeed in doing this I do not know. I will not send it with this mail because it is so difficult that I want to consider it a little longer. I will send it with the next batch, the ones that I received to-day, or, if I should consider it satisfactory earlier than that, I will send it as soon as I get it done. But do not expect anything for two months or more. I am afraid some time more, really, for I am to give the Phi Beta Kappa poem at Commencement at Columbia, and the first thing I do when I finish my operation will be to write that, which will take me some time.

It will amuse you to know that I have been given a degree at a Western University [Baylor] of Doctor of Literature, and I am going there to take my degree the middle of June. Things are funny, aren't they?[1]

I am sorry to appear so slow about doing the poems, but of course my original work takes precedence over everything, and I do not think there is any particular hurry, since so much interest is now shown in Chinese, for translations seem to be appearing every minute (Have you seen Waley's latest book?)[2] and as we cannot be the first in the field, it makes no difference whether we are the hundred and first or not. I am afraid you will think me very slow and stupid at it, but it really cannot be helped. I am almost worked to death now, and it does not help my original work at all to be working so hard, and now I am giving up two months out of my existence. Be sure however that I will send you the new ones as soon as I can get to them.

I told you, I think, in other letters that some of the poems you sent did not seem worth doing; for instance, I cared nothing for the little poem by the young lady seven years old. The old person of sixty might be done, and I will see what I can do with her later. The "Song of

[1] *Ibid.*, pp. 535–37; see also below, Appendix II.

[2] *More Translations from the Chinese* (New York, 1919).

White Heads" I have already told you that I do not think of particular interest, neither the long narrative nor the lyric. I did not care for it in Waley's translation. It seems to me simply dull, and I really think you had better leave it out. There is very little use in my attempting to do anything which I think fearfully uninteresting, because if one does not like it one is very rarely successful, and the chances are that the public would not like it either if I did not. The greater proportion I love as much as you do. These are all the ones that you have sent that I do not want to do. I am sure you will agree with me; we have already agreed about the long narrative one before.

Ever so much love to you, dear Florence.

Affectionately yours,
AMY LOWELL

[SHANGHAI], February 26, 1920

DEAR AMY,

The days go on and on—and still no word comes from You!! It is really most extraordinary—I never felt so in the dark. It seems so futile, in a way, to go on sending poems into space. Something may have changed your mind about doing the rendering at all. But then, I feel sure, you would tell me; it is most puzzling. The last line I have received was a letter which was here when I arrived from Tsingtao, October 1st. That is nearly five months ago.

Well, here is another "batch" of little lyrics. I like the Tu Fu "Excursion" [p. 107] very much. D'Hervey de St Denis [*Poésies des Thang*] has done the first one of the two very correctly. As a matter of fact, in many ways I prefer Tu Fu's poems to those of Li T'ai-po.

We are having such a ridiculous time. A friend of ours, a nice youth, was to be married. His bride came out to marry him, alone—no parents or anything to escort her. We asked her to stay until the wedding. She arrived, and, to our horror and consternation, announced that she did not wish to marry the youth, and had, as a matter of fact, fallen in love with someone else on the way out. It is a nice old mess. The other person is a child of 19 travelling round the world in charge of a "bear-leader"—so she can't marry him until he goes home and gets his parents' permission. I don't know what she will do. In the meanwhile, she is sitting here! No passage back to Victoria is to be had till June or July. I think that, in the end, she will probably marry the original one—who is so infatuated that he still wants her. A most mysterious thing: men where women are concerned are *fools*. He, otherwise, is quite an intelligent youth.

110

I am going to speak before the Asiatic Society on March 25 [26] on "Chinese Poetry and Its Connotations,"[1] using slides to show what the poets are referring to.

Love as ever.

Yours,

FLORENCE AYSCOUGH

[SHANGHAI], March 12, 1920

DEAR AMY,

In the mail which arrived yesterday I had a letter from Mrs. Low in which she said that you were to be operated upon for hernia.[2] I am so very, very sorry, and hope that by now it is all well over. She wrote February 4, so it should be—that is if it was done soon.

I feel rather as though I were pouring water into a sieve—to use a proverbial expression—in sending more poems, but this lot is ready, so off they go. I send also one or two notes which may help to make things more vivid. The Chinese house plan, for instance, is important as it shows how things are arranged. A Chinese home [*Fir-Flower Tablets*, pp. xlviii–l, 223] is always a series of buildings separated by Courts and connected by covered passages. The women live in the "kuei" at the back. Guests—that is men guests—never go through.

[H. A.] Giles is picking Waley's things to pieces in a publication which appears here, called the *New China Review*.[3] They are both very wrong. The number has just appeared in which the poems are compared. I am working at it, as I think it is a profitable thing to do. I will send you some results next time. Waley does not publish the Chinese text, so one cannot tell how correct he is. Giles in this *Review* gives the original. It is interesting to compare like this.

Yours ever, and hoping anxiously to hear that you are well again,

FLORENCE AYSCOUGH

What puzzles me is that I thought the operation you had eighteen months ago was for hernia!! Wasn't it? I can't understand, and am afraid you must have been pretty ill.

---

[1] See *Journal of the North China Branch, Royal Asiatic Society*, LI (1920), 99–134.

[2] Damon, *op. cit.*, chap. xx.

[3] II, No. 1, 25–36: "A Poet of the 2nd Cent. B.C. [*sic*]"; see also II, No. 4, 319–40: "A Re-translation"; see also II, No. 6, 591–97: "A. Waley, 'Notes on the Lute-Girl's Song.' "

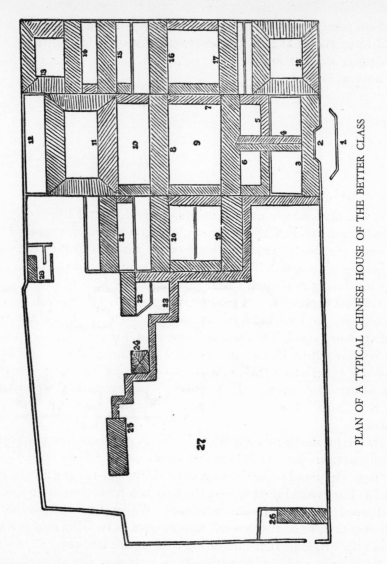

PLAN OF A TYPICAL CHINESE HOUSE OF THE BETTER CLASS

KEY TO PLAN OF A TYPICAL CHINESE HOUSE OF THE BETTER CLASS

Shaded Sections—Buildings.   White Sections—Courtyards.

The house faces South.

No. 1. *Chao Pi.*		Spirit Wall. Built to protect the main entrance from the malign influence of evil spirits: these move most easily in a straight line and find difficulty in turning corners, therefore a wall before the Great Gate is an effective defence.
No. 2. *Ta Mên.*		Great Gate.
No. 3. *Mên Fang.*		Gate-keeper's Room.
No. 4. *Ting Tzŭ Lang.*		Covered passage leading from the Reception Hall to the Great Gate and opening on the street.
No. 5. *Lang.*		Covered passage-way.
No. 6. *T'ing.*		Reception Hall.

112

No. 7. Lang.	Covered passage-way.
No. 8. T'ing.	Inner Reception Hall.
No. 9. Ch'ih.	A stone-paved courtyard. It has no roof and is raised in the centre. On great occasions, such as weddings, birthdays, and so on, it can be roofed and floored, thus being made a part of the house. Trees and flowers are not planted in this court, but are set about in pots.
No. 10. T'ing.	A courtyard. In this second courtyard, to which steps lead down, trees and flowers are planted, making of it an inner garden.
No. 11. Tso Ma Lou.	Running Horse Two-Story Apartments. This is the *Kuei* so often spoken of, the Women's Apartments. It is a building in which the rooms surround a courtyard, and are connected by verandahs running round the court upstairs and down. The space in the centre is known as *T'ien Ching* or Heaven's Well. There are eighteen rooms in the upper story, and eighteen in the lower. The wife uses the front rooms; the daughters, the back.
No. 12. Hou T'ing.	Back Court. It is bounded by a "flower wall," or brick trellis, through which flowers can twine, and is used by the inmates of the *Kuei* as a garden.
No. 13. Nü Hsia Fang.	Women's Lower House. A house for the women servants. As in the house for men servants, No. 18, the floor is actually on a lower level than those of the master's apartments.
No. 14. Fo Lou.	Buddhist Two-Story Apartments. In the upper story, images of Buddhas, and of Kuan Yin, the Goddess of Mercy, are kept. As a rule, it is locked, and only people who have washed carefully and put on clean clothes may enter.
No. 15. Tsê Shih.	Side Inner Apartment. In this house, poor relations may live. The concubines who do not enter the *Kuei* except on invitation also live here. Guests do not go farther into the house than to the wall bounding this building on the South.
No. 16. Tung Hua T'ing.	Eastern Flower Hall.
No. 17. Tui T'ing.	Opposite Hall. This and No. 16 are used for theatrical entertainments. The guests are seated in No. 16, facing South, and the stage faces North in No. 17. A cloth covering is stretched over the courtyard, and a wall divides the two *T'ing* from the rest of the house.
No. 18. Nan Hsia Fang.	Men's Lower House. A house for men servants divided as far as possible from the quarters of the women servants, also placed conveniently near the Great Gate where guests enter.
No. 19. Ta Shu Fang.	Great Book Room. This room is used as a library and study, and in it the teacher instructs the sons of the family.
No. 20. Hsi Hua T'ing.	Western Flower Hall. Here guests are entertained at meals. Flower gardens are placed on either side, and also walls which prevent either the study or the women's rooms from being seen from it.
No. 21. Tsê Shih.	Side Inner Apartment. A building used by the ladies of the house as a study or boudoir, where they embroider, paint, or write. The light is very good, whereas in the *Kuei*, on account of most of the windows opening on the court ("Heaven's Well"), it is apt to be poor.
No. 22. Ch'u Fang.	Kitchen. This is placed conveniently near to No. 20, where the men of the family dine, and No. 21, the dining-room of the ladies.
No. 23. Ch'ü Lang.	Passage-of-Many-Turnings. The superstitious belief in regard to the difficulty experienced by evil spirits in going round sharp corners governs the planning of this strangely shaped passage.
No. 24. Shu Chai.	"Books Reverenced." The study, or students' room.
No. 25. Hsien.	A Side-room or Pavilion. This is a long, low, outdoor passage, where guests sit and amuse themselves.
No. 26. Ma Fang.	Stable. The stable is placed as far as possible from the house. The horses, however, are kept saddled near the Great Gate for a large part of the day, in order to be in readiness should they be needed.
No. 27. Hua Yüan.	Flower Garden. The gardens are arranged with hills, water, and rockeries, to look as much like natural scenes as possible.
No. 28. Ssŭ So.	Privy.

DEAREST AMY,

Your letter of January 24, with a lot of enclosures, reached me just before we started off on a trip to Japan; where, as you see, we still are. I cannot tell you how distressed I am about your second operation! It does seem trying and annoying to have to go through the whole thing again. I do hope that one of your secretaries will write and let me know how you are getting on. Letters do take an eternity to and fro' now-a-days; one cannot imagine what the authorities do with them. It is almost worse than during the War.

I am not going even to mention poetry or translations until I know that you are better and fit to be bothered again. I shall not expect anything more from you till I see it, as you will be fully occupied with the Phi Beta Kappa Commencement poem for Columbia[1]—and then there will be the excitement of "going out west" to take your degree. Many congratulations on both events. I wish that you had told me which University had given you the degree; it is capital.

Japan is most lovely at this season of the year, and we have had glorious weather, which is lucky. The entire population seems to be obsessed with the desire to travel and "see the sights." Every train and tram is full to the top, and every place of interest and every temple simply thronged with sight-seers. They all look so gay with flowers in their hair and gay neck-cloths, each party wearing similar ones—for ease in identification I suppose.

Well, my dear, I hope that I shall soon have a letter saying that you are getting on as you should; in the meanwhile much love—

Yours ever,

FLORENCE AYSCOUGH

NEAR MEDICINE HAT, Sunday, July 25 [1920]

DEAR AMY,

Forgive scrawl—train shakes. So far all is well; to-day is the first hot day. It has been most comfortable.

I enclose the "Ode"—but fear that it will arrive at the same moment as does Mrs. Omori. I wonder if you will remember to tell me of your interviews with her!!?

[1] Damon, *op. cit.*, pp. 531, 535, 634.

Lois[1] joins me in love to you and Ada. She hopes you are better than you were when she saw you.

Much love to you both.

Yours ever,
FLORENCE AYSCOUGH

CANADIAN PACIFIC RAILWAY, EMPRESS HOTEL, VICTORIA, B.C.,

July 29, 1920

DEAREST AMY,

A line as we stand poised for the leap across the Pacific. It is 10:30 P.M. We rise at 6:30 in the morning to embark. This carries my love and a request: please to let me know how you are and how you get on. If you are too busy to write, or rather dictate—and I know you are—can't one of the secretaries send me a line to tell me how things go with your "insides" which you threaten to wear "outside"? No matter whether there are poems to come or not, I do so want to have a word of you.

I send all affection. Love to Ada.

Yours,
FLORENCE AYSCOUGH

SHANGHAI, August 26, 1920

DEAREST AMY,

Safe and sound—and hot—describes the condition of Lois and myself. Frank met us in Yokohama—well, but rather tired. I wish he were getting off this year instead of next. He says that he can't possibly stay away long enough for us to spend even part of the winter in Boston—so that little scheme is knocked on the head. I am sorry.

I wonder how you are. I do hope you will let me know. I have thought of you so much and hoped you would not have to have another operation. I suppose you will be consulting the New York specialist this month.

I have not begun my lessons as yet; intend to do so on Sept. 1—when, one may hope, it will be a little cooler. I wrote Nung and asked him who wrote the "Two-edged Sword" [p. 52]. He says Li T'ai-po—so I am telegraphing you, and hope you will remember that we agreed upon the one word "Yes." In the meanwhile: enclosed you will find a poem or two which I have finished up since my return.

The mails are worse than ever. I received letters two days ago posted in *Boston, June 14.* Isn't it absurd!! I don't know what the U.S.

---

[1] Lois (Grimmer) Wheelock, widow of Geoffrey Wheelock.

people do with them. The only decent service is by the "Empresses" and your secretaries can always find out when those mails are closing by telephoning to the General Post Office.

My best love to Ada, and much to yourself.

Yours,
FLORENCE AYSCOUGH

[SHANGHAI], September 16, [1920]

DEAR AMY,

Mail closing a day earlier than advertised—no time to write.

Yours,
F. W. A.

SHANGHAI, September 24, 1920

DEAR AMY,

A quick mail goes to-morrow, so I send you a few poems which I hope you will like. I do.

I wonder whether you have seen the New York specialist and whether you have decided the question of another operation or not? I do hope it can be avoided!! I also wonder how your plans for next year are shaping. Of course plans are always liable to be altered by a thousand circumstances, but one must make them. Ours are as follows: we sail April 2, and mean to go through to England fairly directly, and return, say, in early July, to St. Andrews. The plan for spending the winter, Frank says, is out of the question. So, I suppose, we shall return here sometime in the late autumn.

As I shall (if nothing happens) be in America during next summer and could read proof, would it be in any way possible to get the book under way to appear in the autumn of 1921? Of course, it all depends on whether you have any time to work or not.

What is your idea about going to England? You did not tell me *when* you meant to go—supposing you *did*. If you go, would it be practical for you to decide on the form of the book before going, then leave it with the publishers, and let me read the proof? The translation seems to be going much more quickly now, and your part goes quickly too. I do not think that now there will be any big alterations such as there were in the first poems, so it should be much smoother. I am starting work on the preface. Have a number of poems—twenty-six to be exact—waiting to be typed. So we could have enough before long. Have you two poems by Li T'ai-po with the same title "Drinking under the Moon Alone" [pp. 39, 40]? With them is a dissertation

116

[pp. xliv–xlv, lxxii] on the degrees of drunkenness referred to by the Chinese. First line of I [p. 39] is "Among the flowers a jug of wine." Of 2 [p. 40] is "If Heaven did not care for wine, The Wine Star would not be in Heaven." I sent them to you but think they miscarried—I cannot remember whether or not your secretary typed them for you or not, and don't want to do the whole thing over again if it is already done. So, will you please let me know? I have an idea she did it.

It is hot, *hot.* I shall be glad when October strikes one. I do hate sitting in a bath of perspiration!! Lois is very well and seems to enjoy herself thoroughly. She just fits into a "sporting set" here and all Geoffrey's friends are doing their best to make life pleasant for her.

I would be very glad if you could let me know what your ideas are. If the book *is* to come out in the autumn of 1921 I would arrange to stop over a fortnight at the end of April (that is if you would not already have gone), if you wanted me to do so.

I am longing to hear how you and Mrs. Omori (was that not her name?) came out over the diaries.[1]

Much love to Ada and to yourself. As the package is rather thick I am putting poems under separate cover.

Yours ever,
FLORENCE AYSCOUGH

BROOKLINE, MASS., 28 October, 1920

DEAR FLORENCE:

Here are a whole batch of poems which, with great difficulty, I have finished up before my operation which takes place to-morrow. I have not time to write about them. I have sent double versions. In some cases there are things in the alternatives which might well be in the preferred versions.

I think I am perhaps sending you the "Ode" a little prematurely, as I have only just finished it. I am keeping back the "Drinking Song" you left here because I am not satisfied with the way I have done it, and I cannot seem to do it to please myself; so I think that I had rather not send it until after I get well. At any rate, you have eighteen poems here which will keep you busy for some time.

I think we can perfectly well get a book ready by next Autumn if things go as they are going now with me. I feel all right except for

---

[1] See *Diaries of Court Ladies of Old Japan*, translated by Annie Shepley Omori and Kochi Doi, with an Introduction by Amy Lowell and with illustrations, (Boston and New York, 1920).

this beastly operation which they all assure me I must have. The New York specialist is coming over and Allie Porter is going to do the actual operating; they think it will be successful this time. I hope so, for they have painted the horrors of my future in such painful and vivid colours if I do not have the operation.

I have left Macmillan and gone over to Houghton Mifflin, and I think, for our purpose, that is a very good thing as Ferris Greens-let is anxious to take every possible chance of making me famous. I know that Macmillan would never have taken *our* book, and I think that Houghton Mifflin will, as I am one of their authors. Ferris Greenslet has already said that he would like an option on it, and I am sure that with your introduction and notes it will be a most important volume.

Mrs. Omori and I got along very well, and everything turned out satisfactorily. I hope the book [*Diaries of Court Ladies*] will see the light of day before long. I will send you a copy when it comes. In the meantime, I have signed a contract with Ferris Greenslet for my legend book to be issued next June,[1] and that I shall have to finish when I get over the operation. That is the only thing that troubles me now, but, as that is over in June, I can work at your poems during the Summer. I am afraid that April will be rather awful for me, as I think I shall just be tangled up with the legend book, the proofs of which will be coming in about then. Couldn't you manage to have your visit here in June and not in April, and then I shall be quite free?

No more for the present, my dear. I shall not be able to sign this but you will understand. My long silence has only been because I have been so drowned in work. The first thing I do when I come out of the operation will be to send out batches of our poems to the magazines.

Affectionately yours,
[*Signed for*] AMY LOWELL
AM[2]

---

[1] *Legends* (Boston and New York, 1921).

[2] Miss Lowell's letter was accompanied by the following note:

BROOKLINE, MASS., 29 October, 1920

DEAR MRS. AYSCOUGH,

I am enclosing a letter which Miss Lowell dictated yesterday. The operation is just over and the doctors say that they have no doubt that it is successful.

The "Ode" which Miss Lowell mentions I am not enclosing, for she was working on it last night, and it is still in her room and cannot be reached. I shall send it along in a few days.

Sincerely yours,
ANNE MORAN
Secretary

Dear Amy,

Yours of October 28 was waiting for me when I returned from Tsingtao a few days ago. I was delighted with the enclosures, but very sad to think that you have had to undergo this horrid operation again. Oh Amy, dear, it makes me feel badly to think how much you are having to suffer. Please thank Miss Moran for her little note which told me that the actual operation was well over. I shall anxiously wait for more news.

Well, Lois wrote you that I had typhoid. It was a nuisance!! I had it mildly, but it takes a long long time no matter *how* you have it. Of course, I was dreadfully disgusted at having to stop the translations. The worst of it is I don't know when they will let me begin again. Not till the New Year, anyway. In the meanwhile, my teacher has been choosing poems and brought me a pile of about one hundred, I should think, when I saw him for the first time yesterday.

It is too trying!!! Well, nothing is to be gained in swearing. We shall just have to see about the book. In the meanwhile Witter Bynner is working away in Peking. He is to be down here, I believe, about a fortnight hence and Mrs. Simeon Ford has written asking if she may bring him to see me. I shall be very discreet about our work.

You will be interested to hear that Lois is engaged. Her fiancé is an extremely nice man. . . . . We are delighted. . . . .

Much love, dear Amy, to you and to Ada.

Yours ever,
Florence Ayscough

Shanghai, January 14, 1921

Dear Amy,

I was so thankful to have your Xmas telegram as it was proof that you were well enough to think of mundane affairs! I hope that you are really yourself again. I am ever so much better and am having massage which helps enormously. The teacher has been coming for the last ten days and we have translated a fair number of poems. I am devoting all the strength I am allowed to use to translating with him and to the taking of copious notes. Am not going to worry about getting the typed copies off to you but will bring all I can with me. Enclosed are some duplicates and two more *tzŭ* of a set. No. 1 went to you before I was ill.

Mr. Witter Bynner has been here. He and Mrs. [Simeon] Ford came to lunch; she talked so much that it was impossible to get in a word with him as to what he was doing. I enclose a cutting which will amuse you, though I do not think he has carried out his idea of going to Siam. He will be here again in February and I shall see him then more tranquilly. In the meanwhile Dr. [John Calvin] Ferguson passed through and I had a long talk with him. He says that Mr. Bynner has translated a T'ang anthology of 300 poems!! Those he had heard he evidently didn't think much of. In any case it is quite impossible that Mr. Bynner can have made so many translations in the short time he has been at it—I mean good ones; especially as he lost his Chinese professor for months, and has been with him only a short time. He has now returned to Peking to try to "finish up."

As I do admire Dr. Ferguson's scholarship, I spoke to him about our analyses of character and he agrees with us. Do it as much as you can. The poems which have "split-ups" in them are much the nicest. Those I send to-day have practically no possibilities, but so many have.

There will hardly be time for anything to reach me after you receive this, except what is sent to Vancouver to meet us when we arrive by the "Asia" on April 18. Address care the C.P.O.S.—passenger, "Empress of Asia." Must go; 1000 thanks for the cable.

Much love, yours ever,

FLORENCE AYSCOUGH

A *tzŭ* of the Crosswise River II [p. 26]. See No. I of same title which I sent you last autumn; that, this, and No. III should appear together.
1. The sea tide flowing to the south passes Hsün Yang.
2. The Ox Ledge from the beginning of time (has been more) dangerous (than) the "Standing Horse Hill," or Mountain.
3. Those who desire to ferry across the Hêng Chiang (i.e. the "Crosswise River") find the wind and the waves most terrible.
4. One stretch of water draws out sorrow 10,000 li in length.

TITLE
Hêng
Chiang
Tzŭ

1.

Hai	Sea
Chao	Tide (Analysis) Water and the sun rising through sea mist
Nan	South
Chu	Goes
Kuo	Pass, go through, go over
Hsün	Name of town to which Po Chu-i was exiled; Waley often refers
Yang	to it. Hsün Yang

2.

Niu	Ox
Chu	Ledge, islet, bank
Yu	Origin, the beginning of things, early time
Lai	Comes, come to; "Yu Lai" means since the beginning of time
Hsien	Dangerous, insecure, an obstruction very difficult to surmount
Ma	Horse
Tang	In, at (the hill called Ma Tang Hill has some resemblance to a horse standing)

3.

Héng	Crosswise, athwart, at right angles to
Chiang	River
Yu	Desire
Tu	Ferry across ford a stream or sea, to go through, a ferry boat
Feng	Wind
Po	Waves (Analysis) water and skin
0	Evil, terrible, vicious

4.

I	One (here used in sense of a piece, or stretch)
Shui	Water
Ch'ien	Pull, haul, connect, draw out
Chou	Sorrow, grief; the autumn heart
Wan	Ten thousand, sense of countless
Li	1/3 of mile
Chang	Long, length

Tzŭ of the Crosswise River III [p. 26].

1. The Sea Spirit passes by—a fierce wind returns (the effect of his passing has been so violent).
2. The waves beat the stone walls, i.e. Cliffs, of the Heaven's Gate Mountains (as if they would force them) open.
3. Can Chekiang in the 8th month equal this? (This is a reference to the extraordinary "Bore," a wave often 20 feet in height which rushes up the Tien Chiang in Chekiang. It is at its best at the autumn equinox; crowds then go to see it. It is one of the Wonders of the World. Would it be possible to bring it into the poem or had it best be mentioned in a footnote? I thought that you could speak of the "Wall of Sea" in the autumn month. You see, Chinese 8th month is generally, and approximately, our October.)
4. Great booming waves are as if they were connected hills.—They spirt forth snow.

Title same as preceding

1.

Hai	Sea
Shén	Spirit, supernatural being
Lai	Come
Kuo	Pass, go through, pass by

O	Evil, terrible, vicious
Feng	Wind
Hui	To return, revolve, come back, curve, bend round and return

2.

Lan	Waves, billows, surges
Ta	Beat, strike, a blow
Tien	Heaven, the sky
Men	Gate, Door-way. Tien Men, name of two mountains, one on either side of the Yangtze River
Tien	Heaven, the sky
Shih	Stone, rock
Pi	Wall, a ridge, a dividing cliff or water-shed
Kai	Open (Analysis) A door, a bar, two hands lifting it

3.

Che	
Chiang	Chechiang [Chekiang] is the name of a province
Pa	Eight
Yueh	Month
Ho	How
Ju	Equal to
Tzu	This

4.

T'ao	Very large waves which make a noise (water and fig. for longevity which is, of course, always synonymous with "greatness")
Tzu	As if
Lien	Connect with, continue, join, a succession of, unite, following, attached
Shan	Hill, mountain
Pen	Spirit, bring forth
Hsueh	Snow
Lai	To come

SHANGHAI, March 24, [1921]

DEAREST AMY,

A line to carry only a belated "duplicate." I have not typed out any more but have devoted myself to translating as many poems as possible and have them in the "rough." Witter Bynner published six of his translations in the local press, so I made the teacher find the original text and have also translated them. It makes me so angry to have him come out and gallop through a T'ang anthology of 300 poems. He simply can't do such a thing—as I told a little reportress. . . . . When one realizes by sad experience and effort that every character carries weight and affects the sense, it is too absurd. Well, as I say, I have the texts and the translations.

122

We sail D.V. Saturday week, April 2, by the "Empress of Asia" and are due in Vancouver April 18th—sailing May 10 from Quebec. I suppose we shall be in Boston for a day or two.

I have been made an Honorary Member of the Asiatic Society. When I look at the scroll and august company that I am in, it makes me rather shiver. I wonder how you are: whether you are perfectly fit again.

Much love, and love to Ada.

Yours ever,
FLORENCE AYSCOUGH

CANADIAN PACIFIC RAILWAY, EN ROUTE,
NEARING FORT WILLIAM, April 22, [1921]

DEAREST AMY,

I was delighted to receive your telegram; have not answered sooner as I was not sure where we were going to stay in Montreal. Our plans are: due Montreal early Sunday; stay Hotel Ritz for a day or two; then come Boston for week or ten days; go New York for a day or two and sail for England, May 10, from Quebec; back again for summer early July; sail for China October 13.

I have a big budget of poems for you; am eagerly looking forward to seeing you. It is delightful to think that you can work at "any time," as your telegram said. I was afraid that you would be too busy now reading proofs; at this rate I expect you can do the rendering while I am in England and we can work over them together when I come back. After all, St. Andrews is not the end of the world; I can come up. I have worked very steadily on the ship, and in the train, getting things ready for you. Have finished all my own translations and am now doing Witter Bynner's—that is, the six he published. . . . .

It is late, Fort William nears; best love to Ada, and, oh, so much to yourself. Hoping to see you next week, Thursday or so.

Ever with love,
FLORENCE AYSCOUGH

Have written Eunice Cruft to get us room at Vendome, Victoria or Somerset.

[Sent to Hotel Vendome, Boston]
BROOKLINE, MASS., 27 April, 1921

DEAREST FLORENCE:

It is so nice to think that I am to see you again soon. When you get in, if you are not too tired, won't you ring me up, and then we can make dates; because, you see, if you do not ring me to-night, I shall not be talkable to until afternoon to-morrow, and it does not make any difference how late you ring me up to-night.

It is a perfect nuisance that this hernia of mine has come back again, but the doctors think that it is merely a slight accident. I will explain it when I see you. My operation will wait until your departure this time. The only thing that troubles me is that I do not see how I am going to work at any of your poems while you are in England; because that is just the time I shall be incapacitated. But the doctor assures me that I shall be able to work again by the time you come back, and, judging from previous operations, I think there is no doubt about it.

I am enclosing a letter which came for you a couple of days ago, before I knew your address, and I thought it better to keep it.

Affectionately yours,

AMY LOWELL

Enclosure

[CABLE]

BROOKLINE, MASS., 14 June, 1921

MRS. FRANCIS AYSCOUGH,
CARE OF HONG KONG & SHANGHAI BANK,
9 GRACECHURCH ST.,
LONDON, ENGLAND.

Bynner has just published "Hermit on Hill" poem in *Post*. Wish to answer in correspondence column with original text, your notes, and my version, and sign your name. Do you approve. Cable answer.

AMY LOWELL

BROOKLINE, MASS., 28 June, 1921

DEAREST FLORENCE:

Where on earth are you! I sent a cable to you some time ago to England requesting an answer, but got no reply. I am just getting round again, but only crawling; as I am having abscesses where the stitches were that have to be out, my progress is slow. I have been down stairs, but lightly clad, for one week now, and in the garden twice; but I have not yet felt up to seeing anybody or doing any work.

I have succeeded in placing a good many of our poems with magazines to be printed this Summer. The July *North American* [Vol. CCXIV] printed "Songs of the Marches" [pp. 1-4], "Parrot Island" [p. 61], "The Battle to the South of the City" [p. 5], and "Autumn River Song" [p. 67]. The *Bookman* [LIV, 56] has "The Lonely Wife" [p. 10]. The *Dial* [LXXI, 438] has "The City of Stones" [p. 120] and "The

Retreat of Hsieh Kung" [p. 55]. I have sent the *Post* "The Sorrel Horse" [p. 48], and I am trying to get Ellery [Sedgwick] to print "The Cloudy River" [p. 135] in the *Atlantic*. So far I have only received payment from the *Dial*, and I shall hold your share until I know that you have got home.

I presume the authorities in St. Andrews will hold this letter until your arrival, whenever that may be. I seem to remember that you were coming back on the 29th of June. The telegraph company reports that the cable has not been returned to them, so I suppose the Hongkong and Shanghai Bank ate it up. Anyway, I am able to turn a wandering eye to business; so do write as soon as you can and tell me if you met Waley and what other things you did. I received from England a copy of Waley's paper on Li T'ai-po, which I think must have come from you. Deary me! you do seem lost. I have the contract here for you to sign, and Ferris Greenslet asks me daily where you are. Lots of love, my dear, from us both.

Affectionately yours,

AMY LOWELL

NEARING QUEBEC, CANADIAN PACIFIC, "EMPRESS OF BRITAIN,"

June 28, 1921

DEAR AMY,

We are steaming up the St. Lawrence and should arrive at Quebec to-night, Montreal to-morrow, and St. Andrews the next day. You are so much in my thoughts and I wonder how you are. Whether you have picked up well and, naturally, I am longing to hear from you. It was such a comfort to have Ada's cable saying that the operation had gone off well. The papers, which met us at Rimouski, speak of a heat wave at Montreal, so I fear that you are frizzling too.

We have had a successful time, in spite of the fact that it was short, and that the coal strike made moving about very difficult.

I have the map; it is certainly clear. I saw Waley, and hope that the copy of his pamphlet on Li T'ai-po has reached you. I told Kegan Paul to send it. He, Waley, is a strange being. He has no *apparent* enthusiasms—is most la-de-da in fact. Very scornful about every one else's work in every line, and absolutely sure of himself in every particular. At least, he doesn't *seem* to have any doubt on any subject. In view of *some* of the "howlers" he makes, it seems strange. I can't imagine the state of mind in which one feels absolute self-confidence—and confess to envying it greatly.

We were in London only a week, so I could not do everything I wanted to do, nor see every one. The man at the head of Constable's, to whom Mr. Scaife gave me a letter, was most charming. I have a good deal of manuscript to send you, if you are fit to look at it, but will not send it off until I hear from you. Love to Ada and, as always, to yourself.

Yours, dear Amy,

Florence Ayscough

Address just St. Andrews, New Brunswick, Canada.

Brookline, Mass., 2 July, 1921

Dearest Florence:

Thank Goodness you are on this side of the ocean! I am enclosing the contracts which seem to me to be all right; you will observe that I have signed them. When you have done so, keep one copy for yourself and return the others to me. I will then keep mine and send the third back to Houghton Mifflin.

I should be getting on very well, except for a series of abscesses that are appearing in the wound, which is holding me back. They have to be dressed three times a day, which is an awful nuisance; and they prevent my wearing my best supporting bandage, and the one which I can wear is not sufficiently strong to make it quite safe for me to poke round the place or even do much walking in the house. As I had already been up and out before the arrival of these abscesses, to have my string shortened again is most annoying. As I wrote you the other day, however, I am quite able to attend to a minimum of work, so you had better send me the manuscript of your introduction and let me run it over. If I ever can get rid of these abscesses, I think I can fix up the book with you in another month. Everything is a little hazy now, for they do not get better as they should.

I got the Waley pamphlet you sent me and guessed that it was sent at your instigation. I am not at all surprised at what you tell me about him. He acts like a conceited man to me. I did not think his translations were as good as ours, to tell the truth.

I am sending you a copy of the *North American Review* [Vol. CCXIV]. You will see how well our poems look in it. I gave the editor all your honours, and why she should have turned you into a professional [instead of an Honorary] librarian [of the North China Branch Royal Asiatic Society], I do not know, but such is the way of editors; they always pitch on the wrong thing.

There has been a little contretemps about the binding. The purple which you wanted was greatly objected to by Mr. Scaife, to my sur-

126

prise. He informed me that he was perfectly convinced, from experience, that red books always sold better than any other colour and that he wanted to bind the book in fire-cracker paper. After considerable bickering back and forth, I telling him of your longing for purple, we made a compromise of having the cover fire-cracker paper and the binding and lettering purple. I have not seen the dummy, which they seem to be holding away from me, probably because it is going to turn out pink and green. Mr. Scaife was a good deal upset because he could not get the real Chinese characters to put on his dummy. I told him that I doubted whether the booksellers could read Chinese, and I thought any characters would do for the dummies and that yours would arrive in time for the publication of the book, which I hope to God they will. You have ordered them—haven't you? He sent me a specimen page, which I criticised by telling him that I thought the lines were too closely spaced and that the book as set up was too broad for its height, with all of which details he agreed and told me that he would change them, but I again observe that no second proof has come. They soothe my ruffled feelings by saying that they can make any change I like, even after the dummy has gone out. As they are paying for the book, I do not like to hound them too much. I think it will look all right; and, personally, I think fire-cracker paper is a good idea.

No more at this writing, as our ancestors used to say. I have finished all the poems that you left me, with the exception of those we mutually discarded and one more which I did not think was worth doing. The others are waiting for you in a bundle in my "To Be Discussed" folder. I think I had better wait until you come down though, and not send them up to you, as it would take so long to make up preferred and alternative versions, and we can do it in a much shorter time when we are together.

Lots of love, my dear, in which Ada joins.

Affectionately yours,
AMY

P.S. Ellery has refused "The Cloudy River" for the *Atlantic*. Silly ass!

[St. Andrews], July 4, 1921

DEAR AMY,

It was nice to find your letter waiting here, when we finally arrived after some delay in Montreal. I am glad you are beginning to creep about, but hate to hear of the abscesses. What a lot you do have to contend with!! As you say that you are casting a wandering eye on business, I send you some papers for your advice and correction. The introduction is not finished; I have not wound it up as I was not sure of several points as follows:

"Written Pictures" [pp. 149–72]. How do you think it would be to print the prose bit I wrote in regard to these, which appeared in *Poetry*, as a separate little "introduction" to a small part of the book? And, in that small part, print only the translations of the "written pictures"—and use the reproduction of one of them as frontispiece to that? If you do not approve of this, I must incorporate what I wrote for *Poetry*, in the remarks I am to make on translation generally.

Portrait of Li T'ai-po. Dr. [later Sir Percival] Yetts, a friend of mine in England, is sending me what he says is a very nice picture of the poet. Do you think it would be well to have this for a frontispiece?
. . . .

In regard to the Examinations [pp. xxxix–xlii]: do you think they should be treated more fully? If so, can you please let me have the data you have? I will insert it in the introduction.

In regard to the laws of versification [pp. lxi ff.]: I enclose a few very short remarks about the forms of poetry in general. If you think this must be much more full, it must wait until I come up to Boston. I have no books on the subject here.

I am now working on the life of Li T'ai-po [pp. lxvii–lxxx], and the notes to the poems.

In regard to my coming up, so that we may put the book together. Would it be possible to wait until the first of August? I must be here from July 16 to August 1. If you think best I will come up at the end of this week, or the beginning of next, and be back here by the 16th, but if it be possible to wait, I would rather come up on August 1st, and do the work then. You would be much stronger, too. Don't you think so? I wonder if you would telegraph me your answer to this? Then I will know how much to hurry. You have no idea how hard it is to collect one's thoughts when one is moving about; it was simply *hopeless* in England.

Has your *Legends* come out yet?

I enclose also the plan of the Chinese house [p. 223], but will bring the precious map.

Is *Fir-Flower Tablets* coming out in England, too? If so, who is to have it? Waley's first book is out of print.

This must go to post—and I will return to Li T'ai-po, and his life! Much love to you and to Ada.

Yours,
FLORENCE AYSCOUGH

Are you *quite sure* that [Cho Wên-chün's] the "Song of White Heads" [Waley, *A Hundred and Seventy Chinese Poems*, pp. 50–51] is dull? I don't feel convinced on the subject, but think your opinion best.

[ST. ANDREWS], July 5, 1921

DEAR AMY,

As I scribbled on the postcard, your letter of the 2nd, came just after mine, of yesterday, had gone. It really is too trying about those old abscesses. Is the heat bad for you and, as a result, for them? It is good of you to send the *North American Review* [Vol. CCXIV]; I look forward to seeing it when it turns up.

Don't worry about my purple binding; I shall be just as happy with the "fire-cracker." Am very pleased that the binding and lettering are to be purple, as I love the two colours together. I wrote for the Chinese characters and posted the letter before we left Boston; so they should be here in a short time now.

You *have* been energetic to have finished all those poems! I never dreamt that you would be able to. You must have worked like a navvy—though that, at the moment, is not a very good simile—to have done it.

Yes, Ellery Sedgwick is a silly ass to have refused the "Cloudy River" [pp. 135–38], but you always say he does choose the wrong things.

There doesn't seem much more to be said at the moment, so—adieu. What a comfort to feel that you should be reading this to-morrow, as ever is, instead of a month hence.

I enclose the signed contracts, and have kept my own copy. I hope that Lowell and Ayscough will have a success, and am fearfully excited.

Shall I send the map, or keep it till I come? Also, would you like to have the photograph of the "written picture" [between pp. 170–71] proposed?

Love to you both,
FLORENCE AYSCOUGH

DEAR FLORENCE:

Your letter and enclosures came this morning, and as you asked me to wire whether I wanted you at once, I wired quite succinctly that I did not. I am by no means up to regularly working yet, but I can read your introduction all right, which I will proceed to do in a leisurely manner and let you know my profound opinion when I have finished it.

I am thankful to know that Waley's book is out of print. Did I tell you that Ferris Greenslet said he knew the booksellers you mentioned in Shanghai and had constant dealings with them? I am getting along upsy-downsy and in a kind of a see-sawing progress. I have told Ferris that he cannot have the manuscript of the book until August, and he has agreed; in spite of which fact, he telephones me every day to know how soon he can have it, but I have learnt that this is one of the characteristics of Houghton Mifflin Company, and I pay no attention to it whatever. I think Basil Blackwell is to handle the book in England. He has done extremely well with some oriental translations by a man named E. Powys Mathers; but it is not settled yet.

No, I do not envy you your nice cool breeze; it is too cold here today. I can seldom have it hot enough to suit me; so you need not commiserate me about the heat. I am longing to get back at work and have the book sent to press, and I really think that in a month I shall be up to full attention thereto.

At the moment, my nerves are a little frazzled by the fact that a continuous stream of coal is pouring into the cellar under my window, and, judging from the rate at which they are going this afternoon, I think it may take some months before they get through, which will be annoying, as we are hurrying it up to get it done before the arrival of Ada's three months' old grandson, Mr. John Amussen, who expects to arrive with his mother in attendance on Monday next. Since this young person is accustomed to every consideration, we feel that coal being put into the cellar is hardly treating him with due respect.

Goodbye, dear Florence, for the moment. You shall have the introduction back in—I dare not say under a week, but somewhere round there.

Affectionately yours,

AMY LOWELL

P.S. I am going to try the *Yale Review* with "The Cloudy River." Do you know who wrote it, or shall I merely say "From the *Book of*

Odes"? If you have got the photograph of the "written picture," you had better bring it down when you come. Keep the map till we meet. Contracts here o.k.

DEAR AMY,

Thanks for your telegram. I am sorry I worried you to send it. As, of course, when your letter came, I realized that you could not be ready until August. It is a thousand times more convenient for me. I send you some more copy, for you to look at, at your leisure. . . . .

Yours with love,
FLORENCE AYSCOUGH

P.T.O.

I made the Tu Fu biography short on purpose; will keep the details of his life for our next book which, I think, had better be Tu Fu *seul!!!!*

ST. ANDREWS, July 10, [1921]

DEAR AMY,

Many thanks for the *North American* [Vol. CCXIV]; the poems *do* look nice. I am amused at being called a "native of Shanghai"—as every one will think I am "Chinoise." Haven't dared to show that to Frank. Thanks, too, for your letter. I hope the coal will be stored before Mr. John Amussen's arrival.

I enclose some duplicates of revised poems, which may be of use to you—and which may save some typing. Miss Moran sent me a bundle when I left Boston and I find that I have these just as they are. Ada must be a proud and happy grand-parent.

My love to you all.

Yours,
FLORENCE AYSCOUGH

Is "Farewell Words to the Guest Ho, Who Returns to Yueh" among the discards? I think so; am not sure.

"The Cloudy River" [p. 135] is by King Hsuan of Chou, B.C. 826—the other date does not come through on my "copy" of the Ode. It must be clear on the copy I sent you, which of course is the "original."

In "The Battle to the South of the City" [p. 5], in the *North American* do you like the vultures' "*mouths*"? Is the "*m*" sound better there than "beak" would be? One does not think of birds' "mouths," does one?

DEAR FLORENCE:

In the first place, thank you very much for these returned poems. They will be convenient when it comes to sending the book in. I am afraid I like the vultures' "mouths" better. The word sounds better the way it is, and we speak quite as much of a bird's mouth as we do of its beak; but I will think it over and let you know after a day or two.

As to the Introduction [pp. xix–xcv]: everything you say is splendid, but I think we have got to change the absolute writing. You see, you love long sentences with a great many parentheses, and that is terribly hard to read. I think you must try to make your writing simpler. Of course, I could write it all over for you—but not without your being here in the first place; and, in the second place, I would rather not have it sound like my style, as it is to be signed with your name.

Another objection is that it is much too long as it is, and I think you must try to condense everything a little more. But the chief things that should be shortened are the account of the history, which instead of being six pages long should be about two, and your biography of Li T'ai-po, which is now seven pages long—and three would be quite sufficient. It is simply a question of condensing everything, not of leaving things out. I do not think it necessary to quote the poems which Li T'ai-po completed. The completions mean very little without a great deal of explanation; it is sufficient to say that he completed the other man's poems. I think it very necessary to give the different examinations and where they were held, and what kind of posts they led to. This, you say, you cannot do where you are, so you can easily wait until you come down. On the other hand, that long explanation about drunkenness should come out. It would be enough to say that the great numbers of cups the poets say they have drunk does not in the least mean what it would in any Occidental country, and then give the size of the cups, as you have done.

But the most important thing of all, after the telescoping, is to try not to have it read as if you had looked it up in the encyclopedia for an examination paper, without any regard for style. The thing after all must be readable, otherwise nobody will read it, and then it is useless to have it. And remember, in your notes, that they must be absolutely condensed. You must not try to give everything you know, and you must not make them cursive, merely statements.

This whole Introduction reads as though you had done it in a great hurry. You had better digest it some more, and try to get a little personal feeling into it. Then, if you will bring it down when you come, we can go over it together. There are many reasons why I do not want to do the absolute writing—one is that I do not feel strong enough, but the principal one is as I have said above.

The dummy came to-day, and anything more beautiful I never saw. It is simply delightful. But they propose to retail the book at three dollars, which I think much too high. They say they cannot print so handsome a book and retail it for less. They are now considering whether a cheaper book which does not look so well, but which would retail for two dollars, would be better or not. I do not know myself. I have told them it should depend entirely upon what they know of the market. I confess I am extremely loth to give up this book as it now is; it is so beautiful. I wish your characters from China would come. We have got some Chinese characters here, just to see how they look, but they may be washing accounts for all I know. I cannot send you the dummy as I should like to do, because Ferris Greenslet has asked me to hold it until they decide whether to have this book or a cheaper one. It would be a thousand pities to change it; but, on the other hand, I fear three dollars will hold off a great number of buyers.

I am returning the Introduction. I do not agree with you as to having a separate introduction in the middle of the book for the "Written Pictures." I think that should be incorporated in the Introduction. These remarks of the Chinese scholar about the difference betwen Li T'ai-po and Tu Fu are excellent, but again must be condensed, but that is easy to do so I will not send them on. The map of the house, with references, is perfect as it is. Your remarks on versification should have nothing historical about them. It is not necessary to have anything historical, merely to give the different names of the kinds of poetry and a slight analysis describing of what they consist.

There you are, my dear. Remember, in shortening up what you have already written, that we have to put in about the examinations and about the versification, and I think that the entire Introduction, including these two things, should be ten pages shorter than the entire Introduction is now, including what you wrote before you went away and the pages I am returning. That will give you an idea of the condensation we have got to make. When you come down, bring your new version and this version with you, just as it is, so that we can compare the two. Getting the book together will be an awful piece of work.

I do not think that we have done "The Farewell Words to the Guest

Ho." I will not take the time to look it up, because it is easy enough to do it if you want it, but I think it is among the discards.

The *Yale Review* has been obliged to refuse "The Cloudy River," because they are a quarterly and the October number was put in press before the editors went on their vacations. They said very nice things about it, however. It is possible that I may be able to get some into weeklies before the book comes out, but of course it is too late for any monthlies now.[1]

A bientôt, my dear. With lots of love from us both.

Affectionately yours,
AMY LOWELL

P.S. You must count one of our typewritten pages as about two of the printed ones, and you will see where we stand.

BROOKLINE, MASS., 14 July, 1921

DEAR FLORENCE:

I am sending you the dummy. I think it is extremely handsome. They expect to have the title on the back stamped in red letters, and on the side stamped in purple letters with the three characters near the edge. These two characters on the title-page are just any old thing to give the effect. As ours are three, I suppose they will have to be somewhat smaller. They intended to have the real characters of the title of the poem over each one in the text, but they cannot afford to do it in colour. This, however, I think is far too expensive, and in some cases the titles may be too long, so I have suggested that they leave out the Chinese characters of the titles of the poems in the text. It is a pity, as they are so very handsome as they are. I think I never saw a more beautiful book, and the title-page is a marvel. Will you please return it to me at once, as Mr. Scaife wants it very badly for his travellers. I am perfectly delighted with the whole look of the thing, and so I persuaded them to let me take the time to send it to you.

This is written after the letter I have just written to you, and they have decided to go ahead with the expensive book, and if they sell out the first edition they will then publish a less expensive one. Our two names are to appear on the back and sides.

Affectionately yours,
AMY LOWELL

P.S. Knowing that you have the Chinese texts of all the poems here, they can cut the characters from your copies at the press if they decide to have the Chinese titles over the poems.

[1] See Damon, *op. cit.*, p. 739, poems listed in lines 7, 10, 14, 15, 21–22, 30–31.

St. Andrews, N.B., July 16, '21

Simply thrilled at idea of seeing dummy; but as it has not come by this last post, which I have come to the post office to see about, I shall not get it until Monday. Will send it back at once. Thanks for the letter.

Yrs.,

F. W. A.

St. Andrews, July 18, [1921]

Dear Amy,

Ever so many thanks for sending the "dummy"; it is *beautiful*. I am delighted. It has just come, and there is time only to write this line and pop the whole thing in the post.

I will write a proper letter for to-morrow's mail.

The colours couldn't be improved upon, to my mind,

Love,

Florence Ayscough

P.T.O.

Can you give me any idea when you will want me? I would be glad to know as soon as possible, as I must arrange things here. I can come any time after August 1.

F. W. A.

St. Andrews, Tuesday, July 19, 1921

Dear Amy,

I hope that the "dummy," posted yesterday afternoon, will reach you to-day. It *is* nice, and I am so pleased to have the two colours I wanted. As you say, the title page is delightful. Two or three points I want to consult you on are:

China Sale. If the "dummy" went out to Kelly and Walsh, so that they could order in time for the Christmas Sale, it would be a very good thing. That is the sort of time that books sell best out there. I think that Kelly and Walsh would make a special effort; in fact, I would see that they did. If the dummy does go out I will write a personal letter to the manager, whom I know quite well. In any case, it seems to me it would be a good thing to communicate with them at once.

Frontispiece. As the book is to be so expensive, do you think that this had better be reproduced in colour? The actual colour of the "Written Picture" [facing p. 170] is beautiful. The paper is a rich brown colour, and of lovely quality. The scroll is in New York. I can send for it, if it is wanted. In the meanwhile enclose a photograph. The writing is fine.

Chinese Characters. I agree with you that these add immensely to the book. If, or rather, as, some of the titles are very long, how would it be to print them in the real Chinese way, which is in a perpendicular line at the extreme left of the page? I enclose a slip with a few written in the Chinese manner.

Introduction. Yes, I know you are right about the length, and will do as you say about telescoping.

Notes. In regard to these, you say that "they should be simply statements—not cursive." It seemed to me that your first idea, that they should be like the notes in the Folk-lore book, was so good, and I have done them like this. I think the best thing to do is to leave them until I come down; then, if you are sure that you want statements, they can be changed. I bow to your judgment, and Houghton Mifflin's, as to what the public wants. But my own experience has been that people do like to know the stories behind the poems. They always seem interested, and of course most of these stories have not been told.

I think that is all. I wonder how you are. You have not said a word about yourself. Are the abscesses healing?

Much love, yours,

FLORENCE AYSCOUGH

P.S. After writing this I went to fetch the picture of the "written picture," and found the others I enclose.

No. 1. Is the writing on the lovely brown paper. The poem itself is an uninteresting fragment about a fisherman who went into the sunset; very dull.

No. 2. Is the "Noble Lord"; it is written by a famous person, Wên Cheng-ming, and is fine calligraphy. The background is creamy, nothing special; so, if the frontispiece is not to be in colour, it might be best to have this.

No. 3. Is an example of a combination of poetry and painting.[1] The writing is in very fine "grass character"; the poem is nothing special.

[ST. ANDREWS], July 19, [1921]

DEAR AMY,

Since closing and sealing my letter, the enclosed slips have come from China. They are the Title—*Sung Hua Chien, Fir-Flower Tablets.*

---

[1] See chapter by Florence Ayscough, "The Relation between Chinese Poetry, Painting, and Calligraphy," in Harley Farnsworth MacNair (ed.), *China* ("United Nations Series" [Berkeley: University of California Press, 1946]).

No. 1 is written in the script known as *Sung Tzŭ* or "Grass" characters, the ornamental script. Personally, I am indifferent as to which
is used. The "grass," No. 2, has more individuality to my eye.

Love to Ada.

Yours,

F. W. A.

Oh, by the bye, shall you be able to put me up when I come down, or
do you want me to arrange to stop somewhere else?

BROOKLINE, MASS., 22 July, 1921

DEAR FLORENCE:

Are you aware that you have already given me at least five frontis-
pieces for the book, which is, I think, perhaps a little overdoing it? I
am inclined to think that the best frontispiece would be either your
map or the portrait of Li T'ai-po, and that one of the written pictures
should precede the "Written Picture" section. These, I suggest, should
follow the classical poems, or we can put this picture in the introduction at the place where you talk about the "Written Pictures." Of the
two, the one with the tinted background is prettier, but I think there
is a certain charm in using a poem which is translated in the book;
therefore, I give my vote for the "Noble Lord." Ferris Greenslet is
dining with me to-night, and I shall submit these things to him and
talk it over. I have unhesitatingly chosen the plain characters, not
the "grass," for the title-page and binding. If, by any chance, they
want the titles of the other poems in character, it will be difficult to
get them done in "grass." Besides, I really like the plain character
better.

Now as to your coming down here, I would suggest that you come
sometime the week of August 8th, if that suits you. It does not really
make any difference, only I think we must be able to hand in our manuscript not later than the week of the 22nd, preferably the end of the
preceding week. I told them the middle of August, which is indefinite
and gives us some leeway.

I am awfully sorry, but I am afraid I cannot put you up. The fact is
that Ada's daughter and her little baby are staying with us, and they
occupy the two rooms downstairs. This cannot very well be helped
as the baby seems to be always taking naps, and nobody can disturb
him, so that he has to have shifting rooms in order that the house-
work may be done, and my other spare room is still occupied by a
nurse, for I have not shed my last one yet, unhappily. I think the best
way would be for you to let me put you up at the Chilton Club, unless

you prefer to go to the Victoria or somewhere, and of course you will take all your meals with us and really live here. I am just as sorry as I can be about the spare rooms, but there doesn't seem to be any other way to manage it. If you would like to go to the Chilton Club, let me know, because I must see about a room for you; and let me know when you decide what date you are coming. I should not think the work would take us more than a week. Putting the book together will take practically no time. The only thing that may take some time is the Introduction and notes.

I have just placed "The Terraced Road of the Two-Edged Sword Mountains" with *Asia* [XXI (October, 1921), 848]. That makes the ninth of these poems that I have been able to place. I may be able to get in some more, but it is getting late. Most of them have not been paid for yet, and I am saving the money I have got to give you when you come.

I rather think that is all at this writing, as our ancestors used to say.

Affectionately yours,
AMY

BROOKLINE, MASS., 27 July, 1921

DEAR FLORENCE:

Mr. Greenslet says that the dummy is going at once by their traveller to Kelly and Walsh [Shanghai] and that if it has not already started, it will shortly start; and he thinks it would be a very good idea if you were to write your letter to the manager at once also, and see that they order as many copies as you can make them take.

Let me know as soon as you can about your coming, because if you want to go to the Chilton Club, I want to be sure to get you a room.

You will be sorry to hear that my abscesses have started up again. Life is full of sorrow!

Affectionately yours,
AMY LOWELL

[ST. ANDREWS], July 29, [1921]

DEAR AMY—

Thanks for your letter of the 22d. I am glad that you have chosen "The Noble Lord" [p. 152], as I am sure it is more interesting to have the photograph of one of the published poems. I will arrange to leave here the night of Monday, the 8th, so should arrive in Boston early on the 9th. Of course, I perfectly understand how impossible it is for you to put me up, with the house-full that you have. I should very much like to stay at the Chilton Club. I *think* Bessie Perkins put me up there in May, but I never used it. Nor did I ever receive my "invitation." Will that make any difference? Perhaps she didn't do it after all—but she did speak of it.

The portrait of Li T'ai-po has come and is very nice.

My love to the household.

Always affectionately,
FLORENCE AYSCOUGH

How is Carli Perkins?

St. ANDREWS, August 2, [1921]

DEAR AMY,

I am more distressed than I can say about the abscesses. It does seem hard lines. I will save you in every way that I can.

Enclosed you will find an old song often referred to in the same way as the "Snapping Willow" [p. 134, also p. 54]. I don't know whether you think it worth while to render it, or whether it can just come in the notes as it stands. It is spoken of.

I enclose, also, a list of place names according to the post-office system; I finally decided it seemed best to use that transliteration for those, and thus avoid confusion. The other spelling is never used on maps, and people will get so hopelessly mixed if places are spelt one way on the map, and another way in the poems. I send it in case you think it is worth while for one of your secretaries to go through the poems and correct the names that need it. If you don't think so, I can do it when I come; but I thought we might save time if she did.

Yours affectionately,
FLORENCE AYSCOUGH

[St. ANDREWS], August 2, [1921]

DEAR AMY,

I enclose a letter which came to-day. Mr. Hopkins is the *one* sinologue of whom I had hopes as an ally—and I thought that if he seemed favorably inclined it would be a good plan to have him review *Fir-Flower Tablets* for something or other. I tried to see him while in England, but he was away from home—so I wrote to get his ideas. We have them!!! Am looking forward to seeing you next Tuesday.

Affectionately,
FLORENCE AYSCOUGH

[Enclosure.]

Dear Mr. Hopkins,

It was a very real disappointment not to be able to see you while I was in England; both because I wanted to meet you and tell you how much interested I am in your work, and because I wanted to talk over, with you, some work that I am doing myself. I should be very glad of your opinion, as I feel that you may agree, in part, at any rate, with my point of view.

I am working at the translation of poetry, and am collaborating with a woman who is very well known, indeed, in America. She is doing the rendering from my translation. We find that it adds greatly to the vividness of the poems, and, I believe, to the sense the poet had in mind when he wrote them, if, sometimes, we analyse the character, and give it in a phrase, instead of in the arbitrary, and often rather poverty-stricken, word provided by the dictionaries. Take, for instance, *yü*, formed of the two radicals, the "wind," and "to speak"; instead of just saying "a gale," Miss Lowell has rendered this "shouts on the clearness of a gale." Again *yuan*, composed of "water" and the present form of the ancient "meeting streams," that she gives, "the whirled water of meeting streams," instead of an "eddy," "a gulf," etc., and so on. We are, of course, sparing of this method, as one must be careful not to exaggerate. But it makes lovely poems, and, to me, seems perfectly legitimate.

I should be very glad of your opinion. Many people, with whom I have talked it over, do not agree at all. Sir James Stewart Lockhart, for an example, was very angry with me, and left my verandah, in Wei-Hai-Wei exclaiming, indignantly "I do not agree with your theory *at all*." I wrote him that I did not think he could call this idea "theoretical," it being based on the actual composition of the character, but that if he chose to disagree with the *method* of translation, of course he was perfectly free to do so.

All the phrases that we give are based on the analysis of the characters as given in the *Shuo Wên*, and the *Lu Shu*. One day I was puzzling over some character or other, I forget which, and turned to the teacher saying, "I cannot think of the right word to give the meaning of this character." He replied, "Why do you trouble? It is made up of three." It has been very difficult to make the Chinese understand what I was trying to do. They generally say, "One side is the meaning, the other the sound." But once they have grasped the idea, they, on the whole, agree; at least that has been my experience. They take in more or less subconsciously the elements of the character, I think.

When Sir James was coming to see me, my teacher said, before his arrival, "Be sure to remind him of the character ——, the bird reaching earth." I said, "Do you think of that when you see the *tzŭ?* His reply was, "It is like this: when I first saw your little dog come into the room, I turned to examine what it was; now, he comes and goes, and I do not think of him, I only know that he is there—it is the same with this *tzŭ*."

I have always wanted to talk this over with you, as it seemed, from your work, that you looked at the character from a different point of view to most sinologues. And it seemed to me that you might agree.

Do you care for poetry, in itself, at all? The more one studies that of China, the more one admires it. The book, of which I am speaking, comes out this autumn. It is to be called *Fir-Flower Tablets*. . . . . I hope that you will be interested in it.

Please forgive me for troubling you like this. I know you have your hands full, but I shall be grateful indeed, if you have time to send me a line in reply.

Yours very sincerely,
FLORENCE AYSCOUGH

BROOKLINE, MASS., 3 August, 1921

DEAR FLORENCE:

I have made arrangements with the Chilton Club for you to have a room there to be ready on Tuesday morning, August 9th. Unfortunately, the by-laws permit you to be put up for a week only. I said nothing about Bessie Perkins, as you cannot be put up for more than a week a year by any member, so let us hope she did not do anything about it. Unfortunately, if you stay over a week, and I think you will have to, you will have to move on to some more hospitable hostelry, as the rules forbid me to put any guest up for more than a week. Telephone out when you get in, and Ada will arrange to have you sent for. I suppose I shall be asleep at that hour.

It will be fun to get things together, but I warn you that I am much more feeble than I hoped to be and shall not be able to put in a great many hours at a time, which is an awful nuisance. But I suppose it is to be expected. The poems will take a very short time to arrange, I know. The only thing I think we may have any real work over is the Introduction and notes.

A bientôt, my dear, with lots of love from both of us.

Affectionately yours,
AMY LOWELL

McADAM, [NEW BRUNSWICK], August 20, [1921]

DEAREST AMY,

I slept the sleep of the very just until the woman in the next section began to tell "Henry" all the experiences of the night in a most strident voice. I "cursed" her—but, as it was almost seven o'clock, had not done so badly!

This is only a line to tell you that, although I sometimes seem unreasonable, I do really appreciate the tremendous benefit and great privilege that it is to work with you.

141

Another thing—if you should want to speak to me, our telephone number is 39 ring 41—(39–41) why, heaven alone knows. Much love.

Yours,

FLORENCE AYSCOUGH

[ST. ANDREWS], Sunday, September 4, 1921

DEAREST AMY—

I wonder if the northerly wind has come to cool you off as it has done here? It is deliciously cool, and swimming this morning was delicious. It has just come over me that I never said "Thank you" to you for sending me backwards and forwards in the car every day as you did. Please forgive me.

I miss you and Ada dreadfully, and I want to know how Sonny Boy goes on, and if John remains perfectly placid. I feel as though I were firmly linked to the family.

Frank has a wonderful whale story to match the one of the shark. The whales are courting and a fisherman came in who had seen a battle royal out in the bay between five males who were contending for a lady. Frank was just starting out, and presently the whales appeared, a gentleman and a lady whale swimming side by side, and two other gentlemen a little way off. All day they swam back and forth in the passage. At intervals the triumphant gentleman would lift himself bodily out of the water—he seemed to stand on his tail—so Frank says, then he would roar and make a tremendous fuss and throw himself down into the sea with a great "gerlumph"!! Frank says it was the most astounding sight.

It occurs to me that it would be a good plan if I had the draft map back—don't you agree?—then I could make additions for the Tu Fu book.

By the bye, can Miss Moran please give me the address of the man in Faneuil Hall market from whom you get that delicious fresh butter. Cousin Lizzie Hinckley wants it. She says that you dined with a Mrs. Powell when you went to Providence. She also says that she knows Mrs. Powell as a most conventional person. Hope Godard *is* Mrs. Iselin. I thought that was her name.

Much love, yours,

FLORENCE AYSCOUGH

Dearest Florence:

Here is the first batch of proof, which hardly seems worth while sending up to you as there is so little Chinese in it; but I think I shall feel happier if you have looked it over. I am not sure that the lines are not too close together for easy reading, but that is Houghton Mifflin's affair, not mine. Things never look so well in proof as they do in printing. I have asked Mr. Bianchi at the press to see if this is the same spacing between lines as was in the dummy. If it is all right, he is not going to notify me; if it isn't, he will. I thought the dummy looked very well; so if this seems close, it is probably the difference between proof and real printing. They are terribly anxious for it back again, so post it by return mail if you can. I am sending this into town and hope it will catch the night train.

Your letter, my dear, fills me with "envy, hatred, malice, and all uncharitableness." What business have you and Frank to be courting with whales as well as watching the courting of whales, while I am slaving over your damned proof here in Brookline? There is just one thing I am determined upon and that is that if some other year you come back to St. Andrews, and I am in reasonable health and not, perchance, in England, Ada and I will come up and stay with you. I will be a good little girl and keep almost reasonable hours, but come I will, and you cannot prevent it—so you had better not come back to St. Andrews, but transfer your boat and your apple orchard to Wei-Hai-Wei.

Lorna found Sonny very miserable indeed. He has a singularly bad case, the doctor says. She has engaged a room outside her flat in the same apartment house for John, and has got a nurse for him, and she is going to be allowed to gaze at him through the door. And her friend, Mrs. King, will be there constantly to see that the nurse, who is a specially trained child's nurse from a child's hospital, is doing all right. Lorna has now had the woman for two or three days and has confidence in her, and Sonny will come home to his parents, as he is not only physically worn out, but terribly homesick and lonely, poor little chap. Ada has heard since his arrival. Lorna says he is a mere bag of bones, but I have every hope that they may be able to bring him up satisfactorily before Winter colds and things set in.

The butterman's name and address are:

W. H. Lerned & Sons
87 Faneuil Hall Market
Boston

Do ask Mrs. Hinckley who Mrs. Powell was before she was married. She was Hope something, I know. You cannot think how we miss you. I was desolate for several days, and we both feel as if you were part of the family. I wish you could come back before you sail.

Well, my dear, farewell. This must catch the post.

Affectionately yours,
Amy Lowell

Enclosure.

I have not read the proof yet. I have changed the line "early return home" to "nothing could equal the joy of going home at once," which I think is better. I will make the change when you return the proof.

Brookline, Mass., 9 September, 1921

Dearest Florence:

Here is another batch of proof. I have not corrected it, but will do so when you return it. I am, for instance, going to put Liao Sea, on page 18, with a capital "Sea," and the same with Aral Sea, on page 24. All Seas which are a part of the name should be capitalized. On page 21, I think there is a mistake. Is it "Passed the generations of Chin"? I have it in the typewritten copy just as it is here in print, and perhaps it is all right. There is no apostrophe, which I suppose is correct too. They are absolutely hopeless on the subject of the marks over the words, as you will see, but we will get these all right now. You mark them, and then they will send another proof and I will send the new proofs up. Get them back as quickly as you can.

By the way, a young lady appeared here, a couple of days ago, who had a letter to you from your friends, the McLeods (if that is the way you spell it). She had been carrying it round China hoping that you would return to Shanghai before she left; then, when she heard that you were here, she was most anxious to find you. Rose Nichols brought her out to me, and she begged me to tell you how sorry she was to miss you everywhere. Now she is sailing for England to-morrow, so that there is no hope of your seeing her, but I have promised to send her a copy of the book. She knows Waley's mother and sister, and is perfectly crazy on the subject of China. Her name is Miss Eileen Power,[1] and she is a lecturer on history and economics at the London University and has been for a long time at Girton, but has moved on.

Affectionately yours,
Amy Lowell

Enclosure.

[1] See Who's Who, 1938 (London), p. 2732.

St. Andrews, September 10, [1921]

Dearest Amy,

No mistakes in Chinese words yet; I think they are "doing noble." The Ch'in dynasty ruled b.c. 255–206; the Chin a.d. 265–420. Ch'in is in the second tone; Chin in the fourth. The sounds are quite different. The text says "generations of Chin," the "house of Chin" being understood. If you think that people will not understand, put in the "house"; but it is not necessary.

I am sorry not [at this time] to have seen Miss Power. Was she nice? I am delighted that she should have seen you.

I have cut my finger, right fore, and it is done up, so please forgive all these "typist's errors." It is strange how having one's finger out of commission throws one out.

Talk about commuting across the Pacific; some friends of ours from Yokohama arrive in Montreal today, and sail again with us on October 13th! He has come on business—so she just came along too, but it is something of a trip.

Hope that the news from Sonny is good.

Love to all my second family.

Yours,
Florence Ayscough

[St. Andrews], September 15, [1921]

Dearest Amy,

A line to say that no proof has come this week. I hope it has not gone astray. More probably they are having to distribute, and then set up again, that hand type that Mr. Greenslet spoke of.

I just thought I would let you know.

With love as ever,
Florence

I felt very humble about that diaresis—please forgive me.

Brookline, Mass., 16 September, 1921

Dearest Florence:

I am sending up another set of proofs in which I want to make various changes which I submit to you.

In "Drinking Alone in the Moonlight II" [p. 40], I want to take out the quotes before "Sages" and "Virtuous Worthies," leaving them simply with capitals, the way we did "Heroes" in the "Shu Road." I also want to take out the quotes round "Great Tao," providing that is not like a title of a book, as it were. Perhaps if I take

145

out the quotes it looks too much as if it were a person, when it means a doctrine; but still we say "Buddhism" in capitals without quotes, so I think this would go better without the quotes.

On page 42, I want to take out the quotes and leave "tzŭ" and "fu" in italics.

On page 44, I want to capitalize "Hill" for I think "Looking-for-Husband Hill" is the name of it, and if we capitalize part of the name, I think we should capitalize all.

On page 48, I want to capitalize "Women's Apartments" because it is capitalized on page 46, and I do not think we can capitalize it in one place and not in the other, and I like the looks of the capitalizing best.

That is all my questions. Are you willing to have me do this? I am hurrying this off in the hope of catching the train to-night.

Affectionately yours,
AMY LOWELL

Enclosure.

[ST. ANDREWS], September 16th, 1921

DEAREST AMY,

The proof herewith. It did not come by the day train yesterday, as there was nothing at the post-office this morning. I send back the envelope in case you care to send it in to the post-office in Boston and ask them to trace where the delay occurred. As you see, it is marked Boston 8 P.M. on September 14th, so it is absurd that it should not arrive here until September 16th at noon.

There is only one correction in the proof, or rather, to be exact, two—a couple of circumflexes have been omitted in the second poem [p. 34] to Ts'ui of Ch'iu Pu. It is P'êng Tsê.

Regarding the word you are going to change: I think you are quite right; as it reads now people would certainly think of the "spring" as a season. My only doubt about the word "well" is that it seems a little too civilized for that poem. One does not think of the writer as being near houses. Would "spring-water," or something like that, do? On the other hand "well" is good because the verb at the top of the line "kuei" means to peep into or under something. Just as you think about it; the word as it stands now should certainly be changed.

There is no time for more. It is the most glorious day. How is Sonny Boy? Love to all.

Yours ever,
FLORENCE AYSCOUGH

It doesn't help matters much if things do come by the day train. It does not arrive here till 10 P.M. and I cannot get the mail it brings until after the early morning train has left at a little after 7 A.M.

[ST. ANDREWS], Saturday, September 17, [1921]

DEAREST AMY,

Thanks for the proof. I absolutely agree with you that when quotes can be avoided they are best left out. I don't know why they look so much more conspicuous in print. Can you tell me? In "Drinking Alone by Moonlight" [p. 40], the Sages and Worthies can certainly be shorn; the Great Tao is not the title of a book, but of a doctrine. It seems to me that the "the" would obviate any idea of its being thought of as a person, I suppose you mean like the Grand Begum—but surely people will not mis-understand like that!!

P. 42. The tzŭ and fu ["of Ch'ü P'ing hang suspended like the sun and moon"] would, I agree, look better in italics.

P. 44. Yes, [Looking-for-Husband] Hill looks as if it needed a capital.

P. 48. Of course, you know, I do like capitals very much, and think that the references to [Thinking of Spring in the] Women's Apartments should be uniform.

Now there is one change that I want to make in the Introduction, it is simply an omission, and I don't know if this is the moment to mention it, or whether I should do so later. Page 10, line 17 [p. xxxiii, l. 1]: I should like to leave out "(his name means to repel injustice)." The part of his name that means that is left out (it is Ch'êng)—and, in any case, there is an argument about the meaning. Legge calls him T'ang "the successful" which I don't like at all, and there are other suggestions. It seems to me it is not a bit necessary in this place and may only give rise to a useless argument. I am very sorry, and hope it won't be an awful bother. Can you tell the people to do it before it is set up?

Much love as always. How is Sonny Boy? Love to Ada.

Yours,

FLORENCE AYSCOUGH

[P.S.] Wasn't it strange, the other day, when the telephone was so bad; the Boston operator and I could hear each other perfectly.

St. Andrews, September 20, [1921]

Dearest Amy,

No proof today, but there are two things I want to ask you about; so here goes.

Firstly, I have written to the Hong Kong bank in London about the cable, and told them to write to you and tell you what happened.

Secondly, can you please tell me the name and address of the woman who keeps the intelligence office where you get your servants? I think it is where Mamma got hers. The waitress I have had this summer wants to go to the States next spring (she can't go now as she is engaged in Montreal for the winter) and asked me for a good reference. It seems to me the best person to write to is the person who keeps the intelligence office. Margaret is a most excellent waitress, and seems a very nice woman. If you still need one when the time comes she might suit you, though I am not sure. She is the one of whom we spoke as being so very "English you know," and so very precise; and you said that you did not think that she would go with your very Irish household. She is accustomed to living in houses where a large staff is kept and is keen about her work; she keeps silver, etc., beautifully, and is always polishing away at the table. She might fit in with the others.

I was amused at the idea of Mr. Bynner as reviewer for the book. I do not think that he would have helped at all!

We leave here for Montreal on October 5, and go straight across the continent. Do you think they will have done the proof by then? I should like to see the map [frontispiece], if it were possible, and it seems to me it would be a good thing if I could see the plan of the "chia" [facing p. 223; also pp. xlviii–xlix]. Those names are so dreadful. We have never seen the title page since the Dummy came. Do you suppose they have put the Chinese characters right side up?

I was so glad to have Ada's good letter with news of Sonny Boy. Poor little chap, he must have been badly neglected, and I should think Lorna would want to take a knife to that woman!

Much love as ever.

Yours,

Florence Ayscough

Brookline, Mass., 20 September, 1921

Dearest Florence:

Here is a new batch of proof. There are one or two th'ngs I want to ask. In the first place, on Page 60, I see that "Ts'ui" is written with an apostrophe. When I used the same name, as I think I did, in the

Introduction, I wrote it without an apostrophe. We may have changed the name in the Introduction; if we did not, shall we put an apostrophe between the "s" and the "u"? "Wu-t'ung tree"[1] is spelt with the hyphen in the text but without the hyphen in the Introduction—which is correct?

On Page 67, "On the Broad Reach" is in brackets. The other times we have used sub-titles; there are no brackets. I suppose we put them in here because it is interpolated—didn't we?

They have sent me a sample page of the Introduction and of the Notes. I did not like the Introduction and undertook to tell them to change it on my own responsibility. The Notes I think are good, and I enclose a specimen page, but I have already ordered them to go ahead and print them.

Affectionately yours,
AMY LOWELL

[ST. ANDREWS], September 21, 1921

DEAREST AMY,

Before I answer your questions I must say how perfectly disgusted I am at the remark you make in your postscript. Do write and say that you are mistaken; you can't have come through!! It is too much—if you have—and there is nothing to say that can possibly express one's feelings in regard to it.

Now to business: Ts'ui with an apostrophe is correct on p. 60 [also p. 34], and the only Ts'ui I can find in the Introduction is on p. 20 [p. xlviii], and that has an apostrophe in my copy. Is there any other?

As to Wu-t'ung tree [p. 34, also p. lviii]: hyphen or not is perfectly arbitrary. I prefer it without, but what have we done in the other poems? In the "Parting Gift to Ts'ui of Ch'iu Pu" [p. 34], my copy has a hyphen. If that is being printed with one, I suppose this had better keep its; and the one in the Introduction have it put in. In which case I Ch'ang Pu should be joined also; unless you think the words in the Introduction can be left as they are—they look so much better—and yet be joined in the poems where they seem to need to run together as one name. That is the reason it is done—merely to let people know that it is one name.

P. 67. The literal title is "Autumn; Broad Reach; Song." It would look better without brackets. Don't you think so?

Those are all your questions. Would it spoil the cadence if, on p.

---

[1] [The Wu-t'ung is the tree on which the Bird-of-Happiness alights.—EDITOR.]

59, line 11, you put The King of Ch'ên, instead of King Ch'ên? It would be more literal. They have omitted the circumflex in any case.

P. 73. In the "Parting from Yang," etc., we have ch'ang p'u with capitals: do you think that it can stay so, because it is the name of a Fairy plant? If it is put in small it should have a hyphen if the Wu-t'ung does. This must fly to post.

Love as always,

F. W. A.

[St. Andrews], September 21, [1921]

Dearest Amy,

I am so sorry, the enclosed page of notes was left behind to-day—and now the mail has gone. I hope it does not matter. I like them very much and am so glad that you decided to do them this way.

I have had such an interesting afternoon. Have been speaking to an audience of country women from the real depths of the woods. They work for an industry here called the Cottage Craft, organized by a Miss Mowat who is trying to revive the arts of weaving—rug making and so on. She is making a great success of it and is creating a real interest among the women on the farms. John's blue blanket came from the shop where the things are sold. Well, she saw a piece of embroidery I had the other day and said that she wished her women could see something like it. So I scraped together all the Chinese things in the house to make a little exhibition of them and then talked about the life of the Chinese—and read some of the simplest poems. Then we had tea and they asked numberless questions. One woman said: "I had to drive five miles to come but I would gladly drive ten times as far"—and they were all thrilled. They really were. It was delightful to talk to them—one felt that unmistakable current of sympathy. They loved the poems.

I can't get you out of my mind with the possibility that that horrid thing has come through again.

I do hope you are mistaken.

Love—yours,

F. W. A.

Brookline, Mass., 24 September, 1921

Dearest Florence:

I am sending you a copy of the map. They did not send me the original draft of it, which we had, so I cannot compare them. I think the "Two-Edged Sword Mountains" should be printed in red. I dislike the colour of the red ink they have used on this map. I think it should be more like the fire-cracker paper on the cover. This I shall see to when you return it. Why should Ch'ang An be in brackets? Loyang is not, but Chinling is. Naturally these all want to be the same. I should take out the brackets if I were you. It looks to me as if the "Two-Edged Sword Mountains" should be lifted a little to the left—a little Northwest, as it were—the name appears to be jumping off the mountains here, but if you think it is all right we will leave it. I think they have put in Tung T'ing Lake and the Three Chasms very nicely. I do not notice anything else, but you will probably find dozens of things. The plan of the house has not come yet.

Affectionately yours,
AMY LOWELL

ST. ANDREWS, September 26, 1921

DEAREST AMY,

I am delighted with the map. Don't you think it is nice? Yes, you are right, the red is too yellow; the fire-cracker colour would be much nicer.

The Two-edged Sword Mts [p. 52, also p. 8] are in black because they still exist under that name; but if you think they would look better in red I shall be quite "agreeable," as they say. I don't think that their position had better be changed, as the first line of the Terraced Road [p. 52] says that one sees them directly south of Hsien Yang, one of the names of the present Sianfu.

The reason Ch'ang An and Chinling are in brackets is that they *are* Sianfu and Nanking, respectively. That is, the earlier names have disappeared and the towns are still large. . . . . And I suppose that, to be consistent, Loyang [p. 54] and the Two-edged Sword Mts. had better be in the same colour Yes, they have inserted the Tung T'ing Lake [p. 156] and the Three Chasms [p. 72] very well. The handwriting is identical.

Thanks for the copy of *Asia*.[1] Did you notice the very garbled story of Yang Kuei-fei under the title "The Loveliest Lady of China"? I wonder who L. Adams Beck is? [S]He can't know much Chinese if [s]he thinks Kuei-fei was her name! [p. 181, n. 23]. The pictures, too, are idiotic. The gate in front of which Ming Huang lies is utterly unlike anything in China, and the Taoist paradise in which Yang Kuei-fei appears is peopled with Buddhist priests with halos. And the big

[1] Vol. XXI, No. 10 (October, 1921).

cassia tree is heavily laden with pears, plums, etc., instead of bearing tiny little sweet-scented blossoms. The whole thing is so preposterously un-Chinese that it is most discouraging. I am going to write to Mr. Ford, in any case, and think I will mention to him that a paper which calls itself *Asia* should be more careful.

Much love.

Yours ever,
FLORENCE AYSCOUGH

ST. ANDREWS, September 28, [1921]

DEAREST AMY,

The enclosed came yesterday, and I have written Mrs. Brigham that, as I am not well up on the procedure of publishing, I have sent it to you—and that you will answer the question. So, can you send her a line direct? What do you think about it? I know that you won't have your own things set to music, but perhaps this is different.

By the bye—is your cable address, "Sevenels," still registered? Mine, as you know, is just Ayscough, Shanghai.

Much love—yours,
FLORENCE AYSCOUGH

ST. ANDREWS, September 30, [1921]

DEAREST AMY,

Chicago has been trying to talk to me and has kept me so long at the telephone that now I must hurry to catch the post. Text of Poems, p. 77: Yes, Golden Valley is better without quotes. P. 79: The Wu here is not the same Wu as the name of the kingdom. As you say, on p. 78, it should certainly be capitalized; but here [p. 79] it is the Wu *dance*. The line reads: "Lo," Spread out, fall; "I," Clothes, or dresses; "Wu," the posturing dance, in doing which very long dresses are worn; "Nu," the women who are dancing; "Chiao" beautiful, lovely. So, I should think that both wu and dance should be without caps.

P. 83. Yes, Official [l. 9] is better capitalized.
P. 85. Yes, Rest-House [l. 2] looks better.
P. 88. Yes, Measure [l. 1] is better.
P. 89. You are quite right: neither "woman speaks" nor "man speaks" is in the Chinese: but don't you think their being in italics is sufficient? Just as you think best. •
P. 93. Yes, Third Month [l. 2] should have caps.

152

Now would you look at the Notes please.

Note 11 [p. 177]. An Lu-shan lacks a hyphen.

Note 25 [p. 182]. Should Wu dance have caps? It is the dance, not the kingdom.

Note 27 [p. 182]. Should Gold Magpie have quotes because it is a story?

Yours with love,

F. W. A.

Better not post here after Monday, but I can be caught at Montreal where we arrive Thursday, the 6th, and spend the day, leaving ten P.M.

BROOKLINE, MASS., Sunday, October 2, 1921[1]

DEAREST FLORENCE:

Everything is here but the last thirty pages of the text, and I am rushing this off to catch the night train. Before I forget it, please tell me opposite which of the written pictures the photograph of the original is to be put? Which is the poem that it is? Also, I want your addresses in Montreal and Vancouver, and your ship, and the proper way to address it.

Now to my queries: First, the Notes.

Note 69. Shouldn't the apostrophe come after the "s" in soldiers? Was she not the cook to all the soldiers, not to one alone?

Note 70. Instead of "has come to mean" put "has become a complimentary expression for."

Note 87. "Embankment" does not seem a terrible enough word, and we have "cliff" farther down. Suggest something.

Note 121. Instead of the "Hsiung Nu chief replied" put "the Khan replied," since he is called "Khan" earlier in the note.

Note 145. You say King Hsüan was the *Emperor* referred to. Shall I say "the king referred to," as further down we again have king.

Note 155. We have "soon after" and in the next line, "not long after." I suggest "immediately" for the first of them.

Note 164. Since there are five sovereigns, had I not better put "*circa* 2697 B.C."?

Key to House. Am going to put the numbers and exdented Chinese names in italics.

No. 23. Think "Passages" should not be capitalized, since it is not the name of them, merely what they are.

Don't you think that, throughout the Introduction and Notes, whenever a dynasty is given with its name as "T'ang Dynasty," for

---

[1] Holograph letter.

instance, "Dynasty" should have a capital, as in the Table of Dynasties in the end? The "Key" and the "Table" are on separate pages; they are merely end on in the galleys for convenience.

Now for the Introduction.

P. LIV. I am putting "Wu-t'ung" with a hyphen and a small "t."

P. LVIII. Instead of "made up of their four tones" put "four poetic tones."

Galley MSS. 25. Instead of "earliest were probably" put "oldest," to avoid echo with "earliest" in first line.

Instead of "volume we know" put "volume known as the *Book of Odes*."

Galley MSS. 31. Instead of "given to very few" put "permitted" to avoid echo with "given" two lines before.

Shu Tai Tzŭ should be "Tzŭ" not "Tzü" according to copy, should it not?

Last line put "departs from his master's house."

Galley MSS. 23. The Ch'u Lai Mountains should have the "Mountains" capitalized? See Min Mountains above. It looks funny with a small letter.

Galley MSS. 4. "Li Ling" or "Li Lung"; both are here.

Galley MSS. 6. Instead of "having arrived there" put "on arriving there."

Text of Poems.

P. 103. I have changed that awful "parallels of latitude traversed by the constellations" to "paths of the planets" which I think is *much* better. I want to change "hear" in the next to last line to "heard." The change from the past to the present does not seem good, for I am sure the whole poem is in retrospect.

P. 113. "City" [literally White Emperor City], I am sure, should not be capitalized unless this is its name, which I do not suppose it was.

P. 115. I suppose this poem cannot have been written by Li T'ai-po about Tu Fu, and you have the title mixed. The "hated army" would seem to point to Tu Fu? Be careful about this, although I imagine you are quite right.

P. 119. Did we add "written in exile" or is it in the original title? If we added it, I think it should be under title in small caps, and brackets.

P. 131. I am putting the "By a descendant" etc., in small caps, as on p. 134.

P. 134. Does it say *bamboo* flageolet in the *original*? If not, might it not be a flute made of the willow branch, a sort of willow-whistle.

Lord! What a rush! I shall telephone before you leave St. Andrews. The motor is at the door to take this, 6 P.M. Heaven send it catch the train.

Yours in haste and fatigue,

AMY

Worked till after 6 this morning to get the damn things done!

154

ST. ANDREWS, Monday, October 3, [1921]

DEAREST AMY,

I wonder if any proof is coming to-day. I will write at once so as to have this part ready if it does come. The train now comes in an hour later, and goes out an hour earlier; so there is no time to spare between getting and sending off the letters. Moreover, there is only one train a day. If you send anything to Montreal, address the Ritz-Carlton Hotel, Sherbrooke Street.

I will ring you up on the evening of the sixth at about six o'clock. Montreal being on a trunk line we should be able to hear properly. I have nothing especial to say, but want to say au revoir by word of mouth. By the bye, I asked Miss Moran to let me know how much the long distance calls I had on the telephone while I was in Boston, came to. I think I had one to Providence, one to Narragansett and one to St. Andrews. She never has done so, but won't she please let me know in Shanghai? Another thing: please let me share all the calls we have had this month down here.

No proof. This must go.

Love,
FLORENCE AYSCOUGH

BROOKLINE, MASS., 4 October, 1921

DEAREST FLORENCE:

Your letter of Monday the third and your telegram have just come. It is funny that you should have said you were going to ring me up and I should have asked you to ring me up, in my letter, at one and the same time. It was simply beastly yesterday; we could not hear a word.

I asked Mr. Greenslet about who was to pay for the map, and he said, just what I feared he would say, that maps and illustrations were part of the manuscript and were always paid for by the author, which means that I owe you £3.5s, which the bank here assures me is, at the present rate of exchange, $12.16. Exactly what it was at the time you paid the bill it is impossible now to say, especially as you paid it in English money, but this seems to me the fair thing to do.

You are very honest, my dear, in wanting to pay for the long distance calls you had while you were here and to share the calls which we have had this month. I will let you know how much they are, if you want; but it seems foolish.

There was one thing which I forgot to send you, but it was of very little importance, as it was so excellent, and that was the plan of the

155

house. It looked perfectly beautiful, and I compared it with your old drawn plan very carefully, and it was absolutely correct. The numeral five was very Chinese in construction, so much so that it was impossible to read it, so I marked on the plan that it was to be engraved more clearly. I am also having "lake" added to Kokonor. There is plenty of room for it, and I think it makes things clearer.

I am horrified to learn from your letter that the proof I posted on Sunday afternoon, in time for the Sunday night train, had not reached you by Monday. I cannot understand it. I suppose you got a big batch to-day; I trust you did.

They have just telephoned me from the press that they have some more pages of the text, but not all. These I will mail to-morrow to Montreal, reading them through to-night and writing any queries I may have. I am afraid, however, that you may not get them, but it is no great matter if you do not, as they are not making mistakes in names anymore, and the only thing of real importance is that I read them through and find things that I want to ask you about.

I am also going to write you a love letter to-night and address it to Montreal, merely to tell you how good it has been doing this with you and what "a angel" you are. In great haste.

Affectionately yours,

Amy Lowell

St. Andrews, October 4, Tuesday, [1921]

Dearest Amy,

The train is so late to-day that it is out of the question to catch the return post. I am sending you a telegram to this effect, giving also the hotel address in Montreal in case the letter I wrote yesterday missed the post. It was very late for it. The train is *excessively* inconvenient now.

My dear, you have been having an *awful* time of it. I am so sorry; the next book we do I will sit at your elbow the entire time! The picture goes opposite "The fishermen draw their nets from the great pool of the T'an River" [p. 170], etc.

We sail October 13, have two nights in Vancouver.

Address: Vancouver Hotel.

Ship: "Empress of Asia," care Canadian Pacific Railway Co., Vancouver, B.C.

The telephone was hopeless last night, I could hear nothing. There was a bad storm raging, so perhaps that was the reason. As I wrote you, and as you suggested in your letter of this morning, I will ring up from Montreal. You had better find out just when the Montreal night mail closes. I am not sure about it. We shall be there all day; so I should receive anything you send. This must go "on the wings of the wind."

Yours,
F. W. A.

I am "thrilled" at the idea of seeing it all—and think you have been a marvel to get it to me.

[EN ROUTE], October 5, [1921]

DEAREST AMY,

Your letter of Sunday which, you poor thing, you had to write out, came yesterday too late to answer—so, here goes:

Notes

No. 69 [p. 195]. Yes, the woman's husband was cook [p. 47] to all the soldiers; so you are right: it should be "soldiers'."

No. 70 [p. 196]. I like your alteration.

No. 87 [p. 201]. It is difficult to find a substitute for "embankment" which I agree with you is too mild. [S. Wells] Williams gives: T'ang—a bund, a dike to resist water, a sea-wall of stone. Could one call it a "water-wall"? Does thesaurus give anything as an alternative to "dike"? I haven't one here.

No. 121 [pp. 209–10]. Yes, I like your alteration, "The Khan replied," etc.

No. 148 [p. 216]. You are quite right: King Hsüan [p. 135, l. 3] should not be called emperor. If you do not want to use King three times, how would Ruler do instead of Emperor?

No. 155. Yes, I like "immediately" [p. 218, l. 14] very much.

No. 164. Yes, the addition of "circa" [p. 221, l. 2] would be an improvement.

Key to House

I think the idea of putting the Chinese names and numbers in italics is good.

No. 23. The actual meaning of Lang is passage. No. 23 is literally Ch'u Lang —Crooked Passage. If this Passage is capitalized I suppose that the "Passage" in Nos. 4, 5, 7, should also be in caps. How do you think Passage-of-Many-Turnings would be?

Yes, I agree dynasty, when used as T'ang Dynasty, should be caps.

Introduction

P. lviii. So glad you are going to alter Wu-t'ung.

P. lxii. "Poetic tones" would be an improvement.

Galley MN 25 [p. lxvi]. Yes, "oldest" and "volume known" are better.

Galley Mn 31. "Permitted" is an improvement. Tzŭ [p. lxix] should have a little "u" over it, not diaresis. "Depart from his master's house" [p. lxx] is better. Do you think "giving up a job" is a trifle colloquial? Would "position" be too pedantic?

Galley ME 23 [p. lxxii]. Yes, Ch'u Lai Mountain with cap looks much better.

Galley MK 4. Li Ling [p. lxxv], is the right name.

Galley MA 6. "on arriving there" is better.

Text of poems

P. 103. "Paths of the planets" is infinitely preferable. I agree about "heard."

P. 113. It is literally "White Emperor City"; but I think as the "City" comes so far before, it had best be small.

P. 115. No, the title is quite clear. "At Heaven's Edge Thinking of Li Po." I must say I think that the "hated your essay" is obscure; but there it is.

P. 119. I took Waley's title. I have not got the Chinese title myself, as the Old Thing wrote it, and often omitted that important item. Waley's is in his *170 Chinese Poems*.[1] I should *think* [rightly] that he added the "in exile," but do not know.

P. 131. I quite agree about "by a descendant."

P. 134. It says just "Hun Ti," literally horizontal flute [l. 4]. But the character has a bamboo radical, and van Aalt gives this instrument in the bamboo category. I do not think that it is a willow whistle. If you would rather call it "flute" or "horizontal flute," pray do.

Now for a few remarks of my own;

Notes

No. 62. You have probably noticed, but in case it has slipped you, "hang" is misspelt in the quotation of the line of the poem.

No. 76. There is a little v at the end of one line. Of course I know this is only galley, but it is so easy to have things slip.

No. 86. K'un Lun, not Ku'un Lun; it is wrong in my manuscript; but that is not corrected, so you probably have it right.

Key to House

No. 11. Do you think "Running Horse Two-Story Apartment" would look better with hyphens, as Running-Horse Two-Story Apartment? It just struck me that it might.

No. 27. Lacks a dieresis over Yüan.

Dynasties [p. 227]

The Sung Dynasty, A.D. 960–1277, is printed too far in. It looks as if it were one of the Five Dynasties. It should be on the line with Yüan. This Yüan lacks a dieresis.

Under the Han Dynasty, where it changes from B.C. to A.D., don't you think that there should be a B.C. after the 206? I think I wrote it "206 B.C.–A.D. 25," but, as I have not a copy of this table, cannot be sure. Perhaps they thought that looked clumsy.

---

[1] It is not! And it took quite a few minutes on a *hot* June day (less rare than Miss Lowell's distinguished cousin implied) when Heaven was trying the Earth, to find "Hearing the Early Oriole [Written in Exile]" on p. 65 of Mr. Waley's *More Translations from the Chinese*.

P. xxviii. Don't you think that "chan tao" would look better in italics? It is the *sort* of road like "corduroy road," not the name of this one.

P. xxix. The Green Sea is also called Inland Sea; and this is what we have called it on the Map, as it was called that in the "Songs of the Marches." Do you think that we should put in, that it is also called this?

P. xxxiii. I should like to omit the parentheses after T'ang's name, I mean delete "(his name means to repel injustice)." You see it is not T'ang which means that, but his sobriquet "Ch'êng," which we do not give. In any case, there is an argument about it. Legge gives it "The Successful," which I think is rotten; but there is no point in stepping into a controversy, if one is not forced to. Is it at all necessary to acknowledge that the passage in quotes is from Legge's *Book of History?*

P. xxxiv. Don't you think that "(Masculine Powers)" looks funny like that? Ought it not to be "Called the Masculine Powers," or something like that? or omitted altogether? It is not important.

P. xlviii. I think the sentence re the *chien*, line 10, is not quite clear. You see it is the buildings which are increased—not the *chien*. It is like this

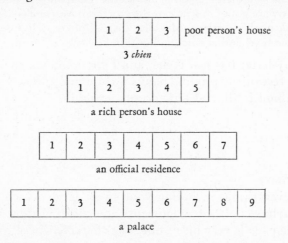

There may be any number of buildings, but each consists of the same number of *chien*, and each building is separated from the next by a courtyard, and has the passages running along the sides of the court. It is not more *chien* that are added, but more buildings of the same *number of chien that the other buildings have.* I enclose a little photograph of one of the Peking Palaces, and, if you look at it with the magnifying glass, you can see the nine divisions, or *chien*, of which I speak.

P. lvi. The Yüan of Yüan Yang lacks dieresis. [And continued so to do!]

P. lviii. Wu-t'ung has hyphen in wrong place.

Galleys MN33 [p. lxiv]. I still think that the (Old Style) and (New Style), in parentheses like that, give the wrong impression, and look as if we thought Ku Shih and Lü Shih, were translated Old Style and New Style. Ku—old; Shih—poem. Lü—Law; Shih—Poem. Nothing is said about style, which is the word "p'ai." If you really think this is right as it is, leave it—but it strikes me every time I read it.

Text

P. 113. This is just a suggestion; as I read the two lines:
The wind clouds at the horizon become confused with the Earth. Darkness.
The myriad chrysanthemums have bloomed twice. Days to come—tears.
It occurred to me that the last might look better printed like the first, that is:
The myriad chrysanthemums have bloomed twice. Days to come.
Tears.
Or else that the first ought to be printed as the second is now:
The wind clouds at the horizon become confused with the Earth—darkness.
This is, of course, the sort of thing that you understand and know much more about than I do. I only felt when I read the lines that they should be uniform.
P. 120. Yü lacks a dieresis. [But—unlike the Yüan above—obtained one.]
P. 126. As we are going to speak of the Northern Measure [p. 88] can we not also speak of the Southern Measure, instead of constellation? This would be like the text, and is much more Chinese.

Your day-letter has just come, and I am delighted that I am going to see the rest of the proof. Thanks a thousand times; you have been an angel about it all, and I am deeply grateful.

Much love, yours,
FLORENCE AYSCOUGH

MONTREAL, October 6, [1921]

DEAREST AMY,

Found everything, including your sweet letter which I will reply to in train; have only a few moments now. Will write you why later.

The title page is very nice—only the characters need to be canted a little. If a straight line is drawn through them the characters should seem to be hung perfectly straight, and right in the middle. Do you see what I mean? The whole thing leans a little to the left now. I enclose the first four characters of the "Written Picture."

Page 136. Yes, Great Decree of Fate [l. 23] is same as Great Decree and should have caps.
Page 141 [l. 2]. Am so relieved that you are going to change that lotus line; it worried me to death. There is no "tall" in text; I think "bent down by day, spread open at night."
Page 143. We added "Plum-blossom Concubine." All that is in the Chinese in the title itself, and Chiang Ts'ai P'in. Do as you think best.
Page 144. Same with this one. All that there is is "Dancing, Yang Kuei-fei." We added rest. So, again, do as you think looks best.

160

Page 152. I think Sun and Moon [l. 12] look better capitalized; and after all they are a certain *kind* of thing. Ten Thousand districts [l. 16] means everywhere—ask Ada!!

Page 155. The city by the river [l. 3] is not its name; it lies there. Can't it be capitalized? I do like caps so much.

Page 156. Does one capitalize "lake" [l. 1], yes, Lake Superior, etc., Yes.

Page 160. Yes, do capitalize Mt. [l. 4].

Page 164. A Chinese word is misspelt: it should be Lêng, not Lung [l. 5].

Page 167. Yes, quotes to Book of Changes [l. 2] should certainly be put.

Page 171. Think joining first two lines great improvement.

Am going to ring you up in a little while

Much love as always,
Florence Ayscough

Didn't we decide that the "Cloudy River" [p. 135] should not be described as *by* King Hsüan?

Leaving Fort William, October 8, 1921

Dearest Amy,

The letter I wrote from Montreal was only a scrap, and the reason was that the time I had kept in which to write you properly was taken up with Mr. Sandwell, editor of the *Canadian Bookman*. I did not know that such a publication existed, but when I saw a copy, and saw that a Canadian Authors' Association had been formed to encourage the cause of literature in Canada, I was determined to see the editor. By dint of telephoning he was discovered. He had already gone back to his home in St. Lambert's, outside Montreal, but he most amiably travelled back, had a cup of tea with me, and a chat which I found most interesting.

He is a lecturer at McGill University, and, as I told you over the telephone, spoke enthusiastically about you and your work. I wish I could remember exactly what he said—but there was so much and all spoken with obvious sincerity. He did say, "I feel that there is no one to-day whose personality has such an influence on the current of literature"; and again, "There is no critic whose word can make or mar a reputation as her's can"—and so on. He spoke of your criticism as being keen, generous and appreciative. As I also told you, he wondered whether you could be induced to take a Canadian tour and said, "Of course, we cannot give her the big audiences she is accustomed to." After all, the population of Canada is very small; not much more in the whole country, than there is in the city of New York. I said that, of course, I could not answer for you, but that I thought you were always glad to do anything you could to increase interest in literature—and the only thing to do was to ask you himself! So, he said he would.

We also talked about the Chinese poems and I showed him some of those I had with me, which, unfortunately, were only "The Cloudy River" [p. 135] and those that came after it. But he was very keen, and said he would like some for the next *Canadian Bookman*. He also said that it did not matter if the book came out in America at just the same time, as it would take it a little while to get up into Canada, and having some poems in the *Bookman* would arouse more interest. I expect by now you have heard from him, but if not could you, perhaps, send him some poems? His address is: B. K. Sandwell, McGill University, Montreal. He is a friend of some people you know, Stringer, Ralph [Robert?] Norwood, etc., and said that he had been talking with them of you a day or two ago.

And now to thank you for your perfectly sweet "love-letter."[1] Amy, dear, I can't tell you how I appreciate it. Yes, as you say, let us keep this intimate feeling of understanding which exists now—whatever comes. You say you are not easy to work with. I do not find it difficult. I really do understand how you feel when you are trying to get the right words, and how horribly nervifying it is. I know that my lack of experience and utter "greenness" must have been fearfully trying, but I will get over that with time. I have learnt a lot, and will be better next time. The one thing you don't quite realize, even now, is the awful difficulty of getting at the Chinese facts. It really is hard; but next time I shall have my notes compiled as I go along and will have the proverbial "chapter and verse."

As soon as I get back I will work on Tu Fu. As to the *Yü Chiao Li*, how do you think it would be to publish a sort of synopsis of the story, taken from Rémusat, with real translations of the poems? You see, a proper translation would take me so long to do, and it does not seem important as some of the other work which there is to be done. Moreover, it is so long and detailed that I think the public would weary of the whole, don't you? Many of the scenes are repetitious, or, rather, are much alike, but the whole is quite delightful. I will get a Chinese copy as soon as I arrive in Shanghai and go .o work on the poems.

---

[1] An excerpt from this letter is to be found on p. 109 of *Firecracker Land:*

"You have been an angel to me. A monument of patience. I am not easy to work with, I know. I get so excited, and I think only of the work and not at all of anyone's feelings. Forgive me for all my many faults and omissions, and please believe how very grateful I am for your wonderful sympathy and understanding. But we must do other books. This is too good to be the only one. So dash into Tu Fu, my dear; we are still almost alone in that field."

Your idea of sending Julia Marlowe a copy of the book appeals to me, but I shall have to trouble you to arrange about it as I don't know where to address her. I enclose a card. I also enclose a letter to Marceau about the photographs as I cannot remember their number on Tremont Street. Thanks so much for the cheque. Will you get the draft of the Map back from Houghton Mifflin, please, so that I can use it for the Tu Fu. I will put in enough places to be able to follow him in his cruisings about. It will be interesting to have it, even if we do not publish it in the book.

Well, there does not seem to be much more to say; we are flying towards the prairies; it is cold, and there has been a little snow—the wheat crop has been most wonderful and the grain elevators are full.

Do you know, I would so much rather have your letters written in pencil on that nice yellow paper than a formal type-written production. Do, sometimes, write to me when you have finished your work after supper, and send it just as it is. I hate to go off and leave my second family, but shall try to come back next year for a bit in any case.

Much, much love,
Florence Ayscough

Don't forget to let me know about the long-distance calls!

Yokohama, October 25, [1921]

Dearest Amy,

We have pitched and rolled, and heaved and shivered across this great stretch of water in the most unquiet manner. We ran into the worst hurricane they have had for years, and the barometer fell to 27, 4 point 88—and the lowest known is 27, 3 point 33. It is quite impossible to describe. The sea was very wonderful, and I wish you had been with us to immortalize it—that is if your brain would have worked under such trying conditions. One really had almost to take to the mode of progression of primitive man, that is on all fours (he *did* proceed on all fours didn't he?) and the sound of it all was—appalling!

I wonder so much what you have done in regard to the *Post* review. As there is no Chinese text with the book, and as not one Chinese scholar in a dozen will have the text, it seems to me far more important to have the review written by someone who knows poetry. [Percival] Yetts is entirely uninterested in it. Of course, if it were possible, I should like to have Mr. Lowes do it; but there was some reason, I forget what, that made it out of the question. It seems to me you said that he wouldn't dare to tackle anything Chinese; but, after all, it is the book from the translated point of view that is being reviewed—that is the main thing, and that he is perfectly qualified to decide upon. Well, you will decide, and I shall be content.

I wonder if the books will be out when this gets you? I can hardly wait to see them. Sir John Jordan ought to have a whole collection of letters after his name—but I can't remember them, so there is nothing to be done. I think that if the books have not gone and they put "K.C.B., etc.," it will do. The "etc." covers a lot of evils. I suppose they will know Bishop Brent's "Rt. Rev.," and so on. Lenox Simpson [*pseud*. B. L. Putnam Weale] is the adviser to the Chinese at the Disarmament Conference, and I thought it would be a good thing for the book to go to the Conference.

There have been some pleasant enough people on board; if it hadn't been so infernally rough one would have got to know them better. One woman met me in the hall this morning and said, "When you are writing, tell Miss Lowell how we read and love her poems, and how sad we feel to know that she has been so ill." She is a teacher of literature, and is the sister of Dr. Drury, head of St. Paul's School. She is thrilled with the poems.

I must go on shore and have a glance at things, and there is a mail out to-morrow, so adieu.

Much love to you both.

As ever,
FLORENCE

CANADIAN PACIFIC OCEAN SERVICES, LIMITED,
R.M.S. "EMPRESS OF ASIA," October 28, 1921

DEAREST AMY,

I saw in the Kobe paper that Sir John Jordan is to go to Washington to the Disarmament Conference, and it struck me that if there is still a review to be written, he *might* do it, if he were asked nicely. Of course, he may be too busy. I do not know how he writes, but he is a devoted friend of China and knows the Far East from A to Z. He began life as a student interpreter in Peking, became Minister to Korea, and then to Peking (1906–1920). His knowledge of China is very great, and he is fond of poetry—though I don't know that he knows much about it. I gave him a copy of Waley when he left the East which he liked. Of course "reviewing" is not exactly his line, but I think that he might be willing if properly approached. (I don't know the etiquette of it all; could you add a personal note?) His name would carry weight in England—and I should think in the U.S. as well—

considering he is a Privy Councillor, a member of the Disarmament Conference *and* a Chinese scholar. I have found a *Who's Who* on board. The proper way to address him is

> The Rt. Hon. Sir John Jordan,
> P.C. G.C.M.G. K.C.B. etc., etc.,
> ℅ H. B. M.'s Embassy, Washington, D.C.

If his copy has not already gone to England, could it please go to him in Washington? Perhaps one had better go there in any case. I have written him a note, now, telling him that I had told the publishers to send him one. Of course I have said nothing about a review. He is a perfect dear, and a great friend of mine.

We arrive at Shanghai, or rather at Woosung, down the river, to-night, and go home to-morrow morning. Nothing to add to my letter from Yokohama.

Love to you all,

FLORENCE AYSCOUGH

Oct. 31. Since arriving I find that Dr. Ferguson (of whom we spoke first for a review) has gone to America to the Disarmament Conference. I am quite sure that he would write a review—but of course it may be too late when this reaches you, and I can't think of a cable that would be explicit. As you may have forgotten his name even, will you please ask Houghton Mifflin to send him a copy of the book and address:

> Dr. J. C. Ferguson,
> ℅ Chinese Embassy,
> Washington, D.C.

Everything is well here, and it is nice to be in our own house.

Yours ever,

F. W. A.

BROOKLINE, MASS., 10 November, 1921

DEAREST FLORENCE:

I was bound I would not write you a line until I could tell you that the proofs were out of my hands. The last few pages seeped away yesterday afternoon. Don't exclaim; you have no idea of the task this thing has been. I had proofs and proofs and proofs. In some cases I had as many as five to a page, and even in the final plate proof there were mistakes; most of them, I fear, owing to my own stupidity; for some you were responsible; for others the press was to blame. We did the thing in too great a hurry, and some little details got left out that should have been put in. For instance, Note 130 [p. 211] simply read "Ch'ü Yüan, the poet and statesman. (See Note 62.)" As a matter of fact, the point of the note was that he had drowned himself in the Mi Lo River [p. 115], which fact was duly recorded in the original analysis. I never should have discovered that it was left out had it not been for the note to the enclosed poem of Witter Bynner's. As the plate was already electrotyped, I had an awful time fixing it, but finally I left out "the poet and statesman" which did not seem to me important, and put "drowned himself in the Mi Lo River." Witter Bynner, you will observe, has Ku Lo,[1] but your analysis had Mi Lo without any doubt, as did the text, so I left it. I hope to goodness you are right.

I am afraid you must expect a bill for several hundred dollars for author's corrections. I will dispute with them when it comes in and get it down all I can, but I am afraid it will be somewhere between three and five hundred dollars. They charge a fearful amount for author's corrections. They charged me . . . . for my corrections on *Legends*.[2] I disputed it and have not yet settled it, for they have not had time to go over the proofs with me. . . . . The press, of course, will pay for their own blunders. It may not be as much as this, but I want to warn you so that you will not get a shock when the bill comes in.

Your telegram made me laugh and weep at the same time. I suppose you think the books are out and circulating freely. Not at all, my dear, the printing started yesterday, and they tell me it will take a week to print, a week to bind, and two or three days for drying; after that you must allow for transportation. I think if the book is in circulation by the first of December[3] we shall be doing well, and that will not help you a bit for the Christmas sale in Shanghai, as I realize perfectly, but I do not think anything can be done about it. I have just this minute rung up Mr. Scaife, and he says he thinks the book will be out in three weeks here, but that it will probably be several months before it can reach China. That would be in quantity for your bookseller, provided he has ordered, or will order, in quantity; your own personal copies will go by mail, if you so desire, and you can judge how long they will take to reach you.

I think the book will be a great credit to us, and I have had a most

---

[1] But see "To Li Po at the Sky's End," p. 150 in *The Jade Mountain: A Chinese Anthology, Being Three Hundred Poems of the T'ang Dynasty, 618–906, Translated by Witter Bynner from the Texts of Kiang Kang-Hu* (New York, 1929).

[2] Published in May, 1921.

[3] It was published on December 14, 1921.

wonderful experience in regard to it. Mr. Telly H. Koo—his real name
he assures me is T'ai Le, he having changed the spelling because his
American friends mispronounced his name when he spelt it in the
usual way—wrote me a letter and asked me to send him either some
of my poems or some of our translations. I replied by sending him
"[The Perils of] The Shu Road"[1] [p. 6] and Tu Fu's "A Desultory
Visit to the Fêng Hsien Temple at the Dragon's Gate" [p. 103]. He
replied to me as follows:

It is hardly imaginable for an American poetess who does not claim to read
and write Chinese to make such a literal and almost exact rendering of some
of the greatest Chinese poems. I can still repeat word by word that poem on
"The Perils of a Szechuan Road." It is a thrilling tale portrayed in a masterly
manner by one of China's greatest poetic geniuses.

In China, there is a well-known classic scholar who does not read a word
of English. He secures the assistance of one of the American educated students, and now the stories of Dickens and Stevenson are being read by thousands of non-English speaking Chinese. It is through men like these, and
ladies like you, that the exchange of intellect is made possible, and that a
better mutual appreciation of the East and West can be effected. You are lending immortality to our poets in this part of the world.

Then he goes on with a long letter in which he says that poetry is
out of fashion in China, that everybody is getting very material.

I asked him if he could tell me any one who knew the rules of Chinese prosody, and he referred me to a gentleman named Dr. Chao, a
quondam Harvard student, who, he says, was Bertrand Russell's interpreter when he was in China. He lives right here in Cambridge, and
I am going to try to get hold of him and see what I can get out of him.
Mr. Koo says that I have just missed one of the best Chinese scholars
of the younger generation, Dr. Tschen, who has been at Harvard for
the last two years but is now studying at Berlin University. I shall
certainly look up Dr. Chao and see what I can find out. I think we
ought to get something appreciable out of it.

I wrote and asked Mr. Koo if he would permit us to use excerpts
from his letter in our announcements, and he replies to-day that we
may certainly do so, that I may tell the publishers that he takes great
pleasure in recommending our new volume and that a good many
Chinese are looking forward to it. He also tells me that he has secured
a competent reviewer in the person of a Harvard educated Chinese
who is a pupil of Professor Babbitt's. As Professor Babbitt hates me
and all my works, I have very little hope for the review. I promptly
suggested to Mr. Koo that you would be an excellent person to write

[1] *Chinese Students' Monthly*, XVII, 114, listed by Damon, *op. cit.*, p. 739.

167

on the value of Chinese literature for English readers, and enclose a letter from him asking you to write such a paper, or, in fact, any paper you want. I have taken the liberty of reading his letter since it came without an envelope enclosed in a letter to me. I have already written him that it will be impossible for you to send him anything by the tenth of December, as you are in China; but that I am forwarding his letter, and that you will doubtless send him an article before long.

I think that Mr. Koo is wrong in thinking of literature as out of fashion—for he lumps China and America together in this. I think it is more and more in fashion all the time, here at least. Richard Le Gallienne, in an interesting article in the *New York Times* "Review of Books" says that modern poetry is coming to take the place of the Bible with many people; it is influencing their thought and even their politics, which I think is very true.

I suppose you subscribed to the clipping agencies as I suggested, for you will certainly want to get everything there is. I will not write more now, my dear, as there are one million things to do, but everything is swimming so far, except the time. They have been perfect centuries in getting the thing through the press, but I suppose we are really more to blame than any one as we got the manuscript in so late, and for that I blame the doctors, and when you get as far as the doctors, the blame seems to trail off into inevitable fate. Your ocean letter arrived safely, and I transmitted its contents to Ferris Greenslet, so I suppose that is all right.

With ever so much love, in which Ada would join only she has gone off to spend two nights with her friend Mrs. Sharp.

Affectionately yours,

Amy

[Shanghai], November 11, 1921

Dearest Amy,

Thanks so much for your telegram in regard to the book. It is too bad that it can't be here for Christmas—but *tant pis*. I am glad that the price is $3.00 not $3.50—as Houghton Mifflin first advised Kelly and Walsh, as with the exchange it makes the price so very high here. The "travellers" don't come out here so the dummy simply arrived by post with no letter from H.M.—just typed extracts from the jacket inside the cover. What was a pity, too, was that on that dummy they put a great splodge of purple on the front, a bad reproduction of a picture from one of Bland's books. This was, I suppose, to show that there were to be names and characters there; but there was no explanation, and Mr. King of Kelly and Walsh was horrified at it. He was much relieved when I told him that this splodge was not to appear. They didn't put it on the dummy they sent you and me or I would have explained it in my letter to Mr. King.

I have been trying, so far in vain, to find the *Yü Chiao Li*. The first thing was to find the characters of the title. You see, the Chinese do not look upon fiction, or drama, as literature; so they do not catalogue it. In the end I found the characters, by chance, in a foreign book, and Mr. Nung has spent one happy afternoon investigating the book-shops. No one has ever heard of it. But he is going to try the book-shops in the [Chinese] "City" which may have some of the old-time books like that.

I am working at Tu Fu,[1] and the commentaries simply make me giddy!! However, I am going to be very "complete," and then we can leave out what we do not need. Translation comes more easily than it did, but it is hard.

Much love, dear Amy, to all my "second family." I wonder if you did not go on your lecture tour? The telegram came from Brookline. By the bye, it does seem a pity to spend so much on my address. "Ayscough, Shanghai" is quite enough; but, if you feel nervous about that, "Ayscough, Scothar, Shanghai," is complete. Scothar being the firm's registered address.

Love as ever,
FLORENCE AYSCOUGH

[SHANGHAI], December 8, 1921

DEAREST AMY,

It seems so strange to be entirely cut off from you after having been working so intimately with you.—And, I may add, not at all pleasant.

The other day the *Literary Review* of October 29th arrived with Witter Bynner's "translations" of Tu Fu. I happened to be working on the one he calls "A Song of Dagger-Dancing to a Girl Pupil of Lady Kung Sun,"[2] and—truly—words fail me. If he didn't call it "translation" it would be quite in order. Paraphrase, if you like.

It is impossible to send you the whole by this post unless I sit up

---

[1] *Tu Fu: The Autobiography of a Chinese Poet, A.D. 712–770, Including an Historical Year Record, a Biographical Index, and a Topographical Note, as Well as Maps, Plans, and Illustrations, Arranged from His Poems and Translated by Florence Ayscough*, Vol. I: *A.D. 712–759* (London: Jonathan Cape; Boston and New York: Houghton Mifflin Co., 1929), and Vol. II: *Travels of a Chinese Poet: Tu Fu, Guest of Rivers and Lakes, A.D. 759–770*, illustrated from etchings by Lucille Douglass (London: Jonathan Cape; Boston and New York: Houghton Mifflin Co., 1934).

[2] See *The Jade Mountain: A Chinese Anthology*, pp. 167–68.

all night—in which case I would get into trouble with Frank—so I send you the preface which I have finished. I think I was rather an idiot not to begin with the poem and let this, which is unimportant, follow. But I didn't, so there is nothing to be done.

It is very simple to work the way Bynner does: what he doesn't understand he leaves out! The Chinese have a proverb—"On a galloping horse, looking at flowers"—which expresses his idea of doing it. I hope you have the page. I must keep mine as I have the other poems and will do them as soon as possible. I don't know whether you will think it wise, or desirable, to print the correct versions, if you will render them, side by side with his, but it would be good for his soul if you did. We have the one "To Li Po at the Sky's End." That isn't quite so bad as some; a mere trifle such as giving the river a wrong name need hardly be noticed. And other little outs hardly count when one compares this with the longer poems. Of course, they are very difficult. The "dagger-dance" is a bad mistake. How could anyone dancing with a little, short dagger, a stabbing weapon, inspire a calligraphist? But, as you will see by the note, Kung Sun didn't dance with a weapon at all: it is only the *name* of the dance which she performed dressed in man's clothes. The poem is very nice and I will send it as soon as ever I can.

I am going up to Peking for a few days to-morrow, to stop with Harriet Monroe's sister, Mrs. William Calhoun, who has come out for the winter. I am looking forward to it very much, and hope I shan't freeze to death.

Yesterday Eunice Tietjens' sister, Louise Hammond, who is a missionary, came to lunch with me. She is working at the "tunes," as she calls them, of Chinese poetry. It is very interesting. She hasn't gone far yet, but is publishing ten with the music she has set them to, and quite a nice little preface explaining her point of view. She puts seven syllables to the line, and rhymes the lines that rhyme in the Chinese; so she gets the effect of the obliques and levels very well. It is very Chinese in sound. Of course she cannot worry too much about sense, or about translating the poem as it stands, but it is nice to have her work at it from this other angle.

I must go and see that my faithful Amah[1] has put in the right things, so—with very much love to all my "second family"—

Yours ever,

FLORENCE AYSCOUGH

---

[1] See *Firecracker Land*, pp. 27, 135–36, *et passim*.

Dearest Amy,

I have done the poem of Kung-sun[1] this morning and will post it at Nanking, so it ought to catch the same post that takes the preface which I did yesterday. Now, if you want to, you can render it and publish it. I think it is quite plain, though the tortoise-shell feast is a new form of hyperbole! . . . . Witter Bynner missed line 20, one of the nicest in the poem. . . . . Of course what he is trying to do *is not possible*. He can't give the poem from Kiang Kang-hu's translation any more than you could render a poem from my free translation. You have to have it as the "pony"; but you get the real sense of the poet from the characters themselves. That is the only possible way.

Both this poem and preface are hard.

Much love, yours ever,
Florence Ayscough

Just for fun, I have been trying to calculate how long it has taken me to get this poem, and the preface, into condition to send to you. The typing and looking up alternative words have taken about seven hours. Getting it into shape with the teacher took about fifteen, or more. I should think I have spent 25 hours on it—and then Witter Bynner thinks he can do three hundred just off the reel.

En route to Peking, December 10th, 1921

Dearest Amy,

I have done three more poems to-day. They are to go up to Mukden, be posted there over Korea to Yokohama, and they *may* catch the same "Empress" that takes the Kung-sun poem and preface. Rather amusing.

It doesn't matter much if they don't make the "Empress"—except that as I went over the Kung-sun poem very carefully to-day I came to the conclusion that my rendering of line 7 was not good. Mr. Bynner's is better. The line is a pair to the one that follows, and refers entirely to the movements being all as powerful as the varieties of thunder: first clap, rumbling, angry roar. I don't think the people's feelings come into it at all.

Do let me know if these all arrive together. These three are also some

[1] See *Tu Fu*, I, 33–36.

of those done by Mr. Bynner. I am numbering all the Tu Fu poems, to keep track of them, and shall put W.B. in the corner of those done by him.

Yours ever,
FLORENCE AYSCOUGH

[SHANGHAI], January 7, 1922

DEAREST AMY,

Your letter of November 10 pursued me to Peking[1] whence I returned about a week ago. I have "a lot to learn," my dear. Of course, I never imagined that you would have to go on worrying over that proof, and am so sorry. But, furthermore, I never imagined that a book *could* be "printed in a week, bound in a week, and dried in a few days"; so, your letter was full of surprise.

Thanks for the enclosure from Mr. Telly Koo. I am writing him that I will send him something, which I will do *via* you, if I may. The experience you have had with him is really remarkable, isn't it? I am so glad. I do hope that the reviewer he has found for you will be capable of appreciating the beauty of your renderings.

I think Mr. Koo is wrong in thinking that literature is out of fashion among the young Chinese. Peking was very valuable to me from that point of view. I met Dr. Hu Shih[2] of whom Witter Bynner speaks in his article in the December *Asia*, which I suppose you have seen. He is quite remarkable and is leading a strong movement among the youth of the country in the revival of letters. I spoke to the students at the [government] University where he is a professor, and to two groups at the [American missionary] Yenching University, and am going to do the same thing here. They are all very much interested. Hu Shih had seen Mr. Bynner, and agreed that he, W. B., couldn't do it the way he was going at it. He said, "I think it is very fortunate that you have made such a combination, and that you, a student, are working with a poet." I showed him the analysis etc., and he was delighted.

There was a Professor Lewis N. Chase there who is teaching Literature (English) in these two universities and I spoke to his classes. He says he has had correspondence with you. I can't remember what his college was when he was teaching in America. Anyway, he is going to lecture on you shortly in Peking.

---

[1] See F. A.'s "Symbolism of the Purple Forbidden City," in *A Chinese Mirror: Being Reflections of the Reality behind Appearance* (London, Boston, and New York, 1925), pp. 257–340, or see *Journal N.C.B.R.A.S.*, LXI (1930), 111–26, and LII (1921), 58–78.

[2] Ambassador to the United States, 1938–42.

I enclose two *fu* which I have analysed in a manner that will, I hope, be clear. Also a translation of another of the poems which Witter Bynner has done. Where, I think, he has made a mistake is in choosing an anthology. In the first place, three hundred poems ought to take him about three hundred years to translate. But the principal trouble is this: an anthology always represents the taste of the people who have picked out the poems, and, in the case of a Chinese collection, it represents the taste of scholars who have an entirely different point of view to ours. As Mr. Nung says, they keep two main points before them:

1. They choose poems with as many historical and literary allusions *as possible*. This is to show the editors' erudition.
2. Then they choose poems that have as many obscure lines as possible. I mean lines which are roundabout. As Mr. Nung says *An, An* the "dark," "obscure," "dim," which is often used for describing the hour of sunset.

The result is that the poems Mr. Bynner has chosen are fearfully difficult, and complicated. One can't put in all the allusions, and, if one leaves them out, why, as Nung again says, "You discredit Tu Fu"— or whoever it may be. As you know, Tu Fu was noted for his great erudition, and certainly the poems Mr. Bynner includes are sufficiently full of allusions to drive one mad.

I can't help being amused when he thinks our poems are going to be too full of colour. It is so impossible to convey one tenth part of the colour that is in them. If he has that bee in his bonnet, no wonder he is so successful in giving "colourless" versions. I was talking to quite an intelligent youth on the train going north, just when I was working on "Kung-sun." I gave him Mr. Bynner's version to read, before I read him a translation, and asked him what he thought of it. He read it carefully and then said, "Why, I think it is very colourless."

The professor of the History of Art from the University of Stockholm, Dr. Osvald Sirén, is here. He has just come back from a journey to Sianfu (on the site of Ch'ang An) and has brought a copy of the "records." I am helping him translate them—or, rather, Nung and I are doing it—and I think that a great deal of it will be useful in the Tu Fu book. By the bye, *please retrieve the map*. Much, much love to you both,

Yours,

FLORENCE AYSCOUGH

173

DEAREST FLORENCE:

I have so many things to write about that I do not know where I am going to begin. In the first place, they got *Fir-Flower Tablets* out very, very late [December 14], only about two weeks before Christmas, and Norreys O'Conor's review in the *Transcript* was not as good as I expected it to be. He was not up to the job, really. I am enclosing it to you, although I suppose your clipping agencies have already sent it. I imagine you subscribe, because that is much the best way of getting things. Le Gallienne's article in the *Times* has not appeared yet. John Farrar had a nice little notice in the *Bookman*. . . . . I have seen no other reviews so far. . . . .

There appeared here the other day a Chinaman, an editor of a news-paper in Shanghai—at least, that is what Rose Nichols[1] who introduced him said he was—but as she went on to say that his paper had the largest circulation of any paper in *Japan*, I do not know what he was. She asked me to meet him, but I was drowned with work, and I was not very enthusiastic because I felt that I might get into a mess if I had anything to do with anybody from China. I thought you had better run that side. Rose reported that he had never heard of either of us, which I do not think astonishing, but I doubt whether I lost anything by not seeing him, although she said he was interested in poetry. I imagine, however, that that was more a polite way of show-ing his interest in her conversation than a reality, because my friend, Mr. Telly H. Koo—do not start, my dear, he spells it that way to avoid mis-pronunciation; he tells me that the form he would naturally use is T'ai Le—informs me that the modern Chinese are all against the literature and arts of former times, thinking that the thing now to be desired is material prosperity and the power of competing with Euro-peans and Americans on their own ground, and that the younger Chinese, if you mention poetry to them, all say "What's the use?"

Mr. Koo has given me the name of Dr. Chao, who is Professor of Chinese at Harvard, and I am going to get hold of him as soon as I get back from the lecture trip I am going on next week, and get him to hammer the versification into my head. But Telly asked me to send him some translations for his Chinese monthly, and I sent him two: "The Perils of the Shu Road" [p. 6] and "Fêng Hsien Temple" [p. 103], and he replied that he had not supposed it possible for an Ameri-can to make such excellent translations, that he had known the "Shu Road" by heart all his life, and that our translations were exact. . . . .

[1] Damon, *op. cit.*, p. 182.

I have had many pleasant remarks made to me on how charming the poems are. Professor Lowes is absolutely mad about them, and says that he wishes now that he had asked to review the book, and I wish to goodness he had. I had the following from Mrs. Colum yesterday. She is the wife of Padraic Colum, the Irish poet, and has a fine taste in literature:

My husband is immersed in your Chinese book, which he carries around with him. As for myself, I have determinedly stuck to Li T'ai-po, and resisted all temptation to go on to Tu Fu. I never read anything so wonderful as Li T'ai-po, or so unponderously wise.

> "Why should one spend one's life in toil?
> Thinking this, I have been drunk all day."

I had influenza at Xmas, but really, though it ought to have depressed me, I got so exhilarated with Li T'ai-po that I did not mind it at all.

I should imagine that the book would make a great sensation and have a deep influence on young poets. If only horses and wine were restored to the world again—Li T'ai-po could never have lived without them. I do not know whether it is you who have made him so wonderful, or if he is like that all by himself. I never could get in the slightest degree interested in Chinese poetry before, though I have often read translations. I feel very grateful indeed to you for this book.

I think it would be a great pity to track Witter Bynner's poems down with the purpose of showing him up. I think we had better ignore him entirely and go ahead with our own work. If some of the poems are the same, well and good, but I certainly should not try to dig his out, nor try in any way to impose ourselves above him. . . . .

There's one thing I wish you could find out, and that is something about the man who taught him, Dr. Kiang Kang-hu, because Witter Bynner is going round blowing like anything, saying that he had no idea until he reached China how highly his collaborator was considered there by scholars, that he is one of the most considerable of present-day Chinese journalists, is, in short, one of the important people in China, none of which do I believe, and I should like some data to be able to refute his statements when people remark that neither you nor I are Chinese.

Also, can you not give me some sort of an account of Mr. Nung— and make it sound as grand as possible—to show that we have a native Chinaman behind us, for, in *Asia*, Bynner said that he did not believe that any one, even though born in China, could really get the nuances of the poems, which was, of course, an attempt to cut the ground under your feet. Apparently he knows nothing whatever about the commentaries, but . . . . he throws round a lot of big names of people he met in China, such as Dr. Hu Shih, whom he calls "an influential young modernist of Peking Government University and author of widely read poems in the so-called 'vulgar tongue'," and "World-of-Jade, otherwise Nieh Shih-chang," who is a young student and who, he says, "piloted me on many trips." Then there is Princess Der Ling, former lady-in-waiting of the departed empress, and Dr. Ku Hung-ming, whom he speaks of as "a conservative in both politics and literature, a monarchist and a classicist," and says that he went to the University of Edinburgh long ago. According to Witter, all these people have greatly praised his work, which I can well believe, for they know nothing whatever of the English language.

Here is what he says of Dr. Kiang, who, apparently, was not one of the people in favour of a revolution in China: "Some years ago he founded a girls' school and gave his own dwelling in Peking to house it: the first girls' school in the country founded by a Chinese. He inherited a fine library and a distinguished collection of paintings. Some of the latter are in museums in Japan. . . . . What was left of the library he has given to the University of California. His share of other property inherited from his father he has renounced in favor of his brothers. When Yüan Shih-k'ai usurped the throne, Kiang risked his life by challenging the act and finally fled to America. Now that he can be of service again to China, he has relinquished academic opportunities in the New World to return to his own people." This sounds beautifully, and may be true, but the position he held here was in Berkeley, California, and not in one of the older universities, and the service he is performing for China is to act as a newspaper correspondent in Moscow.

The name of the anthology they have translated is "Three Hundred Pearls of the T'ang Dynasty." You can, of course, look them up and translate all the poems he has done if you want to, but I think it would be a great mistake to pay any attention to him whatever. I should merely like to know these facts about the people he mentions in order to punch his pretensions to powder in case it may be necessary in some private conversation.

Now, my dear, please do not send me any more poems at the moment. You know I cannot do them now; I told you that I should not be able to look at them for a year. I am doing Keats now, and, as soon as I see these Chinese poems and read them, I immediately begin doing them in my head; and that is just what I do not want to do, for I must not be taken out of the Keats mood until the book is done. This does

176

not mean that I do not want you to write me about them and tell me all your difficulties; it only means that I must not read even the analyses until the Keats book is finished, and that will not be until I get through the proof next Autumn. I realize, of course, what an awful blow this will be to you, and I wish it could be otherwise, but I have hardly time to do the Keats book now. As it is, I must give up going to England because of it, and it is necessary that I stay in one mood entirely while I am doing it. Therefore, I have not read these poems you have sent me, but have put them aside to do later. I do not think we want to rush another book right on the heels of this one, anyway. It took us four years to do this one. I think we may very well wait two or even three years before we publish the Tu Fu book. I know it will be hard for you to do them and just put them aside until I am able to take them, and perhaps I shall be able to glance at some of them when I get a little farther along; but just now I am swamped in material and the collecting of it, and all the hours of my days are not enough. In fact, I am almost desperate with what I have got to do on that Keats book, and, unfortunately, Houghton Mifflin want to publish it next Autumn, and I should think they would. They have already been delayed a year on it, and there really is nothing whatever to do but get it done as soon as possible. Your work will take much longer than mine and there is much more of it, so the harder you can work, and the more you can plough up with notes and comments, the better. You know the poems get themselves done very quickly when once I get at them.

By the way, as to the *Yü Chiao Li*,[1] I never meant to publish it in any way, or any part of it. You must have misunderstood me there. What I meant was that I should like personally to know the analyses of the poems in the book so that I might render them myself for my own amusement and keep them with the French copy of the book. There is no such thing as publishing anything like that to-day, I am convinced, nor should I want to take the time to do it; but it is a very charming tale, nevertheless, and of course the French renditions of the poems cannot bear much if any relation to the originals.

Next week I go off on a nearly three weeks' lecture trip, and do the same thing in the middle of February, and then, towards Spring, I go down to Charleston, South Carolina. I regret having made these dates because they take me away from the Keats work, but that cannot be helped now.

I am quite sure that our book is going to make a very favourable im-

[1] See letter of A.L. to F.A., August 16, 1919.

177

pression. I am afraid of Waley; I am sure he will jump on us in the *Literary Review*, and I am a little nervous about the split-up characters and their effect on the Chinese gentleman who is going to review us for the *Chinese Students' Monthly*, but I am not a bit afraid of people who do not know Chinese and have no preconceived theories about how to translate. You see what Mrs. Colum says about never having liked any Chinese translations before. I think we have done a good piece of work, and that everybody is going to like it, except a few crotchety sinologues possibly. I only wish you were here. There would be plenty of field for your speech and pen if only you were. I wish I dared give a lecture on Chinese poetry,[1] but I am afraid I do not know enough. Somebody would be sure to ask me if I knew some old poet whom I have never heard of; still I think it would make a nice lecture. . . . .

I do wish you were nearer. Your second family misses you. Ada sends lots of love, and so do I.

Affectionately yours,

AMY LOWELL

per F. W. B.

P.S. It is now Monday evening, and this letter, although dated to-day was dictated on Saturday. Prof. and Mrs. Lowes dined here last night. They were both perfectly enchanted with your Introduction, and they cannot say enough about the beauty of the poems; and the Notes are meeting with universal commendation.

They advertised the book with my name in bigger print than yours, and Mr. Linscott wailed when I told him how horrified I was. He said he had done it only because my name was known, and I had a certain clientèle who would buy whatever I had a hand in. As we are not paying for the advertisements, I could not very well stop it, but I have since remonstrated with Ferris Greenslet, and he says it shall not happen again. Another annoying thing happened. I sent both our photographs to the *Transcript* to be published with O'Conor's review, and the pig-headed editor only used mine. Dear Florence, please do not think these things are of my doing. You know that I am not that kind of an animal, but it is the penalty you unhappily pay for this being your first book and my ninth. It will right itself in time. I am writing to Mr. Smyth of the *Times* to beg him if he cannot put in both our pictures, to put in only yours.

Please send me any reviews that come out in Chinese papers, as the agencies will certainly not see them.

[1] See below, Appendix IV; also Damon, *op. cit.*, pp. 602–3.

You said you wished I would sometime write to you in pencil on my yellow block. Well, I am doing so, sitting in my usual chair and thinking of you. How I wish you were in your chair and we could talk of everything instead of writing. I don't care what the bat-eyed sinologues may say if they jump on us; we have done a crackerjack book, and I love it.

This will be typed to-morrow to save your eyesight, but I wrote it with my little pencil all the same. Don't be discouraged at my not being able to do the Chinese poems now. I think you must surely realize, if you think a bit, that it is impossible, and I can do them all the better later when I can soak myself in them.

Goodbye, Dear,

Lots of love,
[Signed for] AMY

Miss Lowell left before signing this letter.

[SHANGHAI], January 13, 1922

DEAREST AMY,

I wrote a few days ago, so have not much to say. Enclosed are translations of the poems Mr. Bynner published in the article in *Asia* for December. He is very scornful about Mr. Mathers—whoever he may be—but, as a matter of fact, Mr. Mathers, though he adds a great deal to the "Song of the Palace" which he has no business to do, gets the idea of the poem far better than does Mr. Bynner. . . . .

Would you please number the two *fu* I sent you as the duplicates which go to-day are numbered. It will save a lot of trouble to have Tu Fu's poems with their numbers, and the miscellaneous ones with theirs.

Much love, my dear. As you may imagine, I am looking forward anxiously to the book's arrival. Love to Ada.

Yours,
FLORENCE AYSCOUGH

[SHANGHAI], February 11, 1922

DEAREST AMY,

You would have heard from me long ago had it not been that a very bad shipping strike in Hong Kong has held up all the mails. The Chinese are learning Western ways with extreme aptitude, and this strike has lasted for four weeks. The ship that is finally going to-day has, I think, a Filipino crew from Manila; she has no cargo, but I imagine that her mail will be enough to sink her. We have felt very "cut off."

Since I last wrote, *Fir-Flower Tablets* has arrived, and I am perfectly delighted with it. It really is a delightful piece of book-making and is very much appreciated. Various people to whom I sent it wrote the moment it came, so they could not say much about the contents, but they all admire the book itself. Dr. Yetts received his copy on Christmas Eve and says, "It is by far the most interesting Christmas token I have received and I am much looking forward to reading it. The first glance shows how admirably the publisher has done his part." R[eginald] F[leming] Johnston, tutor to the baby emperor,[1] who is a most delightful person, wrote a charming letter. He was just going off to the Western Hills when it came and was taking it with him. I shall hope to hear from him again later.

The one thing that Mr. Nung criticizes in the makeup is that the characters on the cover, to look really Chinese, should be set further in. A Chinese book always has its title written on a "tab" of paper which is set about 3/4 of an inch from the side margin and about 1 3/4 from top. I enclose a piece of paper with the characters placed as the Chinese would place them. The following conversation, which may amuse you, took place. I asked Mr. Nung if he had been able to read the book and he replied:

NUNG: Yes, I have enjoyed it. The friend of Madame Ai, has a writing brush which is full of life's movement.

F.W.A.: Your words are a little not wrong! indeed, not wrong! And that is a gift from Heaven. Anyone could do what I am doing with your help; but to write poems like those—*that* Heaven does.

NUNG: Not wrong! But if Madame Ai did not make the poems ten thousand times perfectly clear, her friend could not write with life. We have a saying, perhaps Madame Ai does not know it: "What is the beauty of the peony flower, without its green leaves"!

As for the reviews which I have so far managed to get, they are, I am sorry to say, very dull. Dr. Darroch's is most disappointing. In asking to have him do the one for the *North China Daily News* I hoped to have something of interest, and to that end sent him some of the "texts." He is a very fine Chinese scholar, the only foreigner, as far as I know, who has the *Chin Shih* degree [the third literary degree, approximately equal to Doctor—pp. xxxix-xlii]. Moreover, he spoke very well after I had been reading poems at the Asiatic Society in November, so it seemed likely that he would do well. Well, *tant pis!* Johnston is going to arrange to have it reviewed in the Peking paper, and there are two reviews, one in the *New China Review*, one in the *Chinese Recorder* which should be out soon. The *Journal* [of the North

[1] The Hsüan T'ung emperor, last of the Manchu (Ch'ing) Dynasty. Later known for a period as "Mr. Henry Pu-yi"; still later publicized as "the Kang Te emperor of 'Manchukuo.' "

China Branch, Royal Asiatic Society] does not appear until July. There is another daily paper review which should be out soon. I have written to a man in Tientsin to have it reviewed there; so it should be well advertised, in this part of the world. Of course, I am waiting anxiously for the American reviews.

We have come to a very momentous decision which is this. Frank will retire from the firm at the end of this year. We shall sell this house, and, sometime next spring, will come and make St. Andrews our headquarters. As you may imagine, my feelings are mixed. Nothing will induce Frank to live in England, so he says; nor would he like Boston; whereas he loves St. Andrews. My plan is this: I shall work very hard this year to collect all the Tu Fu, and, I think, Wang Wei, material that I can. I won't send it to you, nor attempt to put it into shape, as that does take such an awful time, but will bring it all with me, to work at in St. Andrews, and then with you, if you will. Then we shall see. We don't mean never to come back to China at all; in fact, I hope that we shall come sometimes for the winters, but we shall give up living here permanently. It may be that when you and I have done Tu Fu, I shall want to go through it with Mr. Nung, but I am taking very careful notes, so perhaps it won't be necessary. Of course one does get better as one goes on. I am not as dependent as I was, but it *is* hard.

Miss Hammond was down from Wusih again this week, and was talking to a Club about her "Poem Tunes," as she calls them, and in the course of her talk she said that to understand poetry is most difficult, that when one takes up a poem although one knows the meaning of each separate character, one can *not* make them make sense until one's teacher has elucidated the poem. I groaned aloud in sympathy, and was thankful to hear her say this. She is a missionary, lives among the Chinese, talks practically nothing else, does all sorts of literary work, and has been at it for eight years. I felt comforted. I do feel such a fool so often. Her "tunes" are really splendid. When she does them, they give precisely the Chinese effect.

Some people from Stanford University have just been passing through—Professor and Mrs. [Payson Jackson] Treat. They were very much interested. She did not know Witter Bynner, but knew of him and said that he has many followers at Stanford. I showed her some of the comparisons of his translations and the text. She was very much thrilled—so much so that I have given her a few of the raw translations to compare with his versions. I hope that this is not a tactical error. It seemed a good plan.

181

I enclose a translation of one more of those which he did and published in the Literary Section of the *Evening Post*. It is the last I shall do. There are one or two more, but they are so hopelessly full of historical allusions that they really are a bore. It seems to me waste of time to go on with them. . . . .

I am doing a most delightful poem by Tu Fu written after he reached home, just after he had been Censor for a month. If you remember, before that he had been in the hands of brigands for nearly two years; so he had not seen his wife and children for a long time. He found them very poor and his description of cutting up his official robes embroidered with Feng Huang, etc., to patch their baize clothes is sweet.[1]

How is Keats going on? Are you working at it? And how are you, yourself, my dear? You have not said one word about your health since I left U.S.A.

My love to Ada. Oh, Mrs. Forbes wrote me that some of your trees had suffered in a bad storm. I am so sorry. Which ones went?

Love as ever.

Yours,

FLORENCE AYSCOUGH

BROOKLINE, MASS., 16 February, 1922

DEAREST FLORENCE:

I am sending you a copy of Waley's review.[2] Mr. Canby wants you to answer it, and I am also thinking of answering it myself. I can answer the question about the *fu*, I think, and there is no objection at all to your answering it also. I can also point out that the Giles version of the poem, "Night Thoughts," is not even accurate in idea.

But listen, my child, I have fallen upon a bit of luck. I think I wrote you that there was a man here, Professor of Chinese at Harvard, whom my friend Mr. Telly H. Koo told me knew a great deal about Chinese poetry. His name is Dr. Chao. He himself disclaims any special knowledge about Chinese poetry, but as he is preparing a new book on rhymes in Chinese—there not having been one for several hundred years, he tells me—I think he must have an interest in poetry. At any rate, the gentleman is dining with me to-night, on which occasion I intend to ask him every conceivable question pertaining to Chinese prosody which I can think of, with the analyses of the *fu's* which you sent me the other day as a base.

---

[1] See *Tu Fu*, I, 273.

[2] See the "Literary Review" of the *New York Evening Post*, February 4, 1922; also Damon, *op. cit.*, p. 592.

I saw another rather impressively learned Chinese in New York, a Mr. Chang [Peng-chun],[1] with whom I had some talk. I asked him about the vexed question of the *tzǔ*, and he said it did not have to consist of several stanzas as we supposed; it might be only one stanza. But apparently you are right in saying that if it consists of more than one stanza, each stanza has to follow the same pattern. He said it was a poem intended to be sung; in other words, it is the old definition of the lyric, which was a poem sung to strings. Hence the reason why so many of them are called by the titles of the tunes they are to be sung to.

Waley is simply ludicrous about the *fu*. He does not know what "polyphonic prose" is, and it makes him mad to think that we have invented anything which has a prototype in ancient China. The analyses of the *fu*'s you sent me seem to prove, alas, that the word "identical" was too strong. The *fu* is not identical with "polyphonic prose," but is very much like it; but I want to talk the whole thing over with Dr. Chao. I have never seen him, only written him and had replies. I do not know at all whether he is an open minded person or not. He appears to be afraid of me; says he hopes he will know enough to answer my questions. Why he should suppose the questions would be so extremely erudite, I do not know. I gave him a brief outline in my letter of the kind of thing I wanted him to answer without mentioning any specific things. It seems to have given the gentleman's feet chills. Anyhow, he is coming to-night, and I only wish you were to be here too. I do not find it easy to understand these Chinamen; nor do they find it easy to understand me.

By the way, Mr. Chang was quite as decided as Mr. Nung on the subject of that frost in "Night Thoughts"[2] being on the floor and not outside the house, but Mr. Chang was by no means as anxious to white-wash Li T'ai-po as Mr. Nung is. He assured me that he thought Li T'ai-po was dead drunk at the time, and hence the sad thoughts of home and mistaking the moonlight for frost. He was very eloquent about the degree of his tipsiness.

I think you had better send the answer to Waley to me, and let me send it on to Mr. Canby, and then I can read it over first and, if it conflicts with anything I have said, fix it up or cut it out. I hate to wait until your article can arrive without making any answer to Waley, so I thought I would take up the question of the *fu* and the question of my own rhythmic sense by myself. But this will depend largely upon

[1] Damon, *op. cit.*, p. 591.
[2] See letter of A. L. to F. A., January 24, 1920.

183

what comes out of my interview with Dr. Chao to-night. I will write you the result of that as soon as it has taken place. I think, however, you had better answer both these questions yourself, also, in your paper; the more we hammer it in the better.

The most amusing thing to me is the fact that Mr. Waley thinks we have mis-translated the next to the last line [in "Ch'ang Kan"] on Page 29 ["I will not go far on the road to meet you, ..."]. . . . Waley, being German, has no sense of humour and does not understand irony. You notice he is afraid to say definitely that it is not properly translated; he simply says that it must be a mis-translation because he could not make head nor tail of it himself. I think, however, that he was very much astonished at the book, and I think he tried very hard to say so. In writing your paper, I should not take too controversial a tone, I should treat him with great courtesy and kindness, but make it quite evident that he is entirely wrong; there is no use in quarreling with one's *confrères*.

. . . . is more of a skunk than ever. I am sending you the last number of *Poetry*[1] in which he has again tried to go for us. I do not understand the man; he seems to me to be a perfect fool, for how a form of eight syllables to a line can be considered the nearest to a form of five or seven syllables is beyond me. He came round to see me when I was in New York, and was as nice to me as possible, at which time he told me that the book did not contain nearly as many "split-ups" as he thought (by the way, you notice that Waley has not spoken of the "split-ups"), and asked me to speak at the Poetry Society Dinner—of which Society he is the president—and when he got me there [January 25] insulted me in his introductory speech.[2] Naturally, I got back at him with an awful slam and left him nowhere. I do not wonder that the man is sore, with everybody saying how uninteresting his translations are, although he has placed them round in a lot of magazines. Of course Harriet Monroe will give him all space and all comforts, she hates me so,[3] but we really killed the man and he knows it.

I am afraid Waley's article is going to do some harm. I had a letter yesterday from a woman, who had also reviewed the book and whose review I had taken some exceptions to, saying that I ought not to mind her review after Mr. Waley's list of our *errata*. But the more edu-

[1] XIX, No. V (February, 1922), 272–78.

[2] Damon, *op. cit.*, pp. 591–92.

[3] *Ibid.*, pp. 356–57, 408, 521, 623, 666; see also Miss Monroe's "Amy Lowell," *Poetry*, XXV, No. I (October, 1924), 32–38; "Rubies in a Gate of Stone," her review of *What's O'Clock*, *ibid.*, XXVII, No. III (December, 1925), 154–58; and "A Keen East Wind," her review of *East Wind*, *ibid.*, XXIX, No. III (December, 1926), 160–63. See also below, Appendix II.

cated think that Waley will do us good rather than harm, as he admires what we have done, and everybody knows he is a rival translator.

I have seen nothing of the February number of the *Chinese Students' Monthly*,[1] which is supposed to have the Chinese gentleman's review in it, so I am afraid it turned out to be a slam from Mr. Koo's not having sent it. I thought it would probably be a slam as his reviewer is a pupil of Professor Irving Babbitt's of Harvard, and if there is anything Mr. Babbitt hates it is I. He stands for the old classical tradition without modification, and of course I am anathema to him. I mean, naturally, the classical tradition in English, not in Chinese. But I imagine that a pupil of his could hardly like anything I do, on principle. It is too bad, my dear, that you are associated with a person who has so many enemies, but perhaps it has another side too.

Get your article off just as fast as you can, for time counts a lot in these things. I should have sent you the review last week, but I have been so jammed that I could not get it off.

. . . . The book is making many friends for itself. I get charming notes on it, and the reviews, as you will see from your clipping agencies, are splendid. It does not matter much what the smaller papers say, so I am not sending them to you—I remember that we agreed that I should not—but Waley and Le Gallienne are fine. Houghton Mifflin are advertising the book in the March *Dial*, a splendid advertisement, and are quoting from Waley and Le Gallienne.

I guess this is all for now. I will write you again after I have seen Dr. Chao, but probably not until I get back week after next, as I am simply jammed this week and I leave on Sunday. . . . . I was particularly interested in what you told me about your visit to Peking and Dr. Hu Shih and his opinion of Witter Bynner's work. Being a born publicity agent, I promptly had these things put in a note and circulated in the newspapers. I enclose a clipping from one of them.

I am telling everyone without reserve that we are doing a book on Tu Fu. I do not mean that I am announcing it to the newspapers, but I have told everybody myself because I think it is a good thing. Mr. Chang was immensely interested to hear it.

Well, farewell, my child, for the moment. Everybody thinks we have done an elegant job, and I confess I think so too. . . . .

Affectionately yours,
AMY LOWELL

[1] XVII, No. 4 (February, 1922), 351–52: review signed "H. H. C." On p. 114 of Vol. XVII, No. 2 (December, 1921), of this magazine "The Perils of the Shu Road" appears.

Dearest Florence:

I saw Dr. Chao last night, but it was a terrible disappointment. The child is a young boy, not long out of college, I should think, who is greatly interested in the new poetry movement in China, the writing of poetry in the vernacular, but has not kept up his classics at all, and all he knows of the ancient poems are those he was forced to learn by heart when he was young. As he says, he learnt to repeat them before he knew what they meant; he admits that the sound still attracts him more than the sense. I wonder if that is not the case with most of the young Chinese.

I am enclosing a nasty slam which came out as a review in the [February] *Chinese Students' Monthly*. I told Mr. Koo, the editor of the monthly, what would be the result if he handed the review to a pupil of Professor Babbitt's. . . . . It is such a silly paper that it could not hurt a flea; besides which, the *Chinese Students' Monthly* goes nowhere except to Chinese students, so far as I know. I have written a somewhat strong letter to Mr. Koo, a copy of which I enclose.[1] I should not take it up with him if I were you, but go ahead with the paper you are writing for him utterly regardless of this review. It is not worth noticing.

I read Dr. Chao "The Perils of the Shu Road" [p. 6], and he said that the words were all right and that the effect was given; but he also evidently greatly missed the sound.

I am enclosing a letter I have just written to Mr. Canby. The remarks about the *fu* were made up from the paper you sent me and some things which I worked out with Dr. Chao last night. I hope it is correct now; it should be. The parallelism, etc., came from him. I do not think he is any authority; I only hope he has not gone too far wrong. I showed him the last line but one in "Ch'ang Kan" [p. 29], which Waley says we have mis-translated, with the analysis; of course I had not the characters. He says the word *tao* cannot mean "road" there because in that case the syntax would be wrong, that it is a verb, not a noun, and means "to say," or something like that. He thinks the line should be translated, "I shall not complain how far I have to go to meet you." I am not at all sure that he is right. In the first place, he was trying to read from transliteration, which is very difficult; in the second place, his English vocabulary is slight. He was considerably puzzled by the negative *pu*, and knew so little of the poem that he said he could not tell whether this was intended to be ironical or not. I

[1] See pp. 189–90.

wish you would take up this line with Mr. Nung and see whether Dr. Chao is right in his suggested translation. He thinks the line with which we have had so much difficulty in "The Perils of the Shu Road" [p. 8, l. 17], and which Waley pitches into me for the cadence of, really means "Oh, to go home at once!" I think myself that a better rendering than any I thought of at first would be, "What a delight it would be to go home immediately!" If you think that is nearer than the one we have got, it is certainly better cadence, and I can have the line changed in the second edition.

After analyzing the *fu* with some care, it seems to me that our expression "almost identical with 'polyphonic prose' " is too strong. I think it would be better to say "The construction is very much like." Also, I shall have to change about the rhymes appearing when and where they will. There are certainly internal rhymes—Dr. Chao and I found a good many last night—but end rhymes are clearly the rule, as your analysis shows. You did not take up the question of internal rhymes with Mr. Nung, apparently. I wish you would. "Internal rhymes" means rhymes in the middle of a line, not necessarily rhyming with the end rhymes, but with other rhymes in the middle of lines, either the same line or others. It is these internal rhymes which give the likeness to "polyphonic prose" more than anything else. There are certainly sometimes two or more together as we have stated; for instance, in "The Shu Road," in Line 34, I am sure the first and third words rhyme, and I think the second rhymes too. Then again, in Line 26, the first and fourth words rhyme, but the place he especially noticed was in Line 21 where the last four words all rhyme. What I should like to know is how much of a practice this is. It seems to be done quite often, and that is really its resemblance to "polyphonic prose" more than anything else. Of course, I cannot tell the tones except in the case of the rhymes where you have pointed it out, and Dr. Chao tells me that words which are in separate tones cannot rhyme. As this is exactly opposite from what Waley says, I doubt whether Dr. Chao knows what he is talking about. He clearly knows almost nothing of the language of the classic period. He admits that it is far more different from present-day Chinese than Chaucer's English is from present-day English, so I think it more than possible that Waley is right and that words in different tones may rhyme, although not at the ends of lines. In other words, that different tone rhymes may be allowed in internal rhyming; in fact, Dr. Chao himself said that this might be the case in internal rhyming. That is the chief thing I want to know now, but the particular line with the four rhymes he himself pointed out with excitement must have been done consciously and not by accident, and he seemed to consider them all true rhymes.

. . . . Chao is a good little boy, but he is only teaching the Chinese language here, nothing to do with the literature; and, in spite of his compiling a new dictionary of rhymes, I do not think he has any literary sense. He told me before he came that he had only the knowledge of the classic literature which any educated non-literary Chinese would have, and that he was non-literary there was no manner of doubt when he arrived. I think he was justified in having his feet a little cool before he came. He was not, by any means, as intelligent as Mr. Chang [Peng-chun]. Dr. Chao was very enthusiastic over Dr. Hu Shih, who, he said, knows a great deal, and I suggest, if possible, that you get Dr. Hu Shih to give his honest opinion of the book and permit us to use whatever we choose out of it for publicity. If you could get Dr. Hu Shih to review the book in some paper over there, that would be the best of all. Make him tell the truth and not hide himself under the kind of politeness which will be seen through by his countrymen. If he does not like what we have done, as the *Chinese Students' Monthly* reviewer evidently does not, let him tell you so frankly, and why, if he is enough of a scholar to know why, and if it is very bad, we need not use it. Also, if it is bad, do not let him publish it. Sound him before you suggest his reviewing the book for a paper. . . . .

I am considerably wrought up over these things and am awfully mad with the *Chinese Students'* reviewer. It gave me a violent headache and a sleepless night. But these things cannot be helped; they are part of the game. All of which proves, what I have always known, that scholars are the enemies of literature. They have nearly killed the Greek for us, and up to date they have killed the Chinese.

Now, my dear, I will not write any more, or my heated feelings will burn up the paper. Please back up my contentions in my letter to Mr. Canby in your article, and, above all things, pitch into Waley for thinking that Giles's translation of "Night Thoughts" is nearer the original than mine. I have not taken up his objections to my cadence because they are nonsense.

Oh, by the way, an interesting thing happened last night. Dr. Chao said that a Chinese reads these poems very slowly and lets the characters sink in with all the meanings and pictures they convey. Whereupon I gave a scream, and jumped up and showed him the page on which we analyzed the characters in your Introduction He was interested and showed no objection to the method; on the contrary, he seemed to agree with it, but he said that he thought "to stand" in your split-up of *se* did not mean that, there; he thought it was merely used to show with what words that word rhymed. I explained to him that even without it the only change I should make in the translation of that particular word would be to leave out "long."

I wish I were not here all alone. I need you every minute. I am not capable of coping with these things as you know, but the two of us together could go far. Please send me all the reviews that appear in Chinese papers, and particularly the native ones, if there are any such. Reviews over there by people who are sinologues, or by Chinese, are of infinite importance to us. I am very much amused to see that the only thing we really feared has not come to pass, for neither Waley nor the Chinese reviewer has taken any exception to the split-ups.

Affectionately yours,

AMY

[Enclosure]

[COPY]

18 February, 1922

MY DEAR MR. KOO:

I have been wondering why you did not send me the February number of the *Chinese Students' Monthly* as you promised to do. Dr. Chao brought it over to me last night, and I now know why you did not send it. I think, however, that it would have been wiser to have kept your promise, with a note telling me what I might expect. You remember that I told you what would be the result of your asking a pupil of Professor Babbitt's to review any book which had to do with me.

My objection to the review is not at all because of its strictures upon the translations of the poems, but because of the tone in which the review is written, which is patronising and sneering to the last degree. As a matter of fact, no translation can ever reproduce the musical effect of an original, and I carefully said in my Preface that it had been no part of my design to endeavour any such reproduction, and this gentleman does not hint that the translations are not correct. I read "The Shu Road" out loud to Dr. Chao last night, and he said that he considered I had got the effect and the words perfectly, but of course the sounds of the original were missing. He admitted that he himself preferred the sound of a poem to its meaning. I do not know whether this attitude is peculiar to the modern Chinese. Certainly, I have never heard any one else of any other nation make such a statement.

When your reviewer pronounces that *vers libre* is queer to an English ear, he talks nonsense, since *vers libre*, although possibly this gentleman did not know it, was even written by Milton in his choruses to "Samson Agonistes." After all, I might reply that no foreigner is in a position to judge whether or not a form is "queer" to a native ear.

Another objection to the style of your reviewer is that it is not his own.

189

He is simply parroting his master, Professor Babbitt. . . . . I have always heard that the Chinese were a peculiarly courteous race, and I confess that this has been my experience with the few I have met personally. I had some conversation with Mr. (or Dr.) Chang Peng-chun the other day and found him most polite and interested, and, at your suggestion, I have met and had some conversation with Dr. Chao. Dr. Chao says he is not literary and has not kept up his classics, which is undoubtedly true, but he was very nice and kind and was able to tell me quite a number of the things I wanted to know. Mrs. Ayscough writes me that Dr. Hu Shih in Peking is extremely interested in our work, and you yourself have already given your opinion, for which I cannot cease to be grateful.

Remember that I explicitly say that it was not any criticism on the part of your reviewer that seems to me unfortunate, but the manner in which it was written. I wonder whether you think such writing is liable to promote a pleasant feeling between our two countries.

Very sincerely yours,

AMY LOWELL

SHANGHAI, February 21, 1922

DEAREST AMY,

Your splendid long letter of January 9 came a few days ago. It enclosed the *Transcript* review which I was glad to see, though it is dull. Several other people sent me the awfully nice one from the *New York Times* by Le Gallienne; so that was satisfactory. I subscribed to Romeike last September; however, there must be some mistake or other, as nothing has come from him. I have written, but it does take an age to get answers. Meanwhile, he will have missed the first reviews. I hope he can look them up.

As far as Kelly and Walsh are concerned: if you cast back in your mind, you will remember that Houghton Mifflin, through you, especially asked me to write to them personally—this I did. As I received no answer in Canada, I went to see them as soon as we arrived, and, naturally, saw the manager of the whole thing, Mr. King. He was most definite in what he said. It doesn't seem worth bothering about any more, but I don't want you to think I was interfering. I was doing only what I was asked to do.

My dear, I know you can't do any translating [i.e., rendering] while you are at work on Keats! We settled that before I left. Besides, I can't possibly be ready with material for ages. I only sent the *fu*, as you asked for them, at once with the Witter Bynner things. It could do no harm to have them lying in your files, and I couldn't tell that you might not want to use them. I wrote you at great length last week . . . . my ideas as to future plans, and they are practically like yours. Great minds do jump! !

Frank is waiting for this, so I cannot write more. A mail goes out to-day. Have you retrieved the map?

Much love to all my second family.

FLORENCE AYSCOUGH

[SHANGHAI], March 24, 1922

DEAREST AMY,

There seems to be so much to write about that I hardly know where to begin. I enclose a copy of a letter which goes to Mr. Greenslet to-day and which speaks for itself. . . . .

In addition to the letter from Mr. [later Sir Reginald] Johnston, asking for a copy of the book for the Emperor, there was one from Lenox Simpson ("Putnam Weale") who wrote *Wang the Ninth* and a number of other books. He is an adviser to the Chinese Government and was at the Washington Conference. It reads as follows:

I have been trying to find time to thank you for your book which reached me safely at Washington and which I read with great interest on the steamer. I think your translations of Li T'ai-po are particularly excellent. I have always loved this poet who seems to embody, as no other, the spirit of China; and the thanks of all literary people are due to you for your labour of love— for I know it was that. I feel that there ought to be some proper recognition of your services and the next time I see the President (as he is a poet himself) I shall take your book in with me and ask that a suitable decoration be given you as a just acknowledgment of your merits.

I wrote and thanked him for his interest and said that it would be very nice to have a decoration. Indeed, it would be quite amusing. When I had the special copy bound for the Emperor I had one bound for the President, too, and sent it up to Lenox Simpson. He replied that he would give it to the President at a suitable moment, but that the political condition at the Capital was such that he didn't know just when that moment would be. For goodness' sake don't say anything about this; I think, as things are at present, it is probable that nothing will come of it. Chaos is worse than ever as far as politics go.[1]

I enclose Johnston's review and one from the French local paper. Next week one is coming out that I think should be nice. Louise Hammond, Eunice Tietjens' sister, is doing it for the *Chinese Recorder*, a missionary journal. I hope that she will appreciate your part at its true worth. It pains me dreadfully, but I am not surprised, that the students of Chinese do not realize what you have done. Of course, no

[1] See Morse and MacNair, *op. cit.*, chap. xxix: "The Washington Conference."

one knows as *I* do, and I talk about it all the time. Perhaps she will see better than they do.

The *China Press*, a very widely read paper, printed Le Gallienne's review *in toto* in their Sunday issue not long ago. That will go all over China. As soon as a new lot of books come I will buy one and give it to the *Mercury* here as I saw the editor the other day and he was much interested. That should be a good review.

And now we come to the review in the *New China Review*[1] which I am sending you. It is acid in regard to *vers libres*, and as to your part of it. I am so sorry. The editor[2] is sick and miserable. . . . . As to my part he makes several criticisms which are absurd. I have marked the margin of the book as I thought that would be the easiest thing for you. I shall answer him about the use of "Son of the Sea" for the Yangtze. He has pointed out two errors which are entirely my fault; they slipped past me. I am dreadfully, *dreadfully* sorry about them. One is P. XLIX (49), l. 7 in the Introduction. The word *chien* should be *chia* (home); and P. 189, l. 25, the name of the river *is* the Ch'ien T'ang, not the T'ien. I don't know whether it is possible to do anything about this. Are the plates going to England? If so, could these corrections be made? Anything that is done is, please, *entirely* at my expense —not that that helps much. I feel badly. I did try so hard and it does seem stupid to have failed like this in detecting mistakes. Please forgive me. Of course, the mere fact of Mr. Couling's giving us so much space in the *New China Review* is a compliment,[3] and his subscribers know what he is like. But I do feel badly that he has been so acid. I am afraid that a certain amount of "race prejudice" creeps in; he is of the type of Englishman to whom everything American is anathema!!

I sent him a copy of Le Gallienne's review, and I wish you had seen the letter he wrote in reply. He reviled Le Gallienne and all his works and said several very rude things (one of his remarks was that he thought Le G. must be paid by the word), so I—not being in any sense a fighter—left his note unanswered. Yesterday, he wrote me very sweetly and sent me a French brochure *Quarante Poésies de Li T'ai-po* by Bruno Belpaire, which seems very interesting. The poems are presented in a crude form—but the translation, as far as I am able to judge in one reading, is accurate.

Now, to go back to your last letter and the questions in it. You ask

[1] IV, No. 1 (February, 1922), 44–51; see also *ibid.*, p. 66.

[2] Samuel Couling. In 1921 he had proposed Mrs. Ayscough as an Honorary Member of the North China (Shanghai) Branch of the Royal Asiatic Society. Mr. Couling died on June 15, 1922.

[3] See Damon, *op. cit.*, pp. 689–90.

about Hu Shih, Princess Der Ling, Kiang Kang-hu, and Mr. Nung. I will take them one by one.

Hu Shih. I have written about him. He is a brilliant young man; only 29. A professor[1] at the Government University, Peking. . . . . I have sent him a copy of the book and have asked him to write me his views about it, but have not heard from him yet. He liked our method very much.

Princess Der Ling. I have always liked her. She seems to me very "straight." I enclose an interview with her. She spent yesterday afternoon with me and I think that she will be very helpful. . . . . She is well educated both from a Chinese and a European point of view. I tried to get a copy of her book for you but it is "out of print." She tells me the publishers, Moffats, have gone out of business, and that the Century Co. has the plates. There seems to be some dispute about the whole thing; she did not agree with the contract they submitted. The book *Two Years in the Forbidden City* is spontaneous, and, I think, bears the mark of truth. She says that she told Witter Bynner she did not agree with his translations and that he kept on quoting Dr. Kiang. Then she said, "*Who is* Dr. Kiang? I do not know. I met him for a few minutes with Mr. Bynner, but I know nothing of him." She has promised to write down what she thinks about our book; I will send it to you. I shall certainly go through with what I am doing now with her as she is a great help. Knowing English as she does, she appreciates the fine points. It is difficult to explain everything when we are so far apart!!!

Kiang Kang-hu. I can't find out anything definite. Mr. Nung knows him but will say little about him. His one remark was, "He can open his mouth very well." When I tried to pump he continued and told me various yarns, which, being only hearsay, I will not repeat; but he did not have a great opinion of the man.

Mr. Nung. As I have told you, Nung is not his real name. He "left his family" and adopted a name which had nothing to do with them as he did not approve of the old ways of going on. He was brought up as the son of a high' official in the old regime. He had a great deal to do with the Revolution, but, because he is utterly disgusted with all the people in power to-day refuses to take part in the Government in any way. Dr. Darroch, who is the only foreigner, as far as I know, who has received the *chin shih* degree, considers Mr. Nung a very fine scholar indeed, and says that he has studied all sorts of things that most scholars of the stereotyped kind have not studied at all. Professor Hu Shih, when he was looking at my manuscript, said, "Your teacher must be a very learned man; he refers here to a book that is not often read." I think he is an unusual person, judged from the stand-point of any civilisation. But that is a common failing as regards Foreigners and their Teachers! Each person thinks his teacher perfect. One great point is that Mr. Nung is ready to look up everything under Heaven to prove a point! I wish there were some way of bringing him to America. I couldn't ask him to come to St. Andrews; he would be so unhappy. But if there were anything he could do such as cataloguing the books in the Widener Library, or doing some sort of work, I would ask him to do it, and I think he would accept. In that case we could

[1] Appointed president in 1945.

have him where he would be quickly available. I wouldn't mind paying his salary, but I could *not* ask him to come to St. Andrews. He is unusual.

Oh, dear, your letter of February 16 with Waley's review, *Poetry*, and various other things have just been brought in—and it is time for this to go to post. It is hopeless. I can't answer anything more by this mail, but will do so in a few days, and then I shall have more reviews to send you. It is funny that Sandburg has never acknowledged the book in any way, nor has Julia Marlowe. Most of the other people have done so in a most complimentary manner.

You never say how you are, nor how Keats is getting on. How is Sonny Boy? and how is Ada? My dearest love to my second family. I feel so badly about the mistakes I make, and feel so jealous when people do not appreciate the work you have done—when I know so well. And when they all say how much they like the Introduction—why, then I want to say "But Amy wrote that," and I can't because, of course, the things said were from me (except your remarks on prosody and that description of Li Po's poetry) and I can't explain all the ramifications. Dr. Ferguson, who will write the review in the Royal Asiatic Society's *Journal*,[1] understands.

Much love, Amy dear.

Yours ever,
FLORENCE AYSCOUGH

SHANGHAI, April 21, 1922

DEAREST AMY,

Your letters of February 16 and 18 were a long time on the way. They reached me just as I was starting to Nanking, ten days ago, where I gave two lectures. You want me to answer the Waley review. It is very difficult—all the things he says are so intangible. I will try to do it, and will send you the result of my labours, but I am not at all sure that it would not be best to let the matter slide. He says that I would not claim a professorial standard of erudition—quite true. He attacks me for generalizing in regard to the language used by the poets. That is the point which tries me most, and the one that is most difficult to reply to, as far as he is concerned. But I shall try to enclose some of the letters in regard to this matter which I have had.

It goes without saying that the colloquial of to-day is further from the poetic style of the T'ang time than was the colloquial of that day. The colloquial of to-day is far indeed from the colloquial of twenty

[1] LIII (1922), 70-83.

years ago; but it is *inconceivable* that people could ever have talked in elaborate "tone patterns," and have used rhymes, and parallelisms in their everyday conversation. Mr. Nung will hardly discuss it. I remarked that Waley's contention was "curious," and he said, "It is not curious—it is nonsense." I wish I could find the Maspero article; as Mr. Morgan says, one would like to know what his contention was. As a matter of fact, I was much surprised that Waley did not tear us limb from limb. If he had taken "Once More Fields and Gardens," he could have done so on the "split ups." You saved our bacon there with your "baker's dozen."

I am sorry not to send the answer to Waley to-day, but I have just this moment finished a very difficult lecture on "The Chinese Idea of a Garden"[1] which I am to give this afternoon, and it has not been possible to write a reply. You may not realize, but the Chinese Garden links up with poetry in the most extraordinary manner.

I hope to send you something—which you may use or not, as you please—by the next mail.

I enclose the Note I have written to the *New China Review*.[2] I wish that you could have written something in regard to poetry—not that I think it would have done any good. The *Review* has not a very large circulation. I am no good whatever as a "fighter," and I think that your fighting quality has been one of the great factors in your success. When you know a thing you are so *convincing*. I recognize my weakness always.

Dr. Ferguson has written a long and very favorable review which will appear in the *Journal of the [North China Branch of the] Royal Asiatic Society*.[3] I do not enclose a copy to-day as I want to write several comments on it, and am going to write to him about one or two things. It does not appear until July.

I am going to Shaohsing (I am sure you have never heard of the place) next week to lecture, and speak here on May 2 on "Chinese Poetry." If only I could find a secretary who could help it would be such a comfort, but there is no one who would be of any use. Even Mrs. —— made many mistakes and she was quite unusual. She has not yet come back, and I do not know if she will.

I will write about Wang Wei next time.

Ever with love to you all,
FLORENCE AYSCOUGH

[1] See "The Chinese Idea of a Garden," in *A Chinese Mirror*, pp. 213–56.
[2] IV, No. 2 (April, 1922), 154–56.
[3] LIII, 70–83.

DEAREST FLORENCE:

I have so many letters of yours to answer that I scarcely know where to begin. I have been away lecturing so much this Winter that I have not written as much as I meant to, and, considering the length of time it takes for letters to go, it is really very trying.

In the first place, Houghton Mifflin Company have used your gift to the Emperor as a note in the Literary Notes in various papers. They have practically copied what you said. . . . .

The letter about the *fu* was duly published in the *Post*[1] but, as Waley has not replied to it, I imagine he cannot. It is very amusing about the split-ups, for no one has objected to them and those were the things we feared, whereas they have all leapt on things we never supposed they would. The prejudice against cadenced verse among the English-speaking residents of China is evidently great, but that does not trouble me. I know they are good translations; but I am more amused than I can say to have Louise Hammond take the very two which I thought were farthest from the Chinese and praise them so highly.

I suppose it is inevitable that I should be stressed in reviews here and that you should be stressed in reviews in China, the reason being, of course, that the magazines know me and are used to cadenced verse and take the book as poetry; whereas the sinologues know you, and understand Chinese, and know no more about poetry than a flea. Waley begs me to learn Chinese and do without you; the Chinese reviewers beg you to let your translations stand as they are and kick me out. I hope you don't agree with them, for, personally, I think our collaboration has been extraordinarily successful and I delight in it.

Mr. Couling's review is negligible, to my mind. I do not know how much Chinese he knows, nor how well qualified he is to speak on the translations as translations merely, but he is quite unqualified by temperament and training to speak on any other side of the book. He is simply a good, old, narrow-minded Colonial Englishman, and nothing in the world is quite as clamped and unintelligent as that. [Sir Reginald] Johnston's review was very nice, I thought, in spite of his not entirely appreciating me. . . . .

Ah, my dear, you are an innocent lamb! You have no idea of the rings of intrigue in this poetry business. The more successful I am the more I am hated. Mr. [George P.] Brett[2] always told me it would be so and I could scarcely believe it, but I am having greater proof of it every

---

[1] See below, Appendix III.

[2] A publisher, later president of the Macmillan Company (see Damon, *op. cit.*, pp. 320, 545).

day. The public is more and more for me, the poets—that is, those less successful than I—more and more against me. I meet with no jealousy from men who have arrived, like Frost, Lindsay, and Sandburg, but I meet with nothing else from those of a lower rank. Meanwhile my books increase their sales, and I had twenty-five hundred people to hear me speak at Ann Arbor two weeks ago.

The mention of Sandburg's name reminds me that you wonder why you have not heard from him. Dear Florence, can you forgive me? I am in the depths of despair about it, but I entirely forgot to send him a copy in your name, and I forgot to send any copy at all to Julia Marlowe. How these things went out of my head, I do not know, except that the work this Winter has been almost killing. I sent Sandburg a copy in my name because I always send him copies of my books, and the fact that you asked me especially to do it in yours went out of my head. When your letter came I hastily hunted up your note to Julia Marlowe and sent it to her with a long apology from me. She will doubtless have written you herself by this time as she acknowledged the book to me. This is abominable of me and I can only say, forgive me. . . . .

Your lectures interest me very much. Just think, I too have had the temerity to give two lectures on Chinese poetry. My only consolation was that I probably knew more about it than my audience, but I shall be thankful when you are settled in St. Andrews and can do your Chinese lecturing yourself.

I do not believe it is possible to get Mr. Nung anything to do at the Widener Library, as you suggest; for, if you paid him the same salary here that you do in China, he would shortly discover that this salary was inadequate, as living costs so much more here. I think that, unless you are very anxious for him, we had better let that drop, as it would be very difficult to manage, and I do not think it would be satisfactory when arranged.

I am waiting anxiously to see Dr. Ferguson's article which you say you are going to send. It seems to me that if it is to appear in the *Journal of the [North China Branch of the] Royal Asiatic Society* that is a very fine place for it to be, because that will get to more people than the merely Chinese papers will get to, will it not?

I have not begun to write Keats yet, if you can believe it. I have been away about two months this Winter lecturing, and although I have collected much material, I have not yet got it in shape to begin the actual writing. However, that is the least effort of the job. I have put off the book for a year and it will not appear until the Autumn of

1923,[1] and I have refused all lecture invitations for this Summer in order to work at it uninterruptedly.

. . . . In your letter you said that you expected to come over "next Spring" for good, and that particular letter was written on February 11th; but, as you have not appeared, I suppose you mean a year from now. I rather expect to be in England next Summer; but you will be working up your Tu Fu material then, and we can go at it in earnest when I get back in the Autumn.

My lecture[2] was largely a rehash of your Introduction with a few little facts that I gleaned outside. I am sending it in case you may like to see it. If you want to do something really amusing in your lectures, compare the poems of [H. A.] Giles which I have quoted with our translations of the same poems. I find this more effective than anything else I can say. I had as large an audience as the ballroom of the Belle-vue Stratford would hold, the first time I gave it for Bryn Mawr, and eleven hundred people at the University of Chicago last week.[3] They told me "they turned them away by hundreds" in Chicago; the hall was jammed.

I guess this is all for now; only do assure me that you are not being pried away from me by the hostile remarks anent my part of our collaboration. That would be a grief indeed, because really, without boasting, I do think that the poems could not have been done better. One of these clippings is very funny, the one from the *New York Tribune*. I think the lady must have got hold of some young Chinese, for it is clear that she does not know what she is talking about but is quoting from some one else. It is marvellously silly.

Now, my dear, I will stop for the nonce. I was much interested in your description of Hsieh T'ao.[4] I rather wish we had put it all in in our introduction. The success of that introduction is marvellous. We certainly made a ten strike there. Ada would send her love if she knew I was writing, but, for the simple matter of her being two thousand miles or so away, I cannot get word to her in time to enclose it in this letter. However, I think you may take it for granted.

Affectionately yours,

AMY LOWELL

---

[1] *Ibid.*, pp. 100, 605, 633–34, 663–71. *John Keats* was not published until February 10, 1925.

[2] See below, Appendix IV.

[3] See Damon, *op. cit.*, p. 603.   [4] See *Fir-Flower Tablets*, p. xcv.

DEAREST AMY,

How do you like my Fir-Flower paper? I won't use it in writing to you as I have consideration for your eyes, but wanted you to see it. The envelope has the fish and the wild goose which carry news from one friend to another, by sea and by land. The goose character is written on the fish in "seal" [character]. It is complete.

I don't know whether or not you have thought that I have dropped out of existence—or whether you have been so busy with Keats that you have not realized I had not written. I suddenly decided to go off up the Yangtze with Mrs. [William C.] Calhoun, and Miss [Anne] Carrere, who is with her, and we left in such a hurry that there was no time to write. I meant to do it en route—but we were so busy looking at everything that there was no time at all.

It was thrilling. We went past the Crosswise River [p. 26], through the Heaven's Gate Mountains [p. 97], to the entrance of the T'ung T'ing Lake [p. 156], and then on to Ichang. There we changed into the ship which took us through the Three Chasms [pp. 72, 113, 201] and on to Chungking. You can see it all on our map in *Fir-Flower Tablets*.[1]

The whole journey was immensely interesting, and the part from Ichang on *amazingly* beautiful. Of course one has always heard of the beauty of the Gorges, but until one sees them one does not realize how marvellous they are. We were especially fortunate. Just before we left Ichang there was a heavy rainfall lasting a good many days; so all the cascades were full of water and made the most extraordinary effect as they were every imaginable shade of colour from a deep blood-red, through deep copper, and light copper, to gold, straw colour, and pure sparkling white. You can imagine how wonderful the whole thing was against a background of soft green mountains all draped in mist.

We passed the village where the Honourable Lady Chao [pp. 62, 198] was born and brought up. Next to it rises the Yang T'ai where the Fairy of the Sorceress Gorge lives, and, just before one comes to it, one passes through the Sorceress Gorge [p. 113] itself. Above the Three Chasms stands Kweichoufu, a city where Tu Fu lived for four years not long before he died, and where he wrote ever so many poems about the Gorges.[2] It is by the site of The City of the White Emperor and above the Chu T'ang chasm. The "Whirling Water Rock"[3] was

[1] See also "The Literary Background of the Great River," in *A Chinese Mirror*, pp. 101–212; cf. also the *Journal of the North China Branch of the Royal Asiatic Society*, LIV (1923), 129–49.

[2] See *Tu Fu*, II, 196 ff.

[3] *Ibid.*, p. 251; see also *Fir-Flower Tablets*, p. 190, n. 46, and *A Chinese Mirror*, pp. 177–97, 210–11.

nearly covered; you see, it is just the beginning of the Fifth Month. When it is covered, the junks do not attempt the passage of the Gorges as, with the water so high, it is too dangerous.

We landed at Kweichoufu and found the place where Tu Fu lived and studied. It is now a school, and Western charts showing all one's internals were pasted on the wall. A little pavilion stands in the middle of a stone-lined pool and in it is a stone table; this is supposed to have been one of his favorite seats. Huge trees, wu-t'ungs and banyans, surround it and the whole place is very peaceful. We had a hard time finding it and were led by a man in a bright blue turban (the Szechuanese, generally speaking, wear turbans—most picturesque) up Moon's Tooth Street, high up the hill to the city wall before we arrived at our destination. As may be imagined, the major part of the population followed us, full of interest.

The next afternoon we spent at Wan Hsien, a most lovely spot. Above the city is a cave in a precipice where Li T'ai-po used to spend a great deal of time; so a memorial temple to him has been made against the face of the cliff. It is kept in perfect repair by the succeeding officials of the place and the statue of Li Po had been newly gilded. It has a delightful expression which I hope will show in the photograph I took of him. Little attendants stand on either side: one holds a wine cup, the other a wine "hu"—that vessel which looks like our coffee pots.

The view from this precipice is magnificent; one can see both up and down the river and far across the country to the north as a valley opens out. It was a perfect afternoon and I shall never forget the scene. Under the temple, under an overhanging bit of cliff, stands his stone chess table with four stone seats around it—all ready for a game. The road leads up a stone staircase and the Boy I took with me remarked when we returned to the ship that we had been over four thousand steps. It was worth it!

The life on the River is so interesting. The way they move the boats against that awful current, which often took our powerful ship absolutely in charge, is astounding. Of course quantities of lives are lost all the time.

I took a good many of Tu Fu's poems with me and it was delightful to read them on the spot. He has written a great many on "Rain"[1]— and one is not surprised after being there, as the mists cling to the hills and come down in showers continually.

It was all hard work—enjoying oneself. One was on deck by 4:45

[1] *Tu Fu*, II, 235–36, 257.

200

A.M.—that is as soon as the ship started (they have to tie up at night; it is so dangerous) and one was kept busy every second looking at something until one tied up at five-thirty or so. Then, if possible, one went ashore, and was very glad to go to bed soon after dinner. As you may imagine I did not do any work at all. But I think that, from the point of view of poetry, it was an exceedingly profitable journey.

Thank you so much for forwarding that delightful review from the *Dial*. I am tremendously pleased with it. The one in the *Tribune* by Grace Phelps is not so interesting. Who is she? She is mistaken about the repetitions of the words coming from the analyses of the character, and does not realize that the Oh-h-h-h you translate is from *Hsi-i-i*, not from the *Ai*, which is a sound of grief.

This is going by a new "Empress," the "Empress of Canada," which is supposed to be going to break all records across the Pacific. Thirteen days from here to Vancouver, so you should receive it June 30 or July 1.

Much love to all my second family. What are Ada, Lorna and the children going to do this summer?

Yours,
FLORENCE AYSCOUGH

[SHANGHAI], June 30, 1922

DEAREST AMY,

I was delighted to have your letter of May 27 enclosing a lot of reviews I had not seen . . . . and also your delightful lecture on Chinese poetry. I am glad you had such splendid audiences. There is only one thing I would suggest—that is that you don't say "Chinamen." For some reason or other the Chinese resent this very much, and as there are probably always young Chinese in your audiences it seems a pity to annoy them without need.

I am thankful you think it too late to answer Waley. Although I have racked my brains, as I wrote you, his review seems too intangible to reply to. The people here who have read it think it simply silly—but one can't say that in reply! . . . .

. . . . As to the people who are trying to pry us apart I pay no attention to them; simply tell them that they don't know what they are talking about. But it is amusing to have Eunice Tietjens say that *your* personality should be subtracted; and people out here tell me that they can hear *me* talking. Of course, what we are both aiming at is to let ourselves come into it as little as possible, and I do think that

201

we have succeeded in eliminating ourselves to a great extent. I am glad it has been so well received. Do not fear that I shall ever feel I can begin to interpret the poems the way you can. . . . .

As far as Sandburg is concerned, it doesn't matter a button who sent the book as long as he got it! I wanted to know what he thought of it. As a matter of fact, I didn't ask you to bother about sending a copy to him, but put his name on the list I left with Houghton Mifflin. I suppose they, seeing that you always sent him a copy of your books, did not send him a duplicate, which was sensible of them.

I send you a few photographs of the Upper Yangtze. If it would amuse you at all I will have some of the others copied, but I have an idea that photographs do not greatly interest you. Please let me know if you would like others. I succeeded in getting some lovely ones, but it was a very difficult proposition.

I will go through the book carefully to see if there are more changes that should be made. I do know of two little ones.

The Princess Der Ling came to lunch to-day. She is going to U.S.A. in about a month and I am going to give her a letter to you. She is very intelligent, and knows the poems well. She is one of the strongest advocates of my doing the whole thing. I tell you this because I want you to convert her. She, naturally, is not a judge of English literary merit though she speaks English fluently. I argued at length to-day to no purpose; but I may say that she did not alter my opinion at all. She said you did some "padding." I said you did *not*. We compared some poems, and she had to admit that you did not add. . . . . She does know the poems in Chinese *thoroughly* and can realize the meaning —even the nuances—in English, but then she does not realize the importance of putting the work of a great poet into great English. Do you know what I mean? It would be impossible—an insult to the poets —to publish my rough translations. And it is when I attempt to improve them that I am entirely at sea. She says: "You give the feeling, you know." Well, I know very well that nothing would induce me to subject Li T'ai-po, and still more Tu Fu, to my renderings. I would like you to charm her and make her know the truth. I am sure that Witter Bynner will do his utmost to gain her approbation. She says that she told him she did not think his work was accurate, and he would not listen to her. She does not think Kiang knows enough English to do the thing properly.

When writing to acknowledge the note from Houghton Mifflin . . . . I asked for the map. Although we shall, I suppose, not use it again, it would be a good plan to enter Tu Fu's wanderings on it, in a general way. By the bye, you have never let me know what I owe you for my share of the corrections. . . . .

I send you Dr. Ferguson's review and a couple of letters which speak for themselves.

You forget how early Spring is here. When I wrote in February it was already in the air; the willows were budding and things were beginning to look green. Yes "next Spring" means 1923, when we expect to come to St. Andrews.

You say that Lorna and the children are to be with you, so I suppose that Sonny Boy is not going to camp again. Give them all my love. I hope they will be well and that all will go smoothly.

And now adieu. Frank is just going down to breakfast and will want this for the post. The amah has finished one side of my hair and I must dress to be ready for Mr. Nung.

Ever yours,
FLORENCE AYSCOUGH

[SHANGHAI], August 12, 1922

DEAREST AMY,

Would you please be an angel and ask Miss Moran to ring up the people who have that delightful "cameo" paper which you use and get them to send me, as soon as possible, three large blocks and three small ones. I brought out a supply with me and find, to my horror, that it is nearly finished. I cannot get any paper here in the least like it, and it is much the nicest I have ever used. It is the creamy yellowish kind that I mean. I am being so economical of what is left that my fine "grassy characters" are turning into little fly tracks which I very much doubt being able to read.

There is nothing much to talk about. It has been *very* hot with no break for the last six weeks: 95 to 100 every day. I am well but do hate being soaking wet all the time. Of course, if one were not soaking wet one would just blow up!

Am working steadily at Tu Fu. He is so utterly different from Li Po. There won't be the least similarity between the two books. Am doing the poems in chronological order. (How do you spell chro—?) and think that a little abstract of the history of that period will have to be the Introduction this time. It is a fascinating period.

Am also building a Chinese country cottage;[1] real country style with mother-of-pearl doors and high roof; so that we can have somewhere to stay when we come out for the winters. I hope that one of Frank's

---

[1] See *Firecracker Land*, pp. 41–89; also *A Chinese Mirror*, pp. 23–99.

partners will live in it the rest of the time and keep the servants together. Of course we don't expect to come out every year but hope to sometimes. That is, I certainly do hope to. This house [Wild Goose Happiness House] is too big to keep for only occasional use, but the Chinese house, with Heaven's Wells,[1] will be awfully nice. I call it my Grass-Hut-by-the-Yellow-Reach[2] and am going to have the "three friends who do not fear winter cold" planted in the first court. In the second court there is a wu-t'ung tree—I am not sure yet what else. And there are to be kuei-hua trees in the small Heaven's Wells which are put to the north of the centre room in each building. I suppose this sounds very confused, but it is going to be *very* nice. . . . . We shall move in as soon as it is built—I think January 1—and then will have time to arrange about the sale of this place at our leisure. We shall sail, I suppose, at the end of April or early in May.

How are you all? My best love to my second family. A typhoon is on the way. It is beginning to blow. There has just been the most awful one down the coast; a really terrible disaster.

Adieu, much love; please don't forget the paper.

Yours,

FLORENCE AYSCOUGH

By the bye, you have never let me know what I owe you for the corrections. Please ask Miss Moran to ask the paper people to send me their bill. It was silly of me to lose their address.

[Shanghai], September 25, 1922

DEAREST AMY,

I wonder if your English Press Cuttings people will send you the *Edinburgh Review* [Vol. CCXXXVI, No. 481] for July, 1922. It has a very long [pp. 99–114] and very nice review of [*A Hundred and Seventy Chinese Poems* and *More Translations from the Chinese* and] *Fir-Flower Tablets* by a Chinese [Chang Hsin-hai]. It is to be had in America of The Leonard Scott Publishing Co., New York. *T'oung Pao* [XXI, 232–42], also, has a long, long review by Pelliot, who is, I suppose, the leading sinologue to-day. It is the number for May–July, and is to be had of E. J. Brill, 33*a* Oude Rijn, Leyde.

It is disappointing from this point of view: instead of treating the matter in a wide manner, as the man in the *Edinburgh Review* does, Pelliot concerns himself with details—as a few years of difference in the date when Liu Yu-si, etc., lived. Dates that I got from the little

---

[1] *A Chinese Mirror*, pp. 26, 82.   [2] *Ibid.*, p. 72.

man in the Art Museum who took them from the Japanese edition of the T'ang biographies. Pelliot says, furthermore, that the Yueh Chih are *not* the Moon Clan. If we choose to translate the character "Yueh," I don't see how he can object. And so on. I shall have to go through it carefully; have only just got it.

It is practically impossible to satisfy the sinologue—and certainly not in a book to be read generally.

No time for more, love to all.

F. A.

Pity the *Times Literary Supplement* review was written by such a dull person.

BROOKLINE, MASS., 7 December, 1922

MY DEAR FLORENCE:

I have not written to you for so long that there seems to be mountains to say, and I scarcely know where to begin. I am enclosing you a copy of a letter I received from Miss Hammond, and which I replied to as per another enclosure.

I have both the reviews you mention, the one in the *Edinburgh Review* and the Frenchman's, but, to tell the truth, I have not had the energy to read the Frenchman's through very carefully yet. I would not worry at all about what these old sinologues say. The more I see of scholars, the more I realize that they have their uses in preparing the ground, but that they know nothing about literature, and that if the fate of ancient literatures were left to them, nobody would ever take the interest to read them. Another thing is that a sinologue is a man who has studied a foreign tongue and is interested in the development of a foreign idiom. He is much more concerned with philology than the native. I would fifteen times rather have the reactions of Mr. Chang Hsin-hai in the *Edinburgh Review*[1] to those of any Frenchman, no matter how erudite the latter may be.

There were certain criticisms Mr. Chang Hsin-hai made which I think are very good. For instance, of course *ch'ing*, as we now know, is simply a brighter colour of any particular colour given. I suppose we started out by saying "green sky" almost by accident, and then I got to like the colour, and I still like it; but I suppose the Chinese really do mean "blue sky" just as we do. I do not think he is right in his strictures on "Night Thoughts" [p. 74], but, on the whole, I thought his criticism was very favourable. Altogether, I think the book has been extremely well reviewed.

[1] "The Vogue of Chinese Poetry," CCXXXVI, No. 481 (July, 1922), 99–114.

I am sending you a copy of the December *Poetry*[1] in which I answered Eunice Tietjens.[2] She wrote some rather nasty things, which I enclose. I think I laid her out rather neatly, myself, and her little answer puts her in wronger than ever.

Witter Bynner's book does not appear, and I do not think it ever will.[3] I think we have given him a dreadful shock. . . . .

I have got your map, and have had it for a long time. They returned it almost immediately, and I told Ferris [Greenslet] not to bother to write you, that I would; and then I delayed all this time, so I suppose you are very much worried. But you need not be, it is all right. . . . .

I am longing to have you come back here. I hoped to go to England this summer, but the Keats book is being so much longer than I expected that I fear I shall be kept here all Summer; but that will have its advantages for we can meet sooner. I am sure that if you stay here you can spend your whole time lecturing on Chinese poetry up and down the country to your heart's content. How is Tu Fu coming along? I hope not too rapidly, for when I finish the Keats book I shall be so exhausted that I shall want quite a long vacation before I attempt anything else. . . . .

There does not seem to be much news here. I am giving my lecture on Chinese poetry at the Brooklyn Institute in February. How I wish it were you that were giving it! I shall resign from every lecture on Chinese poetry when you come over.

Lots of love, my dear, and keep me *au courant* with everything that happens. Your second family misses you all the time, and sends you all their love.

Affectionately yours,

[*Signed for*] AMY LOWELL

---

[1] XXI, No. III, 167–72, "Miss Lowell on Translating Chinese," with reply "Note by Eunice Tietjens." Miss Lowell's letter commented on (Part II of) Mrs. Tietjens' "On Translating Chinese Poetry" in *Poetry*, XX, No. V (August, 1922), 268–74, and No. VI (September, 1922), 328–32.

[2] See Damon, *op. cit.*, p. 636.

[3] See *The Jade Mountain* . . . . , trans. Witter Bynner; see also Eunice Tietjens, "From the Chinese," a review of *The Jade Mountain, Poetry*, XXXV, No. V (February, 1930), 289–92. Of interest, also, is Amy Lowell, "An Observer in China," a review of *Profiles from China* by Eunice Tietjens, *Poetry*, X, No. VI (September, 1917), 326–30. Miss Lowell's review of Mrs. Tietjens' *Profiles from China* was almost as appreciative as Mrs. Tietjens' review thirteen years later of Messrs. Bynner and Kiang's *Jade Mountain*. In reading Mrs. Tietjens' review, the correspondence between the two poets, through the channel cited above, and the publication of *Fir-Flower Tablets* should be borne in mind, as should the choice by Miss Monroe of Mrs. Tietjens as the reviewer of *The Jade Mountain*.

DEAREST AMY,

It was perfectly delightful to have your Christmas cable. I knew that you were busy, and absorbed in Keats, so did not expect letters, but it was a comfort to know that you were alive. It would not seem Christmas if your greeting did not come.

I am working steadily at Tu Fu, and wish that there were time to translate all the 1000 and more poems, with the commentaries, in the edition from which I am working. One would get such a wonderful insight into his life. As it is, I am in volume 16 (there are 21), and shall go through the lot before we leave. At least that is what I am aiming at. And we shall then have a good store of material for the book. So far I have done 376, and, as I told you, am doing them chronologically.

By the bye, *please send me the map*. I want to trace Tu Fu's route of travel on it, whether we use it or not. It can be done here very well; so please ask Miss Moran to foreward it.

This must go; forgive the scrap. My best love to Ada. We are due in Vancouver by "Empress of Russia" on May 7th, and shall go to St. Andrews at once.

Ever yours, my dear,

FLORENCE AYSCOUGH

[SHANGHAI], Saturday, March 23, 1923

DEAREST AMY,

A month from to-day, D.V., April 21, we set sail! As you may imagine, my feelings are more than mixed. We shall go to St. Andrews at once. We shall not be able to move into our own house until the first of July, as all sorts of things are being done to it, so mean to stop at Auntie Belle's house which is being kept as a boarding-house by the cook we had in 1921.

The other day a French doctor turned up who admires *Fir-Flower Tablets* very much, and who had been translating them. He thinks that they would be very popular in France, and asked me if he might publish. Of course, I told him that it was not possible for me to give him permission, but that I would write to you, and ask you to communicate directly with him. Enclosed are several specimens he sent me to send on to you. Will you please write to him:

> DR. JEAN GOURAUD,
>   care Messageries Maritimes,
>   Marseilles.

He is sailing on their ships. He seemed a very cultivated man and was most enthusiastic. If you and Mr. Greenslet approve, it would do no harm to cable him permission. Of course, he is away from the port for several months at a time; a letter might just miss him, which would mean months of delay.

Referring to your letter of December 7: the "green sky" we translate is not the *ch'ing*, which we do generally give as a brightness, or brilliance, of some sort, but the word *ts'ang*, which does mean a green, of sorts. It is also applied to water. In this part of the world one very, very often sees a "green" sky. I like it and think we had better stick to it. Of course, Mr. Thing-a-ma-bob [Chang Hsin-hai], in the *Edinburgh Review* had not the text by him, so his *ch'ing* was a guess.

I shall be very glad to get away from absorbing—or trying to— more and more of Tu Fu, and collect my thoughts. The confusion in my mind is dreadful. Over five hundred poems are done. They give a remarkable insight into his mind and life. I wish I had had time to do the lot.

When I say that the five hundred are done, I don't mean that they are ready for you in any way. They are put into colloquial and checked with Nung. But the most important part of all—at least that is how I regard the analysis—is not touched.

Love to all my second family.

Yours, dear, as always,

Florence Ayscough

Remember—"Empress of Russia" is our boat, due Vancouver, May 7.

[Enclosure]

L'EPOUSE SOLITAIRE
par Li T'ai-Po

Le brouillard est épais, le fleuve largement s'étale.
Les plantes d'eau surnagent mollement.
Pas une lettre: rien.
Ne vient.
Seule la lune brille au travers
Des lourds nuages d'un ciel profond de jade vert.
Il est parti: seule pensée
De ma solitude angoissée
Au long du jour trainant et chagrin et douleur
Au long du jour va ma douleur
Et votre pensée est comme un sceau contre mon coeur.
Le souci
A noué l'arc de mes sourcils.

208

L'arc désormais indénouable.
Toute la nuit, toute la nuit
Je tiens prête pour vous la moitié de mon lit
Et j'attends le retour de mon rêve très doux
De mon rêve divin O Maitre, qui est Vous.
Dans les draps de l'Oiseau-Feu
Et dans le lit de l'Oiseau-Dieu
Faisan d'Amour Crêté d'Argent toutes les nuits
Toutes les nuits je m'endors seule.
Aux chandeliers d'argent fondent les bougies rouges,
Les pleurs de cire coulent coulent
Comme coulent les pleurs de votre infortunée
Intarissablement
Une courte saison et la fleur est fanée
Il neige encore au long des rives de Hsiang.
De l'oreiller où je m'enfouis
J'entends le bruit
Nostalgique et glacé tombant de la clepsydre
Têng! Têng! qui goutte à goutte vibre
Et fibre à fibre
Taille mon coeur.

Je me lève et dans la Salle des Tableaux ils viennent dire:
Les fleurs de neige vont mourir.
Les grands rideaux sont roulés haut
Et je regarde la blancheur scintillante des neiges vernales
Blanchissant tout, couvrant les dalles
Des escaliers et de la cour.
L'air est empli de leur éclat et leurs rafales
De loin paraissent les fumées lourdes d'un grand four
Chaque brin d'herbe est froid et blanc comme le jade des pendants
Et sûrement les Immortels
Sont ivres de vin dans leur Ciel
Pour causer un pareil désordre
Pour saisir les nuages blancs pour les chiffonner et les tordre.

REGRET ET SOUFFRANCE DE PRINTEMPS
PAR LI T'AI-PO

Au levant sur la mer Lao
Un cheval blanc aux rênes d'or.
Je dors
Rideaux de soie à jours ouvrés. Sous la courte pointe
    Brodée
Je dors dans le vent du Printemps.
La Lune se couchant, pend
Tout au niveau de mon balcon
Elle m'épie
La bougie

Est consumée.
Au travers de ma porte une fleur est jetée
Epanouie ...
Et mon lit est vide! Ironie.

LA BATAILLE AU SUD DE LA CITE

Si sombre le champ du combat, jaune si sombre!
Les combattants vont fourmillant grouillant sans nombre
Dans l'air épais qu'à peine il troue
Le Soleil parait une roue
Ecarlate
La pourpre éclate
Pourpre de sang rouge baptême
Sur les pétales du sauvage chrysanthème
Les vautours trainant au bec chairs déchirées.
Les vautours lourds de leur curées
Trainent au sol
Lourds pour l'envoi
Hier sur les murs de la cité vivaient des hommes
Et sous les murs de la cité vont des fantômes
Couleurs des étendards flottant comme des voiles
Etincelant d'étoiles
Roulement des tambours de la cavalerie
La tuerie n'est pas finie.

Dans sa maison La Désolée ...
Epoux et fils sont en allée
Là-bas, d'où vient le bruit des tambours cavaliers.

VISITANT LE PRETRE TAOISTE SUR LA MONTAGNE QUI SOUTIENT LE CIEL IL EST ABSENT

par Li T'ai-Po

Un Chien
Un aboiement de chien
Et puis, le bruit de l'eau qui fuit
Fleurs de pêcher après la pluie
D'un ton profond et si précieuses
Midi. Je n'entends pas de cloches au ravin
Parfois
Entre les arbres je vois
Un daim.
Les sauvages bambous déchirent le bleu-vert d'un ciel ennuagé.
La cascade
Est pendue au long du pic vert-jade ...
Nul pour me dire ici vers où il est allé
Et je m'appuie sur les sapins, coeur désolé.

DEAREST FLORENCE:

I hope you got my wire safely at Vancouver. It *is* good to know that you are in this country again, for I count Canada this country, do not you? It was very amusing when I was lecturing at St. Catherine's this year to hear everybody talk about "your country," as though I lived a thousand miles away instead of just over the bridge across Niagara.

How soon do you intend to come down and make your second family a visit? They are pining to see you. But I am afraid I have doleful news for you in one respect: I have not yet finished my Life of Keats, nor do I believe I shall finish it before the Winter, although I have been working like a perfect Trojan on it; and there is a little volume I have promised to do for the Princeton Press on the modern free forms[1] which must be got out of the way as soon as the Keats book is over. Of course, I supposed I should finish the Keats book about the middle of last Winter and could do the other perfectly well by this Spring, and we intended to go abroad this Summer, but I find Keats is much more work than I expected. The result is that I am extremely tired, so that I am afraid, my dear, (bear up if you can) that I shall not be able to start work upon the Tu Fu book before a year from this Autumn, because I must certainly go to Europe next summer, as Basil Blackwell there, and Ferris Greenslet here, both insist that it is very important, and I think it is. Also, I need a rest if anybody ever did.

I am afraid this will disappoint you, and I am just as sorry as I can be, for, believe me, I want to get all my obligations out of the way and sit down and write poetry; and it is annoying to you to be kept waiting by your coagitator, but it cannot be helped, I fear, just now. I only hope that you have more to do with Tu Fu and can go ahead a little without me, for you know I do these poems very quickly when once I start work on them. Anyway, you come down here and pay me a visit, and we will talk it all over then.

Shall I send the map up to St. Andrews, or would you rather have me keep it here until you come down? I am going to New York on Wednesday for about a week, a new book [*Guzman d'Alfarache*][2] belonging to Keats having been scared up there, making it necessary for me to go and copy the annotations. I do not know how long it will take you to cross the continent and get to St. Andrews, but I am going to ring you up from New York and see if we can have a talk, but you had better wire me your telephone number as you are not yet in your

---

[1] See Damon, *op. cit.*, pp. 610, 635.   [2] *Ibid.*, p. 634.

own house and I do not know what name to call. I do not know the name to put on this letter either, for that matter, but I suppose your name will get you anywhere at the St. Andrews post office.

Please remember us both most kindly to Frank, and let us see you soon, dear Florence. It is a long time since we have met and we have got a lot to say, and the chief of all is a most hearty welcome home. I suppose you have mixed feelings on the subject, but we are altogether delighted that you are on this side of the Eastern water. That kidnapping[1] this morning gives me a chill, but I suppose you were safe at Shanghai.

Ever so much love,

Affectionately yours,
Amy Lowell

On the Prairies, May 11, 1923

Dearest Amy,

Thanks for the telegram, which was most welcome. We had a wonderful crossing, and I heard a perfectly new criticism of the Pacific Ocean, i.e., that it was "too monotonously calm"! Vivid recollections of sundry gales made me simply roar with laughter when the man uttered these words. He should see what it *can* do.

We are due in Montreal on Monday morning; shall stay there at the Ritz until Wednesday evening, and then push on to St. Andrews. The house on Commonwealth Avenue has been sold—the Old Colony informed me by telegraph before we left Shanghai—so I shall probably have to come up to Boston about that before long, but have not made plans yet. The house in St. Andrews is being pulled to pieces and I am longing to see how it is progressing. We shall have to go to Auntie Belle's house, which our late cook is keeping as a private hotel, to start with.

You have never said a word about the Keats book, for ages and ages. Will it appear this Spring, or not until the Autumn? I know that you do not like to have books come out in the Spring. I did not do any work on Tu Fu on the ship—I was too tired, as it kept me hard at it until the day of sailing—but I did make some T'ang history notes which will be useful. They are not very interesting; my hands were like ice, the fog horn was blowing, and the damp fog enveloped me; however, they contain facts, which are very necessary to an understanding of the poems. It is going to be a very difficult book.

[1] The attack on the Blue Express train, May 6 (see Morse and MacNair, *op. cit.*, pp. 676–77; also H. F. MacNair, *China's New Nationalism and Other Essays* [Shanghai, 1925], pp. 214–58).

FLORENCE AYSCOUGH AND YO FEI IN VIENNA

It was hard to leave the Chinese house [the Ts'ao T'ang, i.e., the Grass Hut-by-the-Yellow-Reach][1] and dear Yo Fei. Poor little dog![2] I sent him off to play with Achay's children as the moment of our departure came near, so my last recollection is of a yellow tail wagging cheerfully as he turned out of the back door, and he was spared the pang of seeing us drive away. Achay is the downstairs coolie; his four children, who live in the village by our house, are Yo Fei's dear playmates. It is a great comfort to think of the little house and all the servants as being there—on the spot.

Mr. Nung is going to publish a book—so he will be occupied. It will be useful, I think, as it is a sort of reference book giving the Classical origins of many phrases in colloquial use to-day. You see, the language is changing so rapidly that new sorts of books are needed all the time. I am keeping him more or less in my employ, and he is working at various texts while I am away. That will save much time when I go back, which I hope will be winter after next. Not that there is ever any good in planning so far away, but one does it.

Much love to Ada and your dear self.

Yours ever,
FLORENCE AYSCOUGH

[ST. ANDREWS], May 21, 1923

DEAREST AMY,

In spite of the very poor connection, it *was* nice to hear your voice last night. Not being on a Trunk Line makes such a difference; we heard each other so well from Montreal.

I was awfully glad to have your letter when we came. Keats will be splendid when it is done. Tu Fu ought to be, too; and, of course, as I said last night, we have perfectly new material. Practically none of it has ever been done, so it will be sad if anyone does it before us. That Japanese, Mr. Obata, is the person I am afraid of, as, of course, it is so simple for him—Chinese literature being in a sense his national literature. And, having done Li Po, he will naturally turn to Tu Fu—if his book has been successful. It has been sent to Louise Hammond to review and she had it with her the last time she came to lunch with me. Of course, I could only glance at it—I did see that it had an excellent map. I could not get it in the shops before leaving, nor was it available in Montreal, so I have sent for it and shall look at it with interest.

[1] See *A Chinese Mirror*, chap. i, or *Firecracker Land*, chap. ii.

[2] See *The Autobiography of a Chinese Dog*, or *Firecracker Land*, chap. iv.

A German, whose name I cannot, on the instant, remember is working at Tu Fu, but I do not suppose that German publications count much one way or the other.

As I wrote you, I have a great deal to do to the poems before they are ready for you, so I will just work away, and we will do them as soon as we can. The analysis is not touched. As I said last night, I will try to come up soon, and then we can look the poems over, and talk the whole matter out. Don't bother to send me the map; I have worked Tu Tu out on another one and so do not need that.

Would it interest you to see the slides of the *San Hsia*, the Three Chasms [p. 72], where Tu Fu spent a long time? I have some lovely coloured ones made from photographs which I took last year. If you would like to see them I will bring up my portable lantern, and a box of slides; then you can get an idea of what the Great River looks like. There is a view of the hill at whose foot "The Bright Concubine" [pp. 62, 198–200] was born, etc., etc., etc.

It is very, very beautiful here, quite amazingly so, but of course I do miss many things. Not least of all Yo Fei. Poor little dog! The Ts'ao T'ang did look sweet when we left. The blossoms in the Courtyard were so lovely. Amah[1] looked at the cassia tree in the tiny "Heaven's Well" outside my bed-room window, and, shaking her head, said, "You no smell." She has ruled me with a rod of iron for twenty-four years and more—so we know each other. I have a woman from Montreal who seems nice, but she will never rule me, and that is what I like. Amah is so clever, and, although she cannot read or write, she can tell me historical tales, and talk about the customs of the country in the most delightful way.

Our own house is going to be delightful, but I do not know when we shall be able to move and unpack the forty-three cases of household goods we have brought with us. Not till the end of June at least. The books are what I want most to get at, but there is no place for them yet. We are now going to run down to Eastport, so I must stop.

Are you expecting anyone to stay within the next fortnight or so, or if I just say I can come will it be convenient? Is there any special part of the Keats work that you will be doing so that you don't want to be disturbed? Let me know, and then I can make plans.

Dear love to my second family.

Yours ever,

FLORENCE AYSCOUGH

---

[1] See *Firecracker Land*, pp. 27 ff.

BROOKLINE, MASS., 20 June, 1923

DEAREST FLORENCE:

I am afraid my crimes are hitting me in the face again. I do not believe I ever forwarded the letter of May twenty-third which Miss Rhoades speaks of, but I am forwarding this one which I suppose is a duplicate. I have not dug down through my wire basket for some time, for I have been so frightfully busy with Keats, and I fear the letter to you of May twenty-third is waiting with a number of mine for me to get down to it. This will reach you in time any way. Will you return her letter to me for my files?

I wish, my dear, that you would come down here. Your second family is not merely so in name, it is so in heart, and it feels lonely when it does not see you and realizes that you are on this side of the water. I do not wonder that you balk at leaving the forty-three packing cases; it cannot, of course, be thought of, but please keep in your mind the fact that we want to see you dreadfully and are counting the days until you come.

I have other crimes on my head. I never did anything about the Frenchman who translated us into French.[1] I doubted very much how much he would want to go into it, when he saw all the paraphernalia of contracts and other things which would have to be put through. Moreover, a French translation of an English translation from the Chinese seemed to me to be rather futile. However, I still have his letter, and if you want me to talk it over with Ferris Greenslet I will.

It is looking lovely here, but hot. I suppose you are cool as cucumbers where you are. I must break this off abruptly, for the man has come with the photographing machine to photograph the manuscripts I am going to use as illustrations for the Keats book. Do come as soon as you can.

With lots of love,
AMY

[ST. ANDREWS], July 4, 1923

DEAREST AMY,

I am horrified when I see that the date of your letter is June 20. When one is near at hand one feels that one should answer letters more promptly than when one is so far away that days and weeks seem to make but little difference. Thanks for the letter from Newark; I enclose the one from Miss Rhoades as you asked I should do.

As far as the Frenchman is concerned, I think that it would be a

[1] See *Tablettes de fleur de sapin*, trans. Maurice Thiéry (Paris: Editions Pierre Roger, 1928).

good plan if you would ask Mr. Greenslet what he thinks about it. Chinese poetry is rather popular in France, I think; so, if it could be worked, it would probably be a good thing.

It is sweet of you to say that you want to see me, and, indeed, I do want to see "my second family" very much indeed. But, truly, it is difficult to leave here. Perhaps it will be easier when we are settled. I sometimes wonder if that will ever be. Of course it will, but there is still a lot to be done. It is confusing with noise, and workmen about, so I have not touched Tu Fu.

The Li Po book by the Japanese Obata,[1] is quite good, so it seems to me. I wish I had the command of Chinese that he has of English. It is interesting to see how close in sense his translation of the "Steep Road to Shuh"[2] is to ours. Why he should insert "steep" into the title I do not see. Of course, his transliteration is *awful*—really awful. He follows no known method that I can see, and that only adds to the confusion in regard to Chinese names which is bad enough as it is. I stupidly left my Chinese text of *Fir-Flower Tablets* in Shanghai with some papers there, thinking that if it ever needed revision, I would have to do it with Nung; so, now, I have not the characters to compare with Obata's text. Nor have I the transliterations such as I sent you, and it is difficult to remember accurately. Nor do I think that Li Po's text is among my books. That I can see when they are unpacked. I left a good many things in my study there.

I hope that we shall be able to do Tu Fu before he does, as he will probably go to work at that if this has had success. Impartially, I do think that our work is better than his. Do you know at all how the book has been received?

When does Keats go to press? Do you know at all? I am looking forward to it immensely, as I am sure it will be a fine thing.

It is very beautiful here, and we have had no heat. The days that were described as so overpowering in the cities were as cool as possible here. The forest fires were dreadful, and the smoke reached here in a heavy cloud.

This is an appallingly dull letter but it carries much affection to you and Ada. Lorna and John must be with you, so give them my love too.

Yours affectionately,

FLORENCE AYSCOUGH

---

[1] Shigeyoshi Obata, *The Works of Li Po the Chinese Poet Done into English Verse: With an Introduction and Biographical and Critical Matter Translated from the Chinese* (New York, 1922).

[2] *Ibid.*, No. 74, p. 109.

Could Miss Moran please write on a postcard the name and address of the people who have that nice yellowish paper which you use? Mine has given out and I should like more.

BROOKLINE, MASS., 5 September, 1923

DEAREST FLORENCE:

I telegraphed you last night, so as to reach you more quickly than the mail could, for both Ada and I are absolutely overjoyed at the thought of your coming down here. The latch-string is out whenever you choose to descend upon us, either before or after your Lenox visit. I shall be thankful to be taken away from Keats for a little while; I think it will do the book all the good in the world to go back to it again; I have worked at it so long and so steadily, always feeling the whip-lash of haste descending upon my shoulders, that I am almost distracted by it now. I cannot help thinking that a little rest will do me good, and yet my New England conscience and the absolute necessity for hurry prevent me from stopping without a good cause; so you see you will not only be giving us pleasure in every other way, but proving an absolute benefactor.

Your pamphlets, which I have not had time to read, look extremely interesting.

Please do bring down the magic lantern and the slides that you speak of. We will have a little party and ask a few interesting people to dinner, and we can show them the pictures afterward, if you will. That will be fine; I am looking forward to it.

Poor little Yo Fei![1] I am glad he is better. Of course he would not eat on a great big steamer with nobody who loved him there. No, of course not; no right-minded dog would.

I do wish I were as I once was, for I often think how I should like to come up and spend a week with you. How refreshing it would be! Alas and alack! Was I ever to be what erst I were!

Lorna departed yesterday, so we are only just ourselves. She was dreadfully sorry to miss you.

Ada joins me in love and great expectation. Kind wishes to Frank.

Yours as always,
AMY LOWELL

[1] *The Autobiography of a Chinese Dog,* pp. 100–105.

ST. ANDREWS, September 10, [1923]

DEAREST AMY,

Thanks for your letter. I will plan to leave here the night of Tuesday, the 25th, and be with you on Wednesday—if that will suit you. It will be perfectly delightful to see you both. I will bring the lantern and slides.

Love to Ada,

Yours ever,

FLORENCE AYSCOUGH

ST. ANDREWS, Tuesday, September 18, [1923]

DEAREST AMY,

Thanks ever so much for your telegram. I am looking forward to seeing you and Ada.

My train is due at 8:45 A.M. *train* time. I don't know if daylight saving still holds good in Boston. I shall have two trunks and will not forget my lantern nor the slides.

Ever yours,

FLORENCE AYSCOUGH

ST. ANDREWS, October 12, 1923

DEAREST SECOND FAMILY,

I arrived safe and sound yesterday morning. Frank met me at McAdam Junction, having had to spend the night at the station hotel there with locomotives murmuring at him through the window all night long. He said he considered that a placard marked "devotion" should have been nailed on the door. Everything looks most beautiful and Yo Fei was enchanted to see me. He seems very well indeed, and has covered himself with glory by behaving as a perfect gentleman.

The "River" slides went very well at Elsie's [Mrs. Boylston Beal]; everyone was very nice and enthusiastic. Among others, your charming nephew and his equally charming wife—the George Putnams— were there. He wanted to start off at once for the Three Chasms, and Mrs. Putnam said she knew that, as I had awakened the travel fever, she would have a bad time with him until the crisis passed. He was very nice about *Fir-Flower Tablets*. We lunched with Tinta Codman. Just a few people. Mrs. Tom Motley, Nellie Sears, etc. They all spoke so very appreciatively about your work, especially Mrs. Gardie Lane. Isn't she nice?

I wonder how you progressed with Mr. Greenslet yesterday and whether you have the contract that pleases you. I am so glad that you were so much better before I left. I hated to see you so tired and

218

"stale"—because that was what you really seemed to feel. But the freshness soon comes back when only you give yourself a chance.

I loved being with you both, and feel very much refreshed myself. Thank you a hundred times. I will write soon again. Must go now as we are going off for the day. Much love.

Yours ever,
F. W. A.

St. Andrews, November 13th, 1923

Dear Amy,

I am sure I have to thank you for suggesting that the Women's City Club should ask me to a function. It is very good of you, and very noble of them, and I am much pleased. As they gave me a choice of any day in the first fortnight in December, I have chosen the first week, in order to work in the Duse matinées.[1] I am so anxious to see her again. I have also arranged so speak at Bowdoin College, Brunswick, Me., on my way back, on Sunday evening, the 9th. Next week I am gong to St. John to speak to the Canadian Club, during "Authors' Week," and this afternoon am going up to St. Stephen to read poems from *Fir-Flower Tablets*. So, you see, I am doing what I can in "my radius."

To return to the Duse matinées. Are you going to try to go? If so, will you and Ada go as my guests? If you aren't going, will Ada, anyway? And as it is so impossible at this distance to make arrangements, will Ada be an angel and engage the seats? I do hope we can go together.

We motored over to Halifax to see the fisherman's schooner races. Of course, the result was rather a fiasco, but the sight was simply magnificent. You could have written a grand poem on those two great ships tearing over forty miles of rough sea, neck and neck. They came in less than two minutes apart after sailing four hours and a half. As they rounded Chebusto Head, all sails set, running free before the wind, they seemed to brush the clouds, as Tu Fu would say. It was glorious.

Adieu, love to my "second family," which will, I hope, go to the play with me.

Yours ever,
Florence Ayscough

If Ada can engage the seats, and let me know how much they are, I will send a cheque.

[1] See Damon, *op. cit.*, p. 644.

15 November, 1923

Mrs. Francis Ayscough
St. Andrews
N.B.

Hurrah! I am so glad you are coming down. I did give your name to Mrs. Hopkins for the Women's City Club and I am delighted to know that it materialized. Lucky you are coming the first week in December because I am going to New York to lecture on the eleventh and shall be gone about ten days. Ferris thinks he would like to issue a new illustrated edition of *Fir-Flower Tablets* with some plates from your slides. Better bring all your slides down and we will talk it over. Will get seats for Duse—both performances. Never mind about paying; will give you my little bill when you come down. Lots of love from us both.

AMY

St. Andrews, November 15, 1923

Dearest Amy,

I am absolutely thrilled at the idea of the bare *possibility* of an illustrated edition of *Fir-Flower Tablets*. Do you think I had better bring the slides? They are, of course, coloured and I do not suppose Mr. Greenslet would think of using any *coloured* plates. It seems to me that a better idea could be had from the enlarged photographs which I have. However, if you say so I will bring the slides, too. I am glad that we can go to Duse together; that is "thrilling," too. I will leave here on Saturday night, the 1st, and will go to the Victoria; then in the afternoon I will bring out pictures, etc., and we can go over them. May I dine with you?

Waley's book [*The Temple*] has come. I am hard at it. Have you seen it? If you don't mind, I am going to send you what I write—perhaps I can get off the rough draft by to-morrow—for your criticism. I don't want to be too disagreeable about it, but, really, his translations this time seem to me very bad. I wish that I had studied the texts, but then in 800 words one can't do much in the way of analysis. What it comes to is this, and I am going to end up with this remark, or something like it: "Whatever may possibly be said in regard to the short poems, which contain one simple thought, and, which, if one sticks closely enough to just what the *poet* says, one can give in a sort of way; when it comes to the long, highly ornamented, exuberant compositions they *must be rendered by a poet*, and

220

what's more by a poet who has a very perfect technique, and an absolute command of English." I mean, one who has a very large vocabulary.

I don't suppose that Waley himself would lay claim to being a poet, nor to being a writer of great merit. What he contends is that one needn't be in order to translate; in this book he seems to me to prove, if it needed proof, that one does need to be. He writes some perfect gibberish, and it is rather hard on the Chinese poets to make them responsible for that sort of thing. Is there any such word in the *Oxford Dictionary* as "quogged"? I suppose there is, but it can't be said to be well known. The *Century*, which is all I have here, doesn't give it. "The Temple," p. 107, lines 23 and 24 read:

> Beneath my feet a measureless chasm dropped,
> My eyes were dizzy, hand and knee quogged—

Do you think it admissible to say "eyes were dizzy"? The *Century* does not give anything in that sense. Don't you think one must say "head was dizzy"? I suppose "haunch quaking," p. 68, line 5, is possible, but I don't think it sounds well. Anyway, my whole point is that it is not fair for a person who is not a poet to attempt these long ornate poems. Nothing would induce me to try it. I have far too great a respect for the writers. There is, of course, a lot of the book that is very good—as far as it goes, but, quite honestly, I do not think that it is anything like as good as *170 Chinese Poems*, or as the second book [*More Translations from the Chinese*]. I want so much to know what you think of it.

Best love to you both.

Yours ever,
FLORENCE AYSCOUGH

ST. ANDREWS, November 18, 1923

DEAR AMY,

I couldn't get the rough draft of the review of Waley's book[1] off yesterday (this having one post a day, and none on Sundays, is a curse) so I cut it down a lot and send you the result for your advice and criticism. If you think it "can pass"—to use a pidgin[2] English phrase, please send it to Mr. Canby with *one* of the two letters I enclose. . . . .
If the review needs a lot of changing, please post it to me 216 Germain

---

[1] *The Temple and Other Poems* (New York, 1923).
[2] See *Firecracker Land*, pp. 12 ff.

St., St. John, N.B., care Mrs. Grimmer. I go there on Wednesday, and shall not be back before Friday night or Saturday, and I suppose they want the review in New York. I hope you do not mind my bothering you with this, but don't believe you do.

The other day I had a letter from Mrs. [Gordon] Enders, who is looking after the Royal Asiatic Society Library in Shanghai, and she said, "I have written to the *Bookman* telling them to correct the mistake in the July number about the Introduction to *Fir-Flower Tablets*." I couldn't imagine what they were saying about *Fir-Flower Tablets*, at this late date, but sent for the copy to see. It is an article called "Ports of a Thousand Romances: A Reader's Guide for Round-the-world-travellers" by Fanny Butcher. This passage reads: "Then China. The best thing I have read about Chinese poetry—and poetry seems to me to mean Chinese literature to the Occident—is the introduction to *Fir-Flower Tablets*, an anthology of Chinese poetry translated by Florence Ayscough and Amy Lowell, etc., etc., etc.," . . . . I do not mind an atom, but it struck me that it might be a good advertisement for the book if you wrote about it and seized the occasion to rub in a few of its excellencies in your "own inimitable style"! A forgetful public needs prodding. My type-writer is behaving like the Old Nick. Forgive this mess. I am looking forward to seeing you.

Love to you both.

Yours,
FLORENCE AYSCOUGH

I have no U.S. stamps!

ST. ANDREWS, Tuesday, November 26, [1923]

DEAREST AMY,

It really is awfully good of you to want me to stop, and, of course, I would much rather do so than go to the Victoria; but I don't want you to feel that you must take a "poor wanderer" in. Anyway, this time I will come with pleasure. Train due 9:10, Sunday morning. I will not bring a trunk; two suit cases will do me. Will bring slides and photographs, and negatives. Thanks for sending on the review of *The Temple* to Mr. Canby.

Looking forward so much to seeing you both.

Love as ever,
FLORENCE AYSCOUGH

Have ordered a parcel or two sent to your house; please keep for me.

Dearest Amy,

I arrived safely among the gulls and sardines "in due course" yesterday and found all well. I have a lovely week to look back on and to thank you for. I delight in being with you and Ada, and really feel that it is my second home.

This should arrive just as you are starting for New York,[1] so I will not keep you with a letter but merely say that I enclose a cheque for corrections for *Fir-Flower Tablets*, etc.

I wonder could Miss Moran send me the "Analysis" of "Battle to the South of the City" [p. 5] and "A Desultory Visit to the Fêng Hsien Temple" [p. 103]. I will return them, of course, but want to take the literal Chinese from them. Stupidly forgot to do it, though I meant to.

Again a thousand, ten thousand thanks.

Yours,
Florence Ayscough

St. Andrews, December 18, 1923

Dearest Amy,

I think of you as coming home to-morrow, so send these pictures for you to choose from. I have tried to make them as varied as possible. When you have chosen them, I will send the prints to Miss [Lucille] Douglass and get her to colour them.

Your Christmas parcel came—why *did* you send me anything? I am keeping it until Christmas so as to have a "surprise"; so will write my thanks later.

I hope *Fir-Flower Tablets*, extra-illustrated, looks nice. Please tell me about it.

Thanks for Analyses, which I return.

We expect to leave here about the middle of next week, so please let me have the pictures back as soon as you conveniently can. Was the *New Republic* dinner nice? Did you speak? I wish I could hear all about it.

Have now been asked to speak in Guernsey, while we are over in England. Shall carry *Men, Women and Ghosts* and *Can Grande's Castle* about with me, and, as you say, pass on the good word.

Much love as ever,
Florence Ayscough

[1] Damon, *op. cit.*, p. 645.

January 22, 1924

DEAREST AMY,

In spite of blizzards, gales, and all sorts of bad weather on the four sides of us, we floated across to Liverpool with no discomfort whatever; met a motor there and travelled down by road.

On the 15th the lecture[1] at the [London] Royal Asiatic Society was really a great success. I was much pleased about it. They were very nice to me, indeed, and said such pretty things that I know I turned pink. Apparently when Professor [H. A.] Giles was given the gold medal of the Asiatic Society last year, he spoke of me in his address of thanks, or acceptance—whichever you like to call it. I did not know this and, of course, I was pleased. His son, Lionel Giles, spoke after I had finished, and was very nice and complimentary—so all was well.

I am to speak for the China Society on February 21 and shall do the [Yangtze] River.[2] On February 22 the Poetry and Oriental Circles of the Lyceum Club are going to have tea with me, at the Club, and I shall do Chinese Poetry[3] for them. Then I am going over to Guernsey to speak there.

The weather is very wet, indeed. We have hardly seen the sun; but of course it isn't really very cold—though the houses, as you know, are chilly.

I hope that the photographs of the Yangtze, which I left with you will come soon, so that I can send them on to Miss Douglass. A letter came to-day which had been sent in your care (I am so sorry that people worry you like that), but your secretary forgot to put on Sandhurst which is the name of the town. There are several Sandhursts in England, so the whole long address must be given. [See above.] . . . . I only hope the River pictures have not gone wandering into space.

Love to you both, my dear second family.

Yours,
FLORENCE AYSCOUGH

ON BOARD CANADIAN PACIFIC S.S. "MONTLAURIER,"
April 9, [1924]

DEAREST AMY,

I wonder if you and Ada are in the land of the living? You wretches! Not one word have I heard from either of you since that telephone

---

[1] See "Cult of the Spiritual Magistrates of City Walls and City Moats," in *A Chinese Mirror*, pp. 377–420.

[2] See "The Literary Background of the Great River," *ibid.*, pp. 101–212.

[3] See *Journal of the North China Branch of the Royal Asiatic Society*, LI (1920), 99–134.

conversation the day we left St. Andrews just after Christmas. Now, we are nearing St. John and our principal concern is whether or not we shall manage to get home before Monday, middle day. It seems doubtful. We shall miss the Saturday train which leaves St. John at 6:15 in the morning. Miller has sent us a wireless saying that all the roads are closed; so we can't motor. We are now imploring the C.P.R. people to put on a special to run us from a certain Watt Junction— can be reached on Saturday—and are waiting for their reply.

It is ridiculous that it should seem a hardship to remain away from home an extra couple of nights, but it is. I simply long to see Yo Fei, and to get out of my boxes. Please tell Ada that the parcel with her kimono missed us, so will have to follow us over. It is tiresome. I ordered several things and hoped to get them by the end of March.

We have had a successful time. We found a doctor in London who has done Frank a lot of good. He is a different person which is an immense comfort.

I wonder what you have ever done with the Yangtze photographs? They never came, and now I hear that Miss Douglass is leaving China to be in Scotland this summer, so am afraid that she cannot colour them. Perhaps they could be done from my slides here? There is a youth in St. Andrews who does a certain amount of painting; perhaps he could study the slides and do them. Does Mr. Greenslet still want to do the illustrated edition of *Fir-Flower Tablets*?

I was deeply interested to see by the *Transcript* that you had admitted the authorship of *A Critical Fable*.[1] Did you have a lot of fun over it?

The various things I did in England went well. The Royal Asiatic [Society] people were very nice to me, indeed, and have asked me to speak again next winter. We shall probably be in England again as Frank does not want to go to China, and we *must* leave St. Andrews. He enjoys London. I went down to see old Professor Giles, who was very charming, indeed—quite different to what I expected. For one thing, he is not nearly so old as I had thought and is very alert.

How is Keats? Do you see any end in view? And how are you? tired or fairly rested? Now, Amy dear, *please* do send me a line telling me some of your news. I am lonely for it, and my second family seems very far away. How is Lorna?

You see I know nothing of you at all, at all. Is there any idea of your going to England this summer?

Much love to you both.

Yours ever,
FLORENCE AYSCOUGH

[1] Damon, *op. cit.*, chaps. xxii and xxiii.

Is Duse coming to stop with you? Have you seen her since the week in Boston?[1]

ST. ANDREWS, April 19, 1924

DEAREST AMY,

I am so distressed about your eyes; I can't get it out of my mind. You must feel *frantic*. Knowing your grim determination, I am sure you will put Keats through; but it must be a sore trial to be so hampered.

In regard to Professor Giles' remarks—they were made in his address when he accepted the Gold Medal of the Royal Asiatic Society which was given to him 1922 or 1923.[2] It is most annoying, but my copy of the R.A.S. *Journal* which contained the notice is missing from my set; so I am not positive about the date. I believe it must have gone astray somewhere as I did not know he had ever referred to me. It was not so very much, but in the address he spoke of the younger men who are carrying on work in Sinology such as Pelliot, his son Dr. Giles, [Percival] Yetts, etc., etc., and then spoke of me, as quoted by Dr. Yetts in the cutting I enclose. Yetts himself said a good many nice things which are not reported and which I was too overcome to take in.

The last paragraph is not correctly reported. Dr. [Lionel] Giles (this is the son; he is perfectly charming, and I admire his work very much) never said that the cult [of the Spiritual Magistrates] was essentially Buddhist—he simply referred to the fact, of which I had already spoken, that Buddhist influences had affected it. There was a certain amount of discussion about the origin; it is difficult to prove things that happened four thousand years ago, but a good many Chinese authorities believe that the Ch'eng Huang did have its origin in the cult instituted by King Yao.

Old Professor Giles has the chair of Chinese at Cambridge. I went down to see him there, and he was most charming. He was given a Doctor's degree by Oxford on March 6. I knew that it was to be, as Lionel Giles (Dr., as he is called) had told me so, and said to the old man that I was much pleased he was to have the honour. He answered, "Yes, yes—but I am too old. It does not matter now. I am glad only because of the recognition of the study of Chinese. I wish you were to have it, not me." I told him that I got fearfully discouraged and felt as if I didn't know a thing. He replied, "Why, look at what you have done already."

---

[1] *Ibid.*, pp. 659–60.

[2] See the *Journal of the Royal Asiatic Society of Great Britain and Ireland*, Part IV, October 15, 1922: "Presentation of the Triennial Gold Medal," pp. 642–49.

He can't bear *vers libre* and thinks it is awful not to use verse in translating; so I was rather thankful that he refused to review *Fir-Flower Tablets* for the *Journal* [of the] R.A.S. I found that it had not been done and told Miss [Ella] Sykes, the Secretary, that I wished it might be, and she asked Prof. Giles. As he wouldn't, Lionel Giles has, but I don't think it will be at all satisfactory as he is not in the *least* a poet, and he too dislikes *vers libre;* neither has he studied Chinese poetry. Yetts is the same; and Hopkins,[1] the other sinologue whom they turn to, objects to poetry as such. He told me once, a year or two ago, that he could not see why people ever wrote poetry. "It is the poorest way of saying things" was his feeling.

Cranmer-Byng was very nice to me, indeed, and asked if he might write a review of the book for the *Poetry Review*. He and I got on very well. . . . . I could and did express what I feel very strongly, that by his work with the Wisdom of the East series he has done a great deal to rouse interest in all sorts of Far Eastern questions. On which basis we progressed famously. He really has done a lot, and continues to do it, as he lectures and talks continually. I am a member of the Lyceum Club, and the first time I went there I saw that he was to speak on Chinese poetry that afternoon; so I remained and attended. . . . . After that I met him; then I heard from him from the country several times, and had tea with him and his wife when they came up.

Yetts I saw often. The Taoist book which he and Dr. Lionel Giles are doing has been held up because Yetts has had bad eyes —you can sympathize with him. Sirèn, the art critic and archaeologist, was in London bringing out two books. One, with most lovely photographs, *The Walls and Gates of Peking*, and one on Buddhist iconography. He wants me to do a book on Ch'ang An with him. I can't help being nervous on his account about the iconography book; it is to cost 12 guineas, which seems an awful price. Benn Brothers are bringing it out, but I do not know the terms.

Now, I want to ask a piece of advice. It has occurred to me that various pamphlets I have written might, with their illustrations, make an interesting book.[2] The ones I mean are: The account of the building of the Chinese house. A great deal of folklore, customs, etc., comes into this. It is not written but I have a lot of material. The Cult of the Spiritual Magistrate in as popular a form as possible; The Symbolism of Peking; The Chinese Idea of a Garden; and the T'ai Shan. The pictures for them all are very good indeed. Now, what do you think is

[1] See above, pp. 140–41 (F. A.'s letter to Hopkins).

[2] See *A Chinese Mirror*, etc.

the best way to go about it? You must remember that my only experience of publishers is to sit on a sofa and hear you dictate terms. Do you think I had best write what is to be written, re-write the rest (as that will have to be done, too), and then speak to Mr. Greenslet? Or do you think I could write to him now and ask how he feels about it? Of course, I would rather do other things than re-work the old, if he won't listen to the project at all. Would you mind telling me what method you consider best?

To-day we are wrapped in a blizzard. Yesterday was summer-like and we crossed to our Sacred Island. It was *exquisite*.

Much, much love.

Yours,
FLORENCE AYSCOUGH

ST. ANDREWS, May 18, 1924

DEAREST AMY,

The Duse sonnets[1] are perfectly lovely. How I envy you being able to express yourself like that. You must be so thankful you wrote them. The world has lost its greatest artist. I am so very, very glad to have seen her again. I know you must have felt her death dreadfully. She seemed a part of your life.

When you have a moment would you read the enclosed and see if you think that it is best to write Mr. Greenslet quite simply like that. If you do, would you please forward the letter to him.—If you can suggest a better way I should be grateful if you would.

Although I feel full of qualms at thinking of attempting anything by myself, I do think it would be a good thing for our Tu Fu book if these sketches came out. The more one can make people know about China, the better. I shall be very grateful for advice.

How are your eyes? Can you use them enough to get on with now? Ever with lots of love,

Yours,
FLORENCE AYSCOUGH

ST. ANDREWS, June 8, 1924

DEAREST AMY,

Thanks so much for sending on my letter to Mr. Greenslet. We are corresponding, and I hope that we shall arrange something.

I enclose a reprint for the review of *Fir-Flower Tablets* which has just

[1] See Amy Lowell, *What's O'clock* (Boston and New York, 1925), pp. 235–40; also Damon, *op. cit.*, references to "Duse, Eleanora."

come out in the [London] *Royal Asiatic Journal*.[1] Lionel Giles is the son of the old Professor. He is really a dear, but I do disagree with him so *utterly* about the idiom. Perhaps it is because I have lived among the people and know how they feel and talk, whereas he has not been in China since he was a youth. Funnily enough, that line which he objects to is one of the *most* characteristic. Once, when I was reading in Peking, I read the poem that ends with that line and an elderly missionary lady leant forward with a sigh and said, "Oh how natural that is—I have had it said to me a hundred times." As for the "green" they all pitch into, it is not *ch'ing* which we translate as "green," but another word, *ts'ang*. I am going to write to Lionel Giles and shall tell him.

Did I tell you that I am to speak for the R.A.S. again? We shall be going to England at the end of November, and I am to speak on February 15. I wanted to go to China, but Frank doesn't want to—so we shall go to England.

I am coming down to speak for the North Shore "Garden Club" on July 9, and shall be with Elsie Beal.

Much love, as always.

Yours,
FLORENCE AYSCOUGH

Please tell Ada that her kimono has come. Lois [(Grimmer Wheelock) Dalgliesh] brought it with her, and has it in St. John; so, when I come down, I will bring it, and Ada will be back by then.

F. W. A.

[TELEGRAM]

ST. ANDREWS, N.B., June 28, 1924

MISS AMY LOWELL,
70 HEATH ST., BROOKLINE

Am making plans regarding going Manchester, July eight. If your [Keats] book has gone to press[2] and you are free, will leave here Saturday fifth and stay Boston. If you are still very busy will leave here Monday seventh and go direct Manchester. Please telegraph reply; must make reservations.

FLORENCE AYSCOUGH

ST. ANDREWS, NEW BRUNSWICK, July 16, [1924]

DEAREST AMY,

Forgive me for inflicting you with long hand. The type-writer went to Montreal to be cleaned and has not returned. I had a splendid jour-

---

[1] See Second Quarter, April 15, 1924, pp. 332–33.   [2] Damon, *op. cit.*, p. 663.

ney down and found "all well." . . . . Yo Fei has been behaving like the dickens during my absence. He wouldn't stay at home—but insisted on hunting for me all over St. Andrews.

George and Molly Derby motored up—or would you call it *down?*—from Bar Harbour, arriving last night. They are going on to Quebec to-morrow. I must now take them to see the "sights" of St. Andrews.

Love to you both. I can scarcely wait to see Keats in print.

Yours, dear,

FLORENCE AYSCOUGH

THE GORING HOTEL, [LONDON], March 7, [1925]

DEAREST AMY,

Keats came, and was hailed with joy, a day or two ago. You must be overwhelmed with congratulations, but I must add to the number. It is an immense work, and, as you wish, says the last word on Keats. My dear friend Lady de Sausmarez, who is very well read, writes, "There is something in Miss Lowell's style; it arrests attention and arouses interest at once."

People generally are very much interested in your coming over, and I hope that you will enjoy yourself immensely. The Lyceum Club members are "thrilled" at the prospect of hearing you, and the President of the Poetry circle of the Forum is, I know, writing to see if you have a moment. Mrs. Mends Gibson, who did write a while ago, was disturbed at not hearing from you, but I hope she has by now. She seemed to think that it took about a day and a half for a letter to reach U.S.A. I hope that you can speak for the Kensington society, or whatever they call it. The audiences, as I find them, are very responsive and easy to speak to, and people are enthusiastic, though, I suppose one may say, not as demonstrative as American audiences.[1]

My various appearances have gone very well. The Royal Asiatic was really extraordinarily nice this year, and they had the biggest audience they had had for æons. So I was much pleased. The China Society was equally nice, and Lionel Giles (who is as quiet as a mouse, generally speaking) was quite effusive and said, "I wish I could keep you here all through the year. You draw so." He is the secretary.

What do you suppose my next performance is? I go to Paris to lecture to Les Amis de l'Orient at the Musée Guimet *in French*. It is a truly terrifying prospect for one as retiring as myself, but I hope that it will go through well. I have had a most delightful Frenchman, a Professor Thiéry, to do the translation with me, and this morning we

[1] When she made this reference, Mrs. Ayscough had forgotten for the nonce the occasion on which Miss Lowell had paused during one of her readings to remark to her audience, "If you like my poems, clap; if you dislike my poems, hiss—but, *for God's sake, do something!*"

had a "répétition générale" which was satisfactory—at least he felt that it was. Monsieur Thiéry is a lecturer here and is simply thrilled with *Fir-Flower Tablets*. Literature is his passion, so I think that I will give him a letter to you. I know it would give him great pleasure, and I think that you would like him and find him interesting. Possibly he could be of some use in *some* way. He has made a jolly good translation of the lecture on "Gardens,"[1] though he didn't find it at all easy. It has taken us hours and hours.

Are you going to stay at the Berkeley? Won't you send a line in answer to this at once, and then I shall know. Address here. Our plans are as follows:

I go to Paris next Tuesday, the 10th; stay until 16th. Frank does not come with me. I speak at the Forum Club on 17th; the Lyceum on 18th; and before the Quest Society on the 19th. We go to Guernsey on the 21st; return here the 1st April; stay until the 9th, when we sail from Liverpool to St. John on the "Montroyal." I speak in Guernsey on the 26th.

It is very trying to just miss you; but there it is. Which day do you sail? When we left you had not decided.

Frank has bought the sweetest Sealyham you ever saw to be a playmate for Yo Fei. He is a duck.

We have booked to go to China next autumn, but Frank says that unless the fighting is over he will not go. We shall just have to see.

Needless to say, I have not had time to more than dip into Keats, but, as you know, I think it is beautiful—and so very, very vivid. You are a wonder.

The enclosed is for Ada apropos of a conversation we had when I was with you in December.

Much, much love to you both.

Yours ever,
Florence Ayscough

If you don't bring a secretary and need typing done, I have found a very good place called the Temporary and Permanent Employment Bureau, 42 Lower Belgrave St. The name is a residue from the war—the place is good, and Miss Drevor, who is in charge, *very* good indeed.

Sausmarez Manor, St. Martins, Guernsey, March 25, [1925]

Dearest Amy,

I am *so* delighted to have the invitation for April 4th,[2] and realize that proper appreciation is coming to you. It is thrilling and I would

---

[1] See "The Chinese Idea of a Garden," *A Chinese Mirror*, pp. 213–56.

[2] Damon, *op. cit.*, pp. 694–96.

give anything to be able to take part. It is a wonderful tribute and one so deserved. Apart from your own outstanding work, there is the inestimable assistance and inspiration that you have given to every-thing worthwhile in the way of Art in America. The names of those who are organizing the dinner show that they realize all this *very fully*, and wish to express themselves. It is really remarkable to have such a wide radius. How Ada will weep for joy and emotion!! Now, limitations of time and space prevent my being there—and you and Ada will both be much too busy to write about it—but *please* ask Miss Moran to cut out some of the notices about the dinner and let me have them in St. Andrews. I would like to know who speaks, and know, too, what they say.

I am glad, so very glad. I have no type-writer with me but have tried to write plainly. Much love to you both.

Yours ever,
FLORENCE AYSCOUGH

[CABLEGRAM]

LONDON, 4 April 1925

MISS LOWELL
70 HEATH ST., BROOKLINE, MASS., U.S.A.

Regret unplumbed salt-estranging-sea between us and your dinner. Congratulations and best wishes.

AYSCOUGH

BROOKLINE, MASS., 11 April, 1925

DEAR MRS. AYSCOUGH:

You will be sorry to hear that Miss Lowell is quite seriously ill and has had to give up all idea of the English trip. The hernia has become pinched and everything is kicking up in consequence. She is so very tired, anyway, and has lost so much weight that the doctor thinks it would be utter madness for her to try to go. He is afraid that if she got on the ship and were seasick the hernia might become strangulated, and of course there are no adequate surgeons on a ship.

The dinner was marvellous!!![1] There were about four hundred peo-ple present. It was held in the Somerset ballroom. When I try to think of the decorations all my adjectives seem to turn to superlatives. The doorway was banked with all sorts of spring flowers culled from all the greenhouses in the neighbourhood. Mrs. Bayard Thayer had charge of the decorations and a Mr. [Albert C.] Burrage, whose first name I do not know, sent the most beautiful orchids it has ever been my lot to see. The silver bowl was filled with white orchids and sat on the speak-

[1] See Damon, *op. cit.*, pp. 694–96.

ers' table. And Elinor Wylie, knowing nothing of the presentation of the bowl, and seeing it sitting there in front of her, said in her speech that Miss Lowell reminded her of that silver bowl filled with white orchids—cunning, wasn't it? The speakers' table was on a dais at one end of the room, with Miss Cutting pulling the strings. Mr. Lowes spoke first, and nothing finer in the way of a tribute to Miss Lowell, the *Keats*, and her poetry could possibly have been asked for. He bowled us all over. He and Mrs. Conkling were the high lights of the evening for me, though some of the others were very good. I haven't a programme here so I shall probably get the order mixed a little.

I think, however, that Mrs. Conkling was next with her appreciation of the poetry. She showed a knowledge, understanding, and love of it that really surprised me. I didn't think that anybody in the world who hadn't worked over it could remember different lines which spring out at you from so many of Miss Lowell's poems. But she had nice bits from everywhere and it made up a splendid whole.

Mr. [Edward Burlingame] Hill, according to my lights, wasn't so good. He tried to be very nice, but he is so hesitant in his delivery that it didn't seem to get across at all. He spoke of the rhythms in her poetry.

Mr. [H. S.] Canby and Glenn Frank were both fine, and Mr. Frank had a very ingenious idea about the qualities of Miss Lowell's mind that he had worked out intertwining the poetry with politics, and saying what a clever politician she would make and that he would vote for her for president.

Elinor Wylie is awfully pretty and said lovely things about all of her poetry being inspired by Miss Lowell, but again was not used to the platform I think. . . . .

John Farrar said her life of Keats was so universal that it covered the lives of all poets, which I think was exceptionally nice. Hervey Allen read his tribute from a paper in the most awful Pittsburghian voice, but he said the finest imaginable things. Abbie Brown did very well with a personal note, bringing her home to Boston, and Mr. [A. Edward] Newton was very amusing on the book-collecting end. Mr. [Roger L.] Scaife closed the speeches, and was perfectly splendid. He, much to my surprise, was one of the very best, and gave her a frightful boost. He ended the speeches on a note of sort of affectionate humour, if you see what I mean, that carried over into Miss Lowell's reading "Lilacs" and "A Tulip Garden." Then the bowl was presented, and we all flocked round and shook hands and were generally proud of her.

233

It was a huge success. Everybody has exclaimed over how well it was done, and with what snap the whole event went off. Nobody talked long enough to be boring; everything swept along. There were no reporters allowed, so I haven't anything to send you, but I've done my best to remember things as they were.

I hope you have had a pleasant Winter in England and that you find the small dog well. With all good wishes.

Very sincerely yours,

ANNE M. ALEXANDER

[TELEGRAM]

ST. ANDREWS, N.B., 1000A April 19, 1925

MRS. RUSSELL

70 HEATH ST., BROOKLINE, MASS.

Just arrived; rough passage; how is Amy? Love to second family.

FLORENCE AYSCOUGH

[ST. ANDREWS, N.B.][1]

DEAREST AMY,

It is hardly necessary to waste space in telling you how dreadfully distressed I am at your being so seedy, but I *must* tell you, dear, how badly I feel and how I wish that there were something that I could do, —besides thinking of you all the time. I wish that you might come down here later, and sail and loaf. But, my dear, there are no good doctors nearer than Boston. I expect that at this moment you don't want to move hand or foot. It was splendid to hear from Miss Moran about the dinner. If only I could have been there. How proud you must be.

The book is called *A Chinese Mirror*. It is, as you know, dedicated to you, and I do hope that you will like it. In any case, it will be fairly fresh to you, and you have not seen the pictures. I hated going against your advice, but, taking everything into consideration, it seemed inevitable that it should be produced in England; and, of course, with me it is not quite the same as if I were entirely American. I mean, I do not see how a stigma can attach to *my* publishing, or, rather, printing, in England. Much love, dear.

FLORENCE

[This note is pasted on the backs of two post cards: one the picture of] " 'Cinnabar Walls''—on our island. They are a lovely rose-red—; [the other] A picture of The [yacht] "Wu Yuen" Five-coloured Cloud.

[1] Undated, typewritten letter, pasted in the back of "The Amy Lowell Memorial Meeting" volume.

SELECTIONS FROM THE CORRESPONDENCE OF
FLORENCE AYSCOUGH AND ADA RUSSELL

St. Andrews, April 22, [1925][1]

Dearest Ada,

A thousand thanks for your letter of the 19th which, as you may imagine, I was *thankful* to have. The first hint that I had of there being anything wrong was when my wireless to the "Berengaria" was returned to me with the laconic legend "addressee not on board." We were having very rough weather, with a confused sea, and although the "Berengaria" is so big that she probably would not feel it as we did—she *is* a ship!! How utterly *thankful* you must be that you didn't embark. What a mercy that Amy was taken ill—if she had got to be ill—before starting.

In a way, I can't help being relieved that she is not taking the English trip. At the best she isn't really equal to the effort—I mean physically equal. It—the effort —would all have had to be drawn from the nervous system—and her debit balance there is heavy. Taking her as she was in December, when I last saw her, she was not in a state to adjust herself to all sorts of different conditions physical and mental. There is "no use talking," the mental attitude in England is *very, very* different from that in America, and she is opposed to it anyway—so, apart from the physical, there would have been a violent mental adjustment.

Conditions, too, are utterly different from what they were before the War. I am *sure* that you would have noticed it, and I am *not at all sure* that either of you would have enjoyed it. Therefore, in a way, I am relieved that the journey did not come off. What you say as to

[1] Holograph letter.

235

Amy's condition troubles me dreadfully. *What* is the cause of her losing weight like that—why, 178 pounds is dreadful. I suppose every organ and nerve is tired—and must just quietly rest in order to be able to function properly. It will be lovely for you to have Lorna and "the regiment" for the summer, and I hope that in a couple of months Amy will have gained sufficient strength to enable the plan to be carried out.

I wish that I could suggest Amy's coming down to this lovely air later on, but you see there is no adequate medical attendance within reach *at all*. Nothing nearer than Boston; I mean really first class doctors. If you love me send me a post-card, say, once a week, as I am awfully anxious to know how she progresses; but I don't want to tax you as your hands must be absolutely *full*. What a piece of work the mere cancelling of arrangements must have been. I am glad anyway that she had the joy of the dinner. That must have meant a great deal.

Much love, dear, and all sympathy. Am writing Amy.

Yours

FLORENCE AYSCOUGH

[TELEGRAM]

St. ANDREWS, N.B., 1003A May 14, 1925

MRS. RUSSELL,
70 HEATH ST., BROOKLINE.

Am overcome. Is funeral for family or shall I come up? If it is tomorrow must leave early this afternoon. Dear love, deepest sympathy.

FLORENCE AYSCOUGH

[St. ANDREWS], May 15, 1925

ADA DEAR—

I hardly know how to write—and yet I feel that I must, that I must talk to you—only, what to say? The loss to me is so absolutely *basic*—only you know *how* basic—that I feel as though I had no foundation left, in a mental sense. In one way there was no one to whom Amy meant as much as she did to me. I am, of course, keeping you, in your great affection, and in the wonderful, unique, relationship which you had with her, quite out of the question and in another category. Without her inspiration, and her driving force, and without her faith, I should never have done anything. Only last summer she said, "You must learn to stand alone. You must not depend on me." And I must go on trying to do it; but I feel as though I were groping for her hand.

236

In writing about her loss from the personal point of view, I feel as though I were realizing what it means from the general point of view.

She was unique—no one can begin to take her place or approach the spot she stood. Her own hill-top is hers, and hers only. John Sedgwick expresses it very well when he says she was "a personage." It is not that she was the greatest writer the world has seen, but that, in her, infinitely varied characteristics were combined in a way that made her utterly different from everybody else.

Her keenness of vision, her intuition, her sensitiveness, her swift appreciation, and *above all* her *absolute* sincerity made her a thing apart. These things all the world can know, more or less accurately, according to their own capacity. But what they cannot know of—and what I cannot realize as you and Elizabeth can—is her *heroism*—because she *was* heroic in the way she over-rode physical discomfort and disability. She is the most wonderful example of a mind "triumphant." Her interest and enthusiasm—her love of her art—were so intense, that she could ignore those things to which lesser mentalities would have weakly succumbed.

Ada, she could not have endured the realization of decay of her faculties. Thank God she has been spared all hint of that—not that there should have been any such suggestion, for many years—but latterly she has said so often that she felt weaker—that she had not the same power of recuperation. I could go on writing about her for pages and pages, but I know that you are torn—body and soul—and very, very sad. But, Ada, I cannot stop without saying just simply that I do think I appreciate, in small part at any rate, what you have been to Amy. Quite seriously, I do not think that she could have gone on living without you—you were her prop. Without you, she could never have blossomed as she did—and had you gone away before her she would not have survived.

Do you know, it seems to me as though she had been some beautiful begonia, or other strong plant, that is *too* luxuriant for its stem. The books, and such a vital legacy as they are to the world, are as much yours as hers. No one knew this better than she did—and not only the books but everything that she did was through your aid. Without you her achievement could not have been what it is, and also, I must say, what it has been. It is so hard, so impossible, at this distance to realize that—her vitality is stilled—that she has gone from among us.

You know that I dedicated my book [*A Chinese Mirror*] to her, and the dedication reads: "To Amy Lowell—whose writing-brush is full of life's movement"[1]—and, now—I *must* stop. But one thing more: I have thought of it so much since I heard of Amy's death yesterday morning (of course it was not in Tuesday's *Transcript*—I had a telegram from Anna Carrere yesterday); I was talking while in England with a certain Miss [Ella] Sykes, who is very convinced about the life in the hereafter; and her firm belief is that all the sympathetic souls will come quickly together. It is a beautiful idea at any rate, and I love to think of Amy's soul with Keats' and [those of] all the great poets of every nation—because there will be no racial bars there.

I am coming down to go to New York and Long Island. I shall be in New York, afternoon of May 27 to morning of May 29; in Long Island until Monday, June 1. Where will you be? I want to see you so *very, very* much. I wonder if you could send me a telegram giving me some idea of your plans. The mail from here is so slow.

Much much love,

Yours,
Florence Ayscough

["Sevenels," Brookline], May 17, 1925[2]

My dearest Florence—

I know what a blow it must have been to you—but had you seen her suffering this last month, it would have taken an edge off your despair at her going. Thank God it was quick and painless. After the attack on April 10th the nausea never ceased. So little could she eat and retain that she was down to 159 lbs. We had a consultation last

---

[1] In its complete form the dedication reads:

To

AMY LOWELL

<small>WHOSE WRITING-BRUSH IS FULL OF LIFE'S MOVEMENT</small>

from

<small>FLORENCE AYSCOUGH</small>

Since I wrote the Dedication to this book the sun has risen from out of a sea mist, has climbed to its zenith, and has sunk in the long grass at the edge of the horizon twenty-three times; and yesterday at the hour when her room, high under the eaves, is filled with its slant shining, Amy Lowell laid down her writing-brush for ever.

Scissors cannot cut this thing;
Unravelled, it joins again and clings.
It is the sorrow of separation,
And none other tastes to the heart like this.
[by a Chinese poet *circa* A.D. 950]

F.A.

May, 1925.

[2] Holograph letter.

Sunday—Dr. Porter, Dr. Hugh Williams, Dr. Eastman, and Dr. Lee. They all decided that another operation was necessary in order to save her life. She said she didn't believe it could be successful; to leave her *alone*, and let her die in peace—but it *wasn't peace*, Florence. It was agony to watch her distress when those spells of nausea came—every time increasing the blood pressure and pushing the hernia. The operation was to be on *Wednesday*. From Sunday all through Monday, her depression and hopelessness increased. On Tuesday she was sitting at her table in her room after the travesty of a breakfast—a teaspoon of rice. She telephoned Bessie Putnam—and had such a nice talk. I was sitting close beside her. Then she called Elizabeth and the nurse to put on that day bandage. She was sitting before the mirror trying to pin the band across to one side when she said her hand was *numb*— she couldn't feel the pin. She asked the nurse to pin it. Bunnie was on one side—nurse on the other. I was standing back of the chair—when she said again she was numb. This was her left side; then the right side of her face changed. I saw it in the glass—so did *she*, Florence—and she said, "Pete—a stroke." I said, "*No*, it's just because you are weak and tired." We pushed the chair to the couch, got her on it with pillows under her head, and ice bags. I got the doctor on telephone as soon as we got her on couch. He came out at once—said we had done everything that should be done; less movement the better. The only thing she said after that was when we got her to the sofa she said with difficulty—"Get Eastman." Then she was unconscious from that on, and the breath just grew fainter and fainter until she died at 5:30 P.M.

The doctors tell me I should go on my knees that the going was swift and sudden. She might have lasted for years—like a log, without mind or speech—and she had used her poor body until the last ounce of strength had gone. The only thing that comforts me is that I have so much work to do. I do not know how long I shall be here, but shall have to be more or less here for the sake of the books.

Thank you for your wire and your offer of coming. There was nothing to come for except your love of her—which I know was strong enough to carry you anywhere. She wanted no services, you know, and we carried out her wishes absolutely in every particular. I shall hope to see you, dear, in the near future.

Lorna and the "regiment" will come over here now. They were going West. Mrs. Belmont came at once from New York—The family have been most tender and sympathetic.

Dear Florence, you will have to do your work alone now. I begin the proofs of *What's O'Clock* tomorrow and there are two more books to follow.—I am heart-broken—but would not call her back to suffer. She went at the *peak*—and had that wonderful tribute given her. My dear, my dear!

With love,
ADA

ST. ANDREWS, NEW BRUNSWICK, May 24, [1925][1]

DEAREST ADA—

I said yesterday that I felt as though I wanted to talk to you every day! What a wonderful power of sympathy you have! I suppose that is what made you able to interpret character parts so wonderfully.[2] I haven't anything special to say—and for goodness' sake don't trouble to answer—but I just want to write. You spoke about my work. Frank said he felt badly for me about the Tu Fu book, but I don't honestly think I thought about it at all! I was sick, Ada, and felt too utterly wretched to care about anything. I am one of those unfortunate people who can't cry—so when I am wounded crawl away and hide like a hurt animal. I was in bed for a day or two with fever but am better now, and have been thinking of lots of work. Amy thought that work was the most important thing in life. I know she was right. One thing I have been thinking over is this. You know she was always keen to have an illustrated edition of *Fir-Flower Tablets* come out, and H[oughton] M[ifflin] always stuck out because of the cost of plates. Now I thought that if I could get Miss Douglass to do something in colour (I have written her about it) I would offer to pay for the plates and perhaps we could have an edition as a Memorial to Amy.

I enclose a copy of the postscript I have sent [to London to Jonathan] Cape to add to the Biographical Index which appears in *A Chinese Mirror*.

All this winter it has been borne in upon me more and more that her intuition had provided the key to translation from the Chinese—and I want to show some work that I have done in connection with the Historical Texts to Professor Lowes. I have written asking him when I can see him. I should never have *applied* the use of "split ups" if Amy had not suggested it. I wonder if an article on the Oriental side of her work, for the *Atlantic* would be a good plan?

There is one side of her that is mine, and mine only, and I treasure it—oh infinitely. The mid-night hours of 1921 will always remain among the most precious of my life. One thing is I *did* appreciate it at

---

[1] Holograph letter.

[2] S. Foster Damon, *Amy Lowell: A Chronicle with Extracts from Her Correspondence* (Boston and New York, 1935), pp. 183-84.

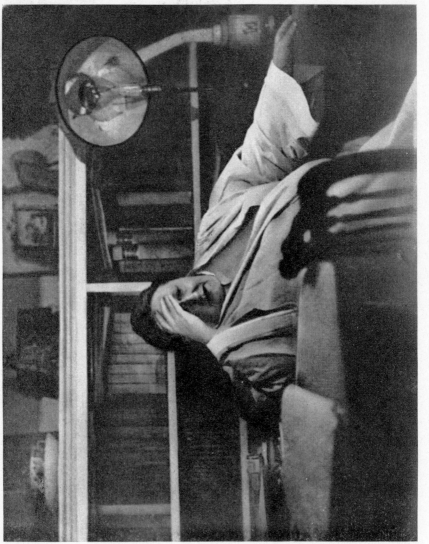

AMY LOWELL IN "HER ROOM, HIGH UNDER THE EAVES," AT "SEVENELS," WHERE
SHE "LAID DOWN HER WRITING-BRUSH FOREVER"

the time—even when we disagreed. I prized the disagreement—if you know what I mean. No one else has collaborated with her; so *that* facet of the jewel belongs to me in its particularity.

How I wish that I had succeeded in getting a good picture of her in her corner. There are certain things about the poor one I did get which are an immense comfort to me now. For one thing her *hand*. Nothing was more individual than Amy's hand, and that is very good, and the whole thing is so natural. If one looks at it from far enough away to miss the *pained* look, it is *very* suggestive. I can't explain to you the curious prophetic feeling that I had when I pressed the lever that took the picture.

The Tu Fu book will have to be done entirely differently. I am glad that at least she and I went through the poems, even at a gallop together.

I pass through Boston from North Station to South Station on Tuesday evening, and unless my train is late will ring you up at about 10 o'clock.

Much love—

Yours,
F. A.

While Amy was alive, I couldn't look at the picture I took—as it still seemed to carry a sort of prophecy—but now it is different—it seems to embody a reality. It is the Keats manuscript beside her, you remember.

4 CADOGAN MANSIONS, SLOANE SQUARE, December 26, [1925]

DEAREST ADA,

I cannot tell you how touched I was by your cable and by the lovely Christmas card. "My home's your inn, and warm and bright Your welcome waits inside." Oh Ada, dear, how you have made me feel that, and how precious the feeling is. It is the sweetest card I have ever seen. I had been thinking, sadly, that there would be no cable from Brookline on Christmas Day this year; so you can imagine how deeply I felt having it come.

We had rather a ridiculous time when we first arrived. I can laugh over it now, but at the time it was trying. We reached London late on a Thursday night to find the flat all "warm and bright" and two very nice maids to greet us. The weather was *very* cold, unusually so. I knew that there was no central heating to the flat, but it never crossed my mind that the building could lack facilities for having electric or gas heating and I was fully prepared to install stoves of one kind or the other, and started out at crack of dawn to see the electric people. That proved out of the question. Light was installed, of course, but electric heating would mean an awful piece of work, so off I went to the Gas Company.

By this time a perfectly black London fog had gathered and I had various adventures reaching "Horse-ferry Rd." where the Gas Company lives; and then I had a series of interviews with bland young men who, one after the other, assured me that it would be days— possibly weeks—before the inspector could come to even *look* at the place. They each began their reply by the question, "Is the flat carcased?" Isn't it a heavenly term? I did not know, of course, and my heart sank lower and lower as the prospect of gas this side of midsummer seemed to grow dimmer and dimmer. However, the last young man I encountered said, "Ring up Inspector Munnings between 4:50 and 5 o'clock this afternoon and see what he can do."

At the precise hour I rang and "cooed" at Inspector Munnings to such good purpose that the dear old thing—as he proved to be—came to see us on his way home after eight that night. He inspected the state of affairs and decided that the flat was *not* carcased. So the carcase had to be ordered.

By the next morning, Saturday, I realized that nothing short of a vacuum cleaning by experts would make the place clean or fit to live in; so I hied me to Harrods to order the big cleaner. When I returned I found Frank in a stew as there had been a bad fall of soot—so that meant sweeps. They came early Monday morning. Tell Sonny Boy, who of course has never seen a "sweep," that they were just like story-book sweeps, as black as negroes and that they came in a pony cart with all their brushes and sacks, just as sweeps should do—and, Ada dear, it is quite impossible to describe to you what it was like! They took away sacks! and sacks!! and sacks of soot!!! The piles that came down the chimneys, there were six in all, were three-quarter way up the chimney breasts, and, of course, a fine black veil of soot enriched walls, curtains, pictures, furniture and clothes.

I fled to the telephone and managed to get the big vacuum that day, but imagine my feelings when the man said cheerfully, "Oh, yes, we did a place the other day where the chimneys had just been swept, and as soon as we finished the soot all came down again. Oh, yes! it often happens, that lady had just had her carpet shampooed, too; oh yes, it was an awful mess, yes, Miss, it was. The carpet had to be shampooed again, yes it did. Yes, Miss, it often happens." At that point I fled, but, thank Heavens, it did *not* happen to us.

242

The next day, however, the gas-men came to "carcase," and when they lifted the planks they found that the floor was laid on a solid bank of concrete, and that, to insert the carcase, little channels had to be chipped—for miles. Well, they chipped and chipped; Frank swore and swore; the weather was colder and colder, and we inhaled more and more of the fine concrete dust which turned everything white where the soot had turned it black. The gas-men perspired and perspired in spite of the cold, and said, grimly, between their teeth, "It ain't often we gets such a job as this 'ere."

Finally, it was done; then the floor polishers came—no, "polisher" is not the right word as, of course, the floors are soft wood stained black—not hardwood polished—and stained all the borders. And then the furniture polishers came and did up the furniture. And then Emma —who came over with us—washed everything she could lay her hands on in gasoline. And *then* we went out and bought some flowers and sat down in a very pretty, comfortable place.

Meanwhile, I had taken a wretched cold which laid me by the heels, and by the time all that had happened and I had recovered, the Christmas rush had begun, and it was impossible to do much or see many people, or make many arrangements.

The *Chinese Mirror* has had a very good press, and is selling as well as such a book can. I mean, it appeals to a limited public, and cannot be expected to have a rush. People are very nice about it. There is talk of a French translation, which will, I hope, come off. I do think that my being here will be good for it.

What's O'Clock is in the Spring list and will appear about March. I am speaking about Amy and showing the slides [of "Sevenels"] at the Lyceum Club on January 20, and shall see what I can do with Mr. Doubleday this coming week. I sent, or rather gave, Elsie Sergeant's[1] article to Cape, and they will reproduce some of it in *Now and Then*. . . . .

I enclose a few memories I have of Amy and copies of the two letters which I have in manuscript and which I shall leave to the "Memorial Room"—unless, for any reason, you would rather I gave them now. . . . .

Has anything materialized about the Biography? And what has been settled about "Sevenels"?[2]

Tell Sonny Boy that the "muffin-man" has just been ringing his bell, in the street below. Isn't that like a story-book? London is a

[1] Damon, *op. cit.*, p. 769.

[2] *Ibid.*, p. 703.

good deal like a story-book in many ways, and, of course, the Portland stone gives it an unreal air in any case.

It is time to wash my hands and prepare tea, so, adieu for the present. I will write again soon and tell you what news I have. As the *Mirror* came out on December 10 in U.S.A., you must have your copy. I hope you like it.

Love to Lorna, the regiment, and yourself—dear, and, again, many thanks.

Yours ever,
FLORENCE AYSCOUGH

Did I give you enclosed photograph? If so, just pass this on to Sonny Boy. If not—Keep it—that is, if you care to—and I will send him another.

CANADIAN PACIFIC, S.S. "MONTCALM," May Day, 1926

DEAREST ADA,

My thoughts are with you so much to-day and I wonder *where* this will find you. I know that when the moment of moving comes it will be a sore wrench.

It is difficult to believe that it is nearly a year since Amy died. The wound seems just as fresh—and *deeper* than ever. I *cannot* get used to feeling that she is not there.

I had the meeting for Amy in the Keats house on April 15th and have a great deal to tell you about it. I went through *many, many* agitations—as to whether there would be a good audience—as to whether there would be too many and so on. Mercifully it was a day with various deluges of rain, so the size of the audience was exactly right, every seat taken and about a dozen people standing. The enclosed invitations speak for themselves. I did not know whether you would like to have John Gould Fletcher[1] or not, but Mr. [Jonathan] Cape[2] thought it would be a good plan to have his name on the card and he was very glad to do it—as was Mr. Drinkwater.[3]

The Chairman was a little bit of a difficulty at first. . . . . Mr. [Francis] Hirst,[4] who is a most delightful person, volunteered and was very keen to do it—so that seemed best and he did it *very well.* Myddleton [*sic*] Murry[5] was away but sent a most charming letter which Mr. Hirst read aloud.

---

[1] Damon, *op. cit.*, p. 753.

[2] *Ibid.*, p. 749. [3] *Ibid.*, p. 752.

[4] Editor (1907–16) of the *Economist* (London); see *Who's Who, 1938* (London), pp. 1591–92.

[5] Damon, *op. cit.*, p. 764; see below, Appendix V.

After we arrived at the house on the 15th, Mr. Howard, who was Mayor of Hampstead when the Keats House was acquired—and who is on the Committee—asked if he might speak—and so did Arthur Severn, Joseph Severn's[1] *son*. It gave one such a curious feeling of nearness to Keats to have the son of his devoted friend there in the room. Mr. Doubleday said that he had sent you the Hampstead paper so you will know these main facts.

I had a stenographer there, so the speeches[2] were all taken down. My idea is to have them all nicely typed—in two copies, one to go to the Keats House (Mr. Doubleday says they would like it), and one to go to Harvard, and put a few photographs with each—as her leather chair—the rare book corner—some garden ones. Would you like this? Everybody was much overcome with the slides—they are beautiful. I think that I can say, with Mr. Hirst, that it was an "unqualified success." I felt very happy about it and think that you would have too. The Keats House is the *sweetest* place.

We have been jammed in *continents* of ice for two days. Made 46 knots in the last twenty-four hours. There has seemed no reason why we should *ever* reach Quebec! but as they have just come and said that all the baggage must be on deck by nine this evening, I suppose there is *some* prospect of our arrival. It is 6:30 now so I must stop. I have lots of extra invitations to the Keats House. I thought that you might like them sent to some people. If you will let me have a list I will send them. An endless ocean of love, dear.

Yours,
FLORENCE

We go to St. Andrews as quickly as may be.

---

[1] Amy Lowell, *John Keats* (Boston and New York, 1925), II, 643, 653–54; see also Sheila Birkenhead, *Against Oblivion: The Life of Joseph Severn* (New York: Macmillan Co., 1944).

[2] See below, Appendix VI.

Appendix I

"SEVENELS," BROOKLINE, MASSACHUSETTS

Amy Lowell

Its name is "Sevenels," and it is a little place of less than ten acres within five miles of the Boston State House. Its chief interest to me is that I was born here; its chief interest to other people lies in the fact that it is an example of landscape architecture and garden-planning of a century ago. Few people, wandering round the meandering paths under the great trees, have the slightest idea of how small its extent really is, for the unknown designer has done as expert a job as, for instance, did Mr. Olmstead in Central Park.

All the way from Boston to Brookline the land slopes up—up—up—in a steady mounting grade, ending at last in a hill upon the southerly slope of which the place lies. Originally it was part of a grant allotted by the Town of Boston to a man named Isaac Grosse in 1638. What sort of land it was of which Mr. Grosse found himself the possessor, one can only guess from the age of the great trees still standing, woods, I should suppose, a portion of which was doubtless soon cleared and turned into pasture. Brookline was very far away from Boston in those days before the mill-dam was built, only the small tongue of land known as Boston Neck connecting the tip of the peninsula with the mainland. Boston Neck ran out over what is now Washington Street, so that the traveller from Brookline was obliged to drive some twelve miles round through Dorchester to get to town. A shorter cut was by boat from the salt meadows bounding the Back Bay, not then filled in, nor to be, for over two hundred years.

A century later, the place, divided in halves, appears as the property of two Tory refugees, a somewhat singular coincidence, as there were only three Tory refugee landowners in Brookline. Once again the Commonwealth took a hand, and in 1781 the estate, still in separate halves (in fact, whether they were originally one is a little doubtful), was allotted severally, only to be finally joined fifty years afterwards.

Now when did this wood and blueberry pasture get itself laid out in formal gardens and plantations? Of that I can find no actual evidence, but I suspect this turning of a farm into a country estate to have been the work of Mr. Stephen Higginson, [who] . . . . bought the place in 1800 and used it as a country residence, living here in a certain state as befitted both his temperament and condition. . . . . I am the more certain of his having been the first to make something beautiful of the place, because his grandson [Thomas Wentworth Higginson] says explicitly that he "built what was then a large country seat in Brookline." . . . .

247

Along with this carriage, it is fair to presume that Mr. Higginson brought back [from England] a love of smooth lawns and patterned gardens, for here they are and here ever since, through successive ownerships, have they remained. My father did not buy the place until 1866, but it is another coincidence that he should have bought it at all, for my great-great-grandmother was a sister of Mr. Higginson, so my father [Augustus Lowell], in losing the long walks and specially grafted fruit trees of his horticulturalist grandfather's place, encroached upon by a railroad, found himself fortunate in falling upon another laid out in somewhat the same, although on a much smaller, scale.

The love of flowers has persisted in our family for very many years, and on Mr. Higginson's admirable ground-plan my father raised up such spaces of flowering beauty as few children can have the good fortune to look back upon. The old colonial wooden house is gone; some vandal of a subsequent owner pulled it down, and, moving to higher ground, built an ugly but substantial brick house which, if pleasant to live in, adds nothing to the charm of the gardens.

It is difficult to describe gardens. They change with the seasons, and colour is their very breath. "Sevenels" makes a corner where two roads join. They are streets now, with numbers, but I remember them as unfrequented country roads. The place is surrounded by a wall of uncemented pudding-stone over which predatory boys have made it impossible to grow vines. There is an entrance on each road flanked by heavy stone posts, and just inside the walls runs a wide belt of trees, mostly elms, but with just enough evergreens to keep the whole inviolate from the eyes of passers-by.

Within this belt of trees is a wide meadow, kept for mowing—in June a glory of daisies and buttercups nodding in the wind, a paradise to a child, as I well remember. On the inner side, this line of trees is brightened by clumps of red-buds and hawthorns; in Autumn two or three copper beeches and several crimson maples keep colour always playing against the wall of green.

Beyond the meadow begins the grove—a little handful of land so cunningly cut by paths and with the trees so artfully disposed that one can wander happily among them and almost believe that one is walking in a real wood. In earliest Spring, snowdrops begin to glisten in the sunny spots under the trees to be followed by such masses of crocuses that I never see them without thinking of Chaucer's "pied mead." These give place to great drifts of daffodils in the hollows, and patches of lilies-of-the-valley, and under the beeches is a colony of painted trilliums. Later in the Summer, the little stars of the potentilla mingle with wild strawberry blooms; and that abominable nuisance, bishop's weed, a great mass of marching white flowers, is really beautiful here, although it must be cut down before it seeds. Under the horse-chestnut trees, by the avenue, monkeywort makes a soft trailing carpet and native rhododendrons are clumped here and there in the shade. One could put the whole grove in one's pocket, but as a child it seemed to me limitless, and many are the Indians I have shot when out scouting with my bow and arrows as they peered for a moment from behind a distant tree-trunk, and, in spite of a little confusion in my mind as to whether I were Robin Hood or the Last of the Mohicans, I delight to record that I never missed my man.

On the lawn beside the avenue grows the largest pink horse-chestnut I have ever seen. I used to call it the bee-tree, for bees frequent it so assiduously that it sounds like a hive in blossoming time.

The house itself stands in the midst of lawns and grass terraces. The South Lawn, fringed by trees and bordered with hybrid rhododendrons and azaleas, drops sheerly down to a path, at one end of which is an old-fashioned arbour covered with wisteria and trumpet-vine, and two flights of stone steps lead into a formal sunken garden. But the real entrance to the garden is by a gradually descending path from the avenue.

I do not know if the garden was artificially blasted out, or if the designer made use of a natural basin, but now it lies some twenty feet below the South Lawn, its surrounding terrace planted with alternate clipped hemlocks and flowering trees. It is so warm, and sunny, and protected here, that everything blooms early and blooms much. But all gardeners will appreciate my difficulties when I say that one can walk entirely round every bed, and that the garden must be kept in perennial bloom from April until October.

On the other side of the house, lawns, shrubberies of magnolia and lilac, and a pine plantation lead to the hot beds (so called because they are cold frames), which is really a cutting and vegetable garden; and a fruit-garden runs up the side of the hill where grow apple and pear trees, more vegetables, strawberries, and all the thousand and one experiments to be set out near the house later on.

Being especially fond of bulbs and not fond of the bedding-out system, one great problem has been how to manage when the bulbs fade. But in two instances I have realized my ideal. In one, narcissus poeticus and foxgloves share a corner, and as the narcissus die down, the foxgloves rise up between them and cover them; in the other, yellow tulips bloom gloriously and give up at last just as the salvia pratensis in the midst of which they are planted is beginning to show signs of flowering.

Having been brought up with flowers, I should know something about them, but alas! I always took them absolutely for granted. Now that I have the ordering of them, I am unreasonably annoyed at both my own ignorance and nature's caprices. Why, for instance, will clematis Jackmani flourish year after year on two of my trellises and die annually on the third? Why will nothing demolish rose-bugs but hand-picking, and why will not the daylight-savers realize that the garden cannot be watered until the sun is down? However, as to this same watering, I offer it as an excellent refreshment to the soul and spirit of anyone addicted to mental work who has neither time nor strength for the labours of weeding and raking. Just past sunset of a June evening with a fine spray on your nozzle, the garden dripping and satisfied with moisture, little flitter-bats in the fading sky and the water bringing out the scent of the roses—that is good. I believe there is nothing better.

It is an old-fashioned garden and it has been my pleasure to keep in it many old-fashioned flowers. Squills, day-lilies, Ladies' delight, bee-balm, snapdragon, old man, night-scented stock, four o'clocks, tree clematis, bleeding heart, mignonette, etc. One whole bed is given to roses, and although standard roses will not grow with us, I have many pillar roses, even the old

249

Malmaison rose, and that quaint variety so seldom seen to-day—the York and Lancaster, striped red and white.

The house is the blot on the place, although a triumphant wisteria vine is yearly doing its best to conceal it. The outside was here and unalterable; the inside I have done what I could to bring into harmony with the old scheme. My architect in the alterations was Mr. Henry Forbes Bigelow, and I owe much of the carrying-out of the designs to that excellent artist and wood-carver Mr. I. Kirchmayer. For very little in the house is old except the furniture, practically everything being made from old designs which I found and had copied. For instance, the fireplace in the music-room is none of it old. The mantelpiece was carved in Cambridgeport from a photograph, but the centre panel could not be clearly enough seen to be copied, so we took the Marlborough Cameo in the Boston Art Museum and copied that. The Chinese-Chippendale mirror was adapted from details of two original mirrors, both of which I liked and wanted combined; it was executed by Mr. Kirchmayer and gilded by Caldwell, New York. In these alterations my period was determined for me by the house and the gardens, the fitting in to it was a work of love for one so wholly enamoured of the eighteenth century as I have always been. But, after all, a library is the heart of a house. Mine is walled with English oak. It contains—books; it also contains flowers, even all Winter long from my very little greenhouse. It is all tiny, as things go nowadays, but it is very cozy and compact, and an object lesson as to what nine and a half acres can be made to do. There is no view, no pond or brook, no long sweep of park land, but I know every tree, every rock, every flower, as only children know these things, and that is something which if forfeited can never be captured again.

Appendix II

SELECTIONS FROM AMY LOWELL'S CORRE-SPONDENCE WITH HARRIET MONROE

BROOKLINE, MASS., 19 June, 1918[1]

DEAR HARRIET:

It will be very nice to have "Appuldurcombe Park" in August, and I hope you will be able to get it in.

In regard to the Chinese poems, Mrs. Ayscough tells me that you want her to write an article about the scrolls for the prose part of the book, and that you will put the poems in the poetry section, of course.

She has just been here, passing through on her way to New Brunswick, and we have had several séances, going over the poems together. She has now taken them away with her to read them all over again with the original characters, for I have made a discovery which I have never before seen mentioned in any Occidental book on Chinese poetry, but which, I think, must be well known in Chinese literature; namely, that the roots of the characters are the things which give the poetry its overtones, taking the place of adjectives and imaginary writing with us. One cannot translate a poem into anything like the proper spirit, taking the character meanings alone. It is necessary in every case to go to the root of a character, and that will give the key to why that particular word is used and not some other which means the same thing when exactly translated. Mrs. Ayscough quite agrees with me in this. This is the key to the situation, and it is the hunting of these roots that she is now doing.

She is then going to send me back the results of her investigation, and I shall finish the poems up on that. They are done already, as far as simple meaning is concerned, but her study may necessitate changes on my part.

As to the lines which you suggest should be long, of course the lines are determined by the cadence and are not arbitrary. I disagree with you that the cadences of Chinese poetry are long. The language is more sliding than ours and may give that impression, but the absolute construction calls for a rather short line—I admit not as short as they sometimes are in an Imagist poem, but I am not concerned in translating Chinese rhythms, which would be quite impossible as so much of the rhythmic effect is got from the vowel sounds of

---

[1] The following excerpts are from the file of correspondence of Amy Lowell with Harriet Monroe in the Harriet Monroe Library of Modern Poetry of the University of Chicago. Others of Miss Lowell's letters to Miss Monroe of interest on the subject are dated: January 29, 1916; February 3, 1916; May 8, 1916; May 4, 1917; May 26, 1917; May 31, 1917; June 15, 1917; November 2, 1918; December 9, 1919; May 28, 1920; and October 25, 1924.

the language itself, and in translating them, not into metre, but into cadence, I am obliged to follow the laws necessitated by the writing of cadenced verse. The lines, therefore, will have to be what cadence requires, whether long or short.

You see I have made an awful study of cadence, and I think I can claim to know a good deal more about it than many people who write it equally well, for first comes intuition and afterwards verification, and for the last few years I have been able to find the reasons for doing things which up to that point I had done instinctively. No such study has been made by any other of the *vers libristes* writing in English. Even Ezra [Pound] has felt and announced his convictions, rather than tabulated, measured, and proved.

So I am afraid that you will have to take Mrs. Ayscough's and my final results as the best we can both of us do in the matter. She knows a lot about Chinese, and what passes her ear will, I am sure, satisfy you. You see she has had much more opportunity to know Chinese than most people, for she was born in China and lived there all her childhood, only coming home to finish her schooling and come out. She married when she was about twenty-two and returned to China, having also spent another Winter in China before that, bridging the time between her two residences there. She has lived there steadily now for twenty years, except for occasional visits to England and America. Chinese is, therefore, to some extent, her native tongue. For although she has only taken up the reading and speaking of it seriously in the last ten years, I think, she has been surrounded by the sound of it, and the feel of it, and the psychology of it, all her life.

I am awfully sorry to hear that you have been worn out, and I trust that you are better now. I am remarkably well.

I am going out to Grand Rapids to speak on November 16th, and it is possible that I may come back via Chicago, although it is in the opposite direction, but of that I am not sure yet. I have no real reason to go to Chicago except to see you all, which I should like to do, for I suppose they are tired of hearing me speak there; but I confess it seems a long time since I have been with you, and I hate to let more than a year elapse.

Mrs. Russell joins me in kindest greetings, and believe me,

Affectionately yours,
AMY LOWELL

[*The critical whimsicalness—or whimsical criticalness—of Miss Lowell's attitude toward Miss Monroe is well illustrated in the two following excerpts:*]

BROOKLINE, MASS., October 10, 1917

DEAR HARRIET:—

You are a wretched, miserable, low side-stepper. The idea of kicking me out of the November issue and then putting it up to me that it is for Sandburg. Just as if I could ever get in Sandburg's way, the dear boy! Of course, give him November, and of course, give Alice Henderson the rest of November, and I perfectly understand about December, and give me the lead in January [for "The Landlady of the Whinton Inn Tells A Story"]. But do you realize that I have not had the lead since August 1916? That is not treating me

252

very well, do you think? Really, Harriet, I am becoming mellow, and sweet tempered, and lovely, practicing my forgiveness on you. I am always having to do it. Now do not strain me too far, there's a good girl. . . . . If you will be sure and get it [A. L.'s "review of Louis Untermeyer's book"] in November, (and now do not side-step again, please) I will forgive you everything *de tout mon cœur*. Particularly after your handsome tribute to my "Bombardment" in your October editorial. . . . .

Of course, the circulation of *Poetry* should be increased, but I do not know how, unless you change your policy of printing new poets because they are new and not because they are good. . . . .

. . . . I am awfully glad Sandburg has done a splendid thing. I greatly admire that man, and I am willing to admit that you were right about him in the beginning, and I was wrong. There is a famous admission for you! . . . .

Affectionately yours,
Amy Lowell

Brookline, Mass., 22 October, 1918

Dear Harriet:—

It is quite obvious that you have died, a fact which upsets me considerably; but on the chance that you may gaze from the Empyrean and see a little letter addressed to you lying on your quondam desk, I am sending this. . . . .

Affectionately yours,
Amy Lowell

Brookline, Mass., September 15, 1914

My dear Harriet:

. . . .

I wish I could have come out to Chicago with my friend, Mrs. Russell, who has been abroad with me all summer. . . . . You ask about the quarrel between Ezra and the rest of us. It is not a quarrel now, it is a schism. It is a very long story, and I do not know quite how to tell you all of it by letter.

Do you remember, Ezra was very anxious for me to run an international review, something on the lines of the *Mércure de France?* He came to me at once as soon as I got to London, and it then transpired that he expected to become editor of said review with a salary. I was to guarantee all the money, and put in what I pleased, and he was to run the magazine his way. We talked over the cost of expenses, and we both thought that $5,000 a year was the least that such a magazine could be run on. As I have not $5,000 a year that I can afford to put into it, I based my refusal upon that fact, and it was most unfortunate that Ezra apparently did not believe it. Like many people of no incomes, Ezra does not know the difference between thousands and millions, and thinks that anyone who knows where to look for next week's dinners is a millionnaire, and therefore lost his temper with me completely, although he never told me why; and he accused me of being unwilling to give any money toward art.

In thinking over what I could do to help the poets less fortunate than my-self, and also to help myself in somewhat the same manner that a Review would do, it seemed to me that to re-publish the *Imagiste Anthology* with the same group of people, year after year, for a period of five years, would enable us, by constant iteration, to make some impression upon the reading public. And I thought it would be interesting for people to see the work of the same group of poets brought out year after year, and it is a method which the edi-tors of *Georgian Poetry* have found most satisfactory. I mentioned this first to the Aldingtons because I saw them first after I conceived the idea. I suggested that the last little book was too monotonous and too undemocratic, in that certain poets were allowed much more space than others, and I suggested that in the "New Anthology" we should allow approximately the same space to each poet, and that we should get a publisher of reputable standing, and I offered, in case we could not get any publisher, to take the risk of the volume itself, and pay for its publication.

The Aldingtons were exceedingly enthusiastic over the idea, as have been the other poets we have asked to join us. Only Ezra was annoyed. He accused me of trying to make myself editor instead of him, and finally tried a little blackmail by telling me that he would only join us on condition that I would pledge myself to give $200 a year to some indigent poet. I told him that the $200 a year might be managed should anyone in stress of circumstances need such a sum, but that I absolutely refused to be intimidated into doing any-thing, or to buy his poems at the expense of my self-respect. I also told him that I would not have suggested the anthology had I known that he would not like the idea, and that it was intended to benefit him, quite as much as the rest of us.

He was perfectly furious for some time, and sent for the Aldingtons, and told them they must choose between him and me, which was awful for them, as he is a very old friend, and has done much for them, and I was only a new friend. They behaved with the utmost honour in the matter. They told Ezra it was not a question of me at all, but a question of the principle, that they felt it only fair to let the poets choose their own contributions, and to give each poet an equal space. He then tried to bribe them, by asking them to get up an anthology with him, and leave me out. This they absolutely refused to do.

We had many consultations on the subject, in which [Frank Stewart] Flint, [D. H.] Lawrence, and Ford Madox Hueffer [Ford] joined us, and we all agreed that Ezra could not expect to run us all his own way forever, and that if he chose to separate himself from us, we should be obliged, although most regretfully, to let him. [John Gould] Fletcher is coming in, and a few of the poets in the last volume who have not been producing much in the interval, have been struck out.

The new anthology will consist of seven of us, viz: The Aldingtons, Flint, Fletcher, Ford Madox Hueffer, D. H. Lawrence, and myself, and the harmony and kindly feeling which we have all displayed toward each other has been very marked. In order to save Ezra's feelings as much as possible, we have written a preface, in which we have explained that Ezra has left us from artis-tic reasons, owing to a slight difference in the interpretation of the word "imagiste." We have changed the name of the anthology, in order to let him bring out another of his own under that title, should he so desire. Our anthology is to be "Some Imagiste Poets."

I think Ezra is regretting his action a little, for he became very nice about it toward the end, and offered not to bring out his volume if it would interfere with ours, but we told him that we had no idea that it would. As a matter of fact, he has no one for his volume except himself and a man named Rodker, unless he rakes up somebody in the interval.

The truth is, Ezra has ducked and draked his reputation with his last work. His poetry is too indecent to be poetical, and even when it is not indecent it is too often merely vituperative. Please do not tell any one that I said so, but I think that he is in a very bad way as far as his work is concerned. Mr. Prothero, the editor of the *Quarterly* who has just accepted from him some of the Fenellosa manuscript, told me that the trouble with Ezra was that he had nothing to say, and I am afraid that is really true. "Blast" will give you a good idea of what Ezra has been obliged to descend to in order to keep his name before the public, and he admitted in a speech at the Imagiste Dinner that it was nothing but advertising.

He looks very ill, and has a bad cough, and I am afraid that he is tuberculous. It has even been hinted that this may have attacked his brain. No one knows anything about it, and this is merely surmise. The fact remains that where his work is concerned he is failing every day, and except for *Poetry* and the *Egoist* there are no magazines that will take his poetry, if I except an occasional contribution to *Poetry and Drama*, and he has only sold two prose articles this year. One, which was mostly Fenellosa, appeared in the *Quarterly*, and an article on "Vorticism" in the current *Fortnightly*. He had a chance, in his articles on French authors in the *New Age*, a year ago, but the work was so superficial and slapdash that it did him harm rather than good.

Ezra has always thought of life as a grand game of bluff. He never has learned the wisdom of Lincoln's famous adage about "not being able to fool all the people all the time." Advertising is all very well, but one must have some goods to deliver, and the goods must be up to the advertising of them. Now that Ezra has ceased to be a youthful phenomenon he must take his place in the steady march by which young men of talent gain to a real reputation, and he finds himself falling back at every step, and this naturally makes him exceedingly bitter. He is very brilliant, but he does not work enough, and his work lacks the quality of soul, which, I am more and more fain to believe, no great work can ever be without. At any rate, that is the situation about the Imagistes. It is not a quarrel; in one sense it never was. I have spared no efforts to keep them all on good terms with each other, even offering to leave the anthology myself, if it would heal the breach. Ezra and his wife dined with me a few days before I left, and we had a very pleasant and perfectly amicable evening, and it would not surprise me if he came into one of our Anthologies later on, but of course, I have not suggested this possibility to him.

The great thing which my summer has done for me is bringing me the intimacy of the Aldingtons. They are a perfectly charming young couple, and I think Hilda's last work an advance on her other, don't you? I am very glad indeed that you accepted the poems she sent you with the exception of "Sea

Iris," in returning which I cannot help thinking you made a mistake. I enclose a subscription blank for my old governess in England, who is very much interested in seeing your book.

Don't be discouraged that the subscriptions are not increasing. A magazine devoted to poetry can hardly expect to increase its subscription list hand over fist. Poetry is looking up, but I do not suppose it will ever be really popular, and I think you are doing a great deal to change public opinion and raise the standard in this country. . . . .

Very sincerely,
AMY LOWELL

BROOKLINE, MASS., 7 July, 1919

DEAR HARRIET:—

. . . .

I see by the current number [of *Poetry*] that Ezra has left the *Little Review* also. I think the truth is that the world has left Ezra. A letter from Hilda Aldington this morning tells me that he has gone to the southern part of France, which I suppose means that, as he can do nothing in London, he has gone into retirement to hide his confusion. Is the *Criterion* really coming off, do you think? And who is the backer? I do not imagine that it will be any more successful than his other ventures in the periodical line have been. Poor Ezra, he had a future once, but he has played his cards so badly that I think he has barely a past now.

Affectionately yours,
AMY LOWELL

BROOKLINE, MASS., 7 January, 1919

DEAR HARRIET:—

. . . .

You will send me proofs of Florence's and my Chinese things in the next number, of course? I am just getting over a sharp attack of the "flu," and what a beastly thing it is.

Affectionately yours,
AMY LOWELL

BROOKLINE, MASS., 9 January, 1919

DEAR HARRIET:—

. . . .

I do not like your changes of title for the Chinese poems, and I simply detest the "done into free verse" business, so if you have no objection we will leave it as originally planned, which is the only thing I like at all. Florence and I went very carefully over the "translateds" and "put into poetry" wording before we found what suited us, and this does suit us both and is the only thing that does. I have not, of course, received the proofs yet, but I will send them on as soon as I can after I get them. . . . .

Affectionately yours,
AMY LOWELL

256

Dear Harriet:

As I telegraphed to you to-day, I do not think "Chinese Poem Pictures" means anything, because any poem that contains a picture is a "poem picture." The point is that they are written to hang on the wall, and the calligraphy is an integral part of the art. I have therefore kept my suggestion of "Chinese Written Wall Pictures." . . . . It may seem heavy, but it is what they are, and it is what Florence's article speaks of them as being. By the way, where is the proof of her article, as I ought to go through that? I believe you said that we should be the first thing in this number of *Poetry*—didn't you?

Affectionately yours,
Amy Lowell

Brookline, Mass., 18 January, 1919

Dear Harriet:

. . . .

Your fine spanking came this morning, and I should feel dreadfully about it were it not that I am guiltless. You have no idea how the mails come, out here in Brookline. They are sometimes over twenty-four hours longer than those to Boston. In fact, I find in the summer when I am in Dublin that I get Western mail over a day sooner than I do in Brookline. . . . .

I am sorry you do not like the title. Personally, I like it very much.

In this proof of Florence's prose part, you have made a good many minor changes which doubtless seem to you good, and which I am not prepared to dispute, but I think it a little hard that you should have left out the fact that Florence's originals are on exhibition in Cincinnati since anybody reading these poems who lives in Cincinnati might wish to compare them with the originals. It might, therefore, be important to her that this sentence be left in. . . . .

Affectionately yours,
Amy Lowell

Brookline, Mass., 18 May, 1920

Dear Harriet:

What a joke that we are going to the same place to get the same degree! . . . .

You ask me what is the proper proceeding when one is invested with an honorary degree. My experience is entirely with Harvard . . . . and nobody ever does anything except sit in silence on the platform until their turn to be eulogized and receive their degree arrives. When your name is called, you stand up and stand perfectly quietly and silently while the president of the college says about two sentences detailing what you have done and how elegant you are; and, at Harvard, where no hoods are given, you just walk up to him and receive a scroll upon which is written your degree. Where hoods are given, as in all the smaller colleges in imitation of England, and I suppose Baylor is no exception to the rule, my brother Lawrence tells me that, at the crucial moment, just before the degree is given, two individuals walk up behind you and throw the hood over your head. Professor [John Livingston] Lowes informs me that it is never done to a woman without pulling off her hat and down her hair in the process, but I have nothing to fear from that, for they cannot pull my hair off, though they may slightly disarrange it. Then you sit down again and wait while the other fellows get their degrees. There will probably be a lot of marching round the campus, which I cannot do because my operation has not left me spry enough to march. . . . . I imagine that there will be something or other after the degrees are given, probably a luncheon. . . . . As there are going to be a great many functions in Waco—at least so the Dallas paper says—I imagine we shall all have to make speeches more or less, but not at the time the degrees are given. . . . .

Affectionately yours,

AMY LOWELL

Appendix III

TO THE EDITOR OF THE "LITERARY REVIEW"
of the "New York Evening Post"[1]

To the Editor of the "Literary Review"

SIR:

Mr. Arthur Waley's review of Mrs. Ayscough's and my *Fir-Flower Tablets* was so interesting, and raises so many questions of importance to Chinese translation in general, that I am going to ask for a little space to answer such of his remarks as come within my particular province.[2] Mr. Waley takes exception to Mrs. Ayscough's statement that the Chinese poetical form called a "fu" is a prototype of "polyphonic prose." Possibly Mr. Waley is not quite certain of the laws governing "polyphonic prose"; possibly he has not carried his examination of the "fu" beyond the matter of rhyme. I think a brief analysis of the two forms will help to clear the air. Although I cannot read the Chinese characters, I have analysed a number of "fu" in transliteration with Mrs. Ayscough, and have lately talked the matter over at some length with a Chinese professor connected with one of our Universities, so I think I may make some claim to know whereof I speak.

The base of "polyphonic prose" is the tenet that the style of any particular part of the poem must follow the emotion it represents. "Polyphonic prose" is a form in which all the voices proper to poetry are brought into play: metre, cadence, assonance, alliteration, rhyme, and return. These voices are confined to no set pattern, but are employed wherever the emotion calls for them. The rhymes may be at the ends of the cadences, as in ordinary verse, or may appear within the cadences (what is known as internal rhyming); they may even be used one immediately after the other. On the other hand, the cadences may be left entirely blank (that is, rhymeless) at will, and as long as such cadences seem desirable. "Polyphonic prose" differs entirely from the usual "rhythmical prose," so often confused with it, on account of the employment of the various voices I have named.

The Chinese "fu" is an irregular form of differing line lengths. The number of syllables to a line is determined by no fixed rule, giving the form almost the appearance of prose to the eye. The rhymes do usually come at the ends of the lines, but internal rhyming is frequently employed, and many lines are left entirely blank. Since Chinese prosody is based on so many syllables to a line,

---

[1] See A. L. to F. A., May 27, 1922.

[2] See issue for February 4, 1922, pp. 395–96, for Mr. Waley's review; same journal, p. 538, for Miss Lowell's reply.

and the rhyme-scheme is exact in pattern in verse proper, this will show, by its departure from the usual practice of Chinese verse, how far the "fu" is a free and independent form.

Again, the rhyme tones of a "fu" are not obliged to conform to the strict alternation insisted on in other types of verse. Chinese poetry lays much stress on parallelism: the image, or idea, of one line is exactly duplicated, in different words, in the next. This device is familiar to us in the Psalms, for Hebrew poetry was built upon it; but Chinese prosody carried "parallelism" to almost impossible lengths. The parallel, or antithesis (for both were used), was even duplicated in syntax, a noun for a noun, a verb for a verb, etc., and duplicated farther in the order of the tones. The parallel of idea was much employed in "fu," but it was not carried into either syntax or tone, which again marks a freedom. Of course, the tone pattern of Chinese poetry is something for which we have no analogy, and need only concern us here to show that it was departed from in the "fu." Here, then, is a form employing the devices of poetry, but in an entirely different way from their usual employment, a form so irregular as to seem almost like prose, but yet clearly not prose, for it makes use of rhyme, line, and parallelism. Where prosodies differ, departure from them must also differ, but is there not something analogous in the way these two forms differ in their adherence and departure from their particular prosodies? The only radical difference between the "fu" and "polyphonic prose" is that although in a "fu" the phrases may be long or short, many or few, the rhymes in each group of phrases must be the same, and this particular rhyme cannot be used again. The Chinese have six rules for the "fu," which may be roughly given as follows:

1. A "fu" must be full of colour.
2. It must display high literary ability.
3. All subjects are proper to it, but all must be treated in a poetical or literary manner.
4. It must set forth aims, desires, and ambitions.
5. It must be stirring and passionate.
6. It must excite emotion.

It is also said that "the words must flow naturally from the lips," which is merely to imply that they must be as easily fitting as in an improvisation. I think all this proves that if the "fu" is not "almost identical" with "polyphonic prose," as Mrs. Ayscough stated, the two forms are, at least extraordinarily alike in many ways, more alike, certainly, than either is to any other form known to-day.

Mr. Waley's second contention, as far as I am concerned, seems to be that a "flawless lyric" should be translated into a flawless lyric. With this, I heartily agree. But, how is the thing to be done? A flawless lyric is a combination of idea and sound. Now the exact sounds of one language cannot be carried over into another when these sounds must also represent a single, definite idea. The great question by which all translators are confronted is, shall the sound be striven for, or the meaning and effect? I believe all good translators aim at the latter. What sort of idea of the original would a foreigner receive if Verlaine's well-known lines:

260

```
                         "Les sanglots longs
                          Des violons
                          De l'automne,
                          Blessent mon cœur
                          D'une langueur
                          Monotone"
were rendered as:
                          The sad, low songs
                          Of queer old gongs
                          Autumn blown.
                          Breasts astir
                          At their whir
                          Moan in tone?
```

Here is the same vowel pattern as in the original, but nothing else. The translation is not only inane; it is lacking in both delicacy and languor; the sounds are retained but the meaning and feeling of the poem are lost.

No, I cannot agree with Mr. Waley that sound is so indispensable a necessity in translation. In Li T'ai-po's "Night Thoughts," Mr. Waley admits that I have reproduced the idea of the poem, but prefers Mr. Giles's metrical rendering because, forsooth, he believes it "closer to the original," when, as a matter of fact, Mr. Giles's poem has only the vaguest Victorian resemblance to what the original poem is about. I was talking about this poem with a learned Chinese gentleman the other day, and this is his paraphrase of the "idea" of the poem: Li T'ai-po has gone to bed after an evening of conviviality. He wakes in the night, cold and somewhat confused, and seeing the bright moonlight upon the floor wonders if it can be frost. The chilly air, the lonely silence of the moon, bring upon him, in his somewhat maudlin state, a sharp attack of home-sickness, in which he thinks with longing of the garden of his childhood. Neither Mr. Giles nor I have been able to reproduce the music of Li T'ai-po's poem, but which of us has most nearly reproduced its effect? I leave it to your readers to decide.

What Mr. Waley says in regard to translation proper is not my affair; but my collaborator, Mrs. Ayscough, will doubtless attend to that as soon as distance permits.

AMY LOWELL

Appendix IV

THREE CHINESE POETS[1]

Amy Lowell

When the subject of this afternoon's talk was proposed to me, it bore the alarming title: "Chinese Literature." Now it did not take very long for me to persuade the powers that preside over these Chinese lectures that this was too large a subject for anyone to deal with in a single lecture, so my task was considerately narrowed to "Chinese Poetry." But, suppose that English poetry were in question, could any lecturer, however agile, run over a list of English poets from Chaucer's day to our own—with citations—and leave anything but a confused jumble of names in the minds of his audience? Chaucer lived in the latter part of the fourteenth century and we live very early in the twentieth, so that the discussion would only be obliged to scan lightly the poetical production of something over five hundred years. But what is five hundred years in the history of China? Chinese poems dating from about two thousand B.C. may still be read, and, what is more, may be read in an English translation. From the twentieth century before Christ to the twentieth century of our era is a span of four thousand years, and all this time China has been composing poems, and these poems have been the base upon which her whole civilization rests. Considering this, I think you will agree with me that a single hour is scarcely long enough for anyone to attempt any clear presentation of the subject as a whole, and you will forgive me if I have felt obliged to compress it still farther. What I shall speak about to-day, then, will be Chinese poetry in general, and in particular the work of three of the most famous poets of the T'ang period—Li T'ai-po, Tu Fu, and Po Chü-i.

I think we must, however, give these three famous men some sort of background; we must give them somewhere to stand, both historically and geographically; we must set them in their social milieu in order that their work may be understood; and we must consider, very briefly, something of the technique of Chinese prosody so that we may realize why the poets of China did certain things and not others.

An interesting study for someone, sometime, to undertake would be to trace the idiosyncratic reasons which determine the poetical practice of nations. Why did the Anglo-Saxon base his poetry on alliteration; why do we base ours on metre and stress? What causes some peoples to delight in rhyme, and others to weave a pattern of counted syllables? Is the Latin quantity, lost to us, entirely a matter of tongue, and what has mere language to do with

[1] See A. L. to F. A., May 27, 1922.

262

Hebrew parallelism? Here is a subject made to the hand of the energetic Ph.D. seeking a new theme. Awaiting the arrival of his brilliant monograph, however, it will be enough for us to-day to note how China has chosen to build her verse.

The obvious thing about poetry is that it must have a more noticeable pattern than prose. This pattern, in fact, is the chief reason for its being. Poetical ideas may be expressed in prose, but the addition of pattern certainly heightens and impresses them. Prosodies start when some man feels the need of sweeping his emotions up to a climax greater than can be achieved in prose. That is the first inception of pattern, and, of course, the type of pattern is determined by the kind of speech of which any given language is composed. Now, until recently, Chinese was a monosyllabic language, and this fact made the rhythms of stress and cadence impossible to it. We all know the staccato effect of Chinese speech—well, that staccato quality is due to its monosyllabic structure, and it is as true of prose as of poetry. How then make a pattern except by the arbitrary control of these syllables into lines? Prose might run on indefinitely, but verse, to be verse, must submit to being cut short at intervals in the interest of pattern; and, as pattern implies repetition, these intervals must be of prescribed lengths. This is precisely what the early Chinese poets saw, and exactly what they did; they limited the lines of a poem to a given number of syllables, and, as each syllable meant a word and each word was a character, their prosody quickly assumed the form of so many characters, or words, to a line. More elaborate elements of pattern-making were invented as time went on, and these I will explain when I come to them, but rhyme, that familiar apparatus of most prosodies, seems to have been present from the beginning. In the earliest specimens of Chinese poetry which have come down to us, the number of syllables to a line was less standardized than it afterwards became, but four words to a line (a form afterwards largely abandoned) was very common.

When the first Chinese singers hit upon this device of counting and regulating syllables must have been in the dawn of time. The Chinese, who have a legend for everything, have a charming one about the invention of writing. Its originator is said to have been one Ts'ang Chieh, a minister of the mythical Yellow Emperor, who reigned in the alarming antiquity of the twenty-seventh century b.c. The legend records that this same Ts'ang Chieh, having "observed the shapes of things in the heavens, and the forms of things on earth, also the foot-prints of birds and beasts on the sand and mud" (I quote from the original Chinese), suddenly conceived the idea of pictographic writing. However this may be, we do know for a certainty that by the sixth century b.c. the Chinese were in possession of a written language which was perfectly adequate for the purposes of literature. In fact, it differs very little from the present Chinese script.

It was in exactly this sixth century b.c. that Confucius conceived the idea of gathering together a number of the poems of past ages which tradition still preserved and combining them into a volume, the famous "Book of Odes."

Confucius was not only a great teacher; he was a great scholar and indefatigable in preserving the scattered writings of the ancients. Before compiling the Book of Odes, he had collected various historical documents into a work known as the Book of History, a small part of which was in verse. These two works, with the Book of Changes, the Book of Rites, and the Spring and Autumn Annals, make up the Five Classics, which, until modern times, every Chinese had to learn by heart before he could hold an official position or be admitted to the privileges of an educated man; and in China this was no mere phrase, as we shall see presently.

The Book of Odes consists of three hundred and five rhymed ballads in various metres, of which the most usual is four words to a line. It is probable that the earliest of these pieces date back to about 2000 B.C., and the others were composed at varying times until the sixth century B.C. The ballads are arranged in four groups. The first consists of ballads sung by people in the various feudal states. It will show us how close the bond between Chinese poetry and Chinese statesmanship has been in China to realize that these ballads were forwarded by the provincial nobles to the Court, where they were submitted to the imperial musicians who determined from them the condition of the populace in the states from which they came and the good or bad government of the vassal rulers, by which means they were enabled to advise the emperor on any given course of action in regard to these states. The second group is composed of odes sung at ordinary entertainments given at Court; the third, of odes sung on grand occasions when the nobles met together; and the fourth, of panegyric and sacrificial odes.

These poems are simple and straightforward, and often of a strange poignance. Some deal with war, many with agriculture and hunting, many are love poems, others are complaints of officials. At least this is what they purport to be, but generations of Chinese commentators have cudgelled their brains to turn them into political allegories. This is no unusual method with scholars. If literature stands in grave danger of perishing without the aid which scholars have exerted to preserve it, it stands in no less danger of perishing because of their very interest in it. The ideal would be a scholar with an artist's perception, but where is such a miracle to be found? Confucius was one of these rare miracles, certainly, for he attached great importance to the Odes. There is a story that on an occasion when he asked his son if he had learnt the Odes, and the boy replied that he had not, Confucius told him that until he did so he would be unfit for the society of intellectual men. But the followers of Confucius were not the Master; they had neither his insight nor understanding. They could no more appreciate the beauty and simplicity of the ballads than they could refuse to be guided by their Master's direct expression of opinion in regard to them. So, with admirable patience, they set about reading moral and political meanings into them. No one knows whether there is any grain of truth in their harvests of suggestions, but whether there is or not is of small significance, as the Odes do very well as they are. Mr. Giles has a pregnant sentence in this regard in his *Chinese Literature*. He says: "Native scholars are, of course, hide-bound in the traditions of commentators, but European students will do well to seek the meaning of the Odes within the compass of the Odes themselves."

I am going to read you a few of these poems. Here is one which purports to be an account of life at some period even earlier than the time when it was written, which was during the twelfth century B.C. There are eight stanzas; I shall read only two. This is from the translation of the Book of Odes by the well-known sinologue, Mr. James Legge:

> "In the seventh month the Fire Star passes the meridian;
> In the eighth month are the sedges and reeds.
> In the silkworm month they strip the mulberry branches of
>   their leaves,
> And take their axes and hatchets,
> To lop off those that are distant and high;
> Only stripping the young trees of their leaves;
> In the seventh month, the shrike is heard;
> In the eighth month, they begin their spinning;—
> They make dark fabrics and yellow.
> Our red manufacture is very brilliant,
> It is for the lower robes of our young princes.
>
> In the fourth month, the Small grass is in seed.
> In the fifth, the cicada gives out its note.
> In the eighth, they reap.
> In the tenth, the leaves fall.
> In the days of our first month, they go after badgers,
> And take foxes and wild cats,
> To make furs for our young princes.
> In the days of our second month, they have a general hunt,
> And proceed to keep up the exercises of war.
> The boars of one year are for themselves;
> Those of three years are for our prince."

This next complains of an official, and again I am using Mr. Legge's translation:

> "Lamb's fur and leopard's cuffs,
> You use us with unkindness.
> Might we not find another Chief?
> But we stay because of our fathers.
>
> Lamb's fur and leopard's cuffs,
> You use us with cruel unkindness.
> Might we not find another Chief?
> But we stay from our regard to you."

The following is an ode of lamentation. Its authorship is uncertain, although all the old Chinese commentators agree in ascribing it to a certain Jëng Shu, an officer of the court of King Hsüan, who reigned for the amazing period of ninety-five years from 876 to 781 B.C. Opinions differ as to the exact date of the great drought to which it refers, but the standard chronology places it in the sixth year of King Hsüan's reign, which would make it 821 B.C. This translation is from Mrs. Ayscough's and my *Fir-Flower Tablets.* (Quote: "The Cloudy River," *Fir-Flower Tablets*, p. 135.)

The last poem from the Book of Odes which I will read to-day is so slight and charming that, for weeks after I did it, I could not get it out of my head.

265

It was probably written about 600 B.C. The lady is supposed to have been the daughter of the Lord of Wei and the divorced wife of the Lord of Sung. On the death of her husband, her son succeeded to his father's position as feudal chief of Sung, but, because of her divorce, the unhappy woman, who was deeply attached to her son, was forbidden to enter Sung where he lived. She is greatly extolled by the Chinese for her strict adherence to this propriety, but it evidently cost her much. (Quote: "The Great Ho River," *Fir-Flower Tablets*, p. 147.)

The next important step in the art of poetry is represented by one man, Ch'ü Yüan, who lived in the third century B.C. He was a famous statesman and poet who wrote an excitable, rhapsodical sort of verse, in which the primitive rules of the time were discarded to be replaced by the needs of the emotion alone. Critics often speak of his "wild, irregular metres," which were, in fact, his natural expression, as his followers found to their cost. He is chiefly known for one long poem, the "Li Sao," or "Falling into Trouble." This deals, in the form of an autobiographic love poem, with his rise and fall in the favour of the king. The poem is so full of allusions, historical and mythical, as to make it very difficult to understand, in spite of which, it is one of the most famous of Chinese poems.

After this, the next development which must be noticed is the invention by Su Wu, who lived at the end of the first century B.C., of the five-character poem. These poems were written in *Ku-shih*, literally "Old Poem." To make this intelligible, I must pause for a moment to explain a little more about the prosody of the Chinese. I will be as brief as I can. The Chinese have a strange quality in their language, namely tone. There are so few sounds possible to a monosyllabic tongue that speech would be extremely restricted if some way of augmenting these sounds had not been discovered. This augmentation was found in the introduction of tone. That is, a sound might rise or fall at the end, it might be dwelt upon or spoken staccato, etc., and each one of these inflections would change the meaning of the sound, so that there would soon come to be as many words to one sound as there were inflections, and each would be represented by a different character in writing. Now, as these inflections cannot be reproduced in transliteration, a poem so written is difficult to read, even for a Chinese. Tone is not identical in all the various tongues of China; for instance, the Mandarin dialect has four tones, the Nankingese five, the Cantonese nine, etc. Only two chief tones are used in poetry, the "level" and the "oblique," but the oblique tone is subdivided into three. In the early Chinese poetry, the tones were practically disregarded; later they were regulated with the utmost deliberation. When I say that Su Wu wrote in Old Style, I mean that he wrote poems in which the tones were not considered, but his adopting the five-word metre as a norm for poetry was an effort in the direction of a more marked pattern than had heretofore prevailed. At almost the same time, also, the seven-word line came into being. It is said to have been first composed by the Emperor Wu of Han, who reigned from 140 to 87 B.C. From this time on, five or seven words to the line became the normal measures for verse, although some poets continued occasionally to write in the Old Style with its wider range of metres.

A word should be said of the strange Chinese form called "fu." It partakes of the nature of both prose and poetry, being written in lines of irregular length, but possessing both rhythm and tone pattern, and also leaning heavily on parallelism, a device beloved of Chinese poets. It strongly resembles "polyphonic prose" in its structure. "Polyphonic prose," as you may not know, is a poetic form written in a block-like prose, but in which all the voices of poetry are brought into play. These voices are: metre, cadence, assonance, alliteration, rhyme, and return. The "fu" also makes use of all the voices of Chinese poetry, but in most cases differently from the way they are made use of in verse proper. An analysis of a "fu" by Ou-yang Hsiu, a poet of the Sung Dynasty, sent me by a Chinese professor, the other day, has twenty-four end rhymes, thirteen internal rhymes, nine internal rhymes between successive words, twenty-five alliterations, and four assonances. The greatest writer of "fu" was the one-eyed Emperor Yuan of the Liang Dynasty, in the middle of the sixth century A.D. There are six rules for a "fu": first, it must be full of colour; second, it must display high literary ability; third, all subjects are proper to it, but all must be treated in a poetic or literary manner; fourth, it must set forth aims, desires, and ambitions; fifth, it must be stirring and passionate; sixth, it must excite emotion. A number of the poems in Mrs. Ayscough's and my book are "fu"; but, of course, in my renditions of them, I have made no attempt to reproduce their form, any more than I have attempted to reproduce any of the other forms of Chinese poetry. I shall read you one or two of these "fu" presently, and you can judge how well they follow the six rules.

The next advance toward standardizing prosody came with the introduction of *lü-shih*, or "Poems according to Law," during the reign of [the Empress] Wu Hou, early in the T'ang period. In *lü-shih*, the tones are crystallized into an exact pattern, so that strictly regulated poems in Chinese consist of lines of either five or seven words, of rhymes used precisely as our rhymes are, and of a tone pattern which, unlike rhyme, is not confined to the end words of lines but runs throughout. As every word was either level or oblique in tone, the pattern was made to complement or juxtapose itself line by line throughout the entire poem. A *lü-shih* poem proper should be of eight lines, although this is often extended to sixteen. There is, however, a longer form, called *p'ai lu*, which may continue to any length. Tu Fu is said to have written *p'ai lu* of two hundred lines. A briefer form, always translated as "short-stop," cuts the eight-line poem in two. These are the only forms permitted to regular verse, or *lü-shih*. Irregular verse follows the writer's inclination within the natural limits of all Chinese prosody.

If we keep in mind the hard and fast laws which govern Chinese versification, and consider how hard it is for a Chinese to break through a convention once established, we shall see that it was only natural that the Chinese became more and more the slaves of *lü-shih;* and we shall at once realize the answer to the often-asked question: Why have the Chinese no epics? They have no epics simply because their prosodaic rules were so narrow and inelastic that they absolutely precluded the writing of long poems.

I shall skip over the many poets who flourished during the next six hundred years and pause for a moment at a remarkable figure, T'ao Ch'ien, also known by the name of T'ao Yüan-ming which he bore in early life. T'ao

267

Ch'ien, who lived from 365 to 427 A.D., is the ideal of the retired scholar. Confucianism laid great stress on the duty of public service, but China possessed another system of philosophy in which this duty was denied. Taoism, sprung from the teachings of Lao Tzŭ, inculcated the belief that "by bringing himself into harmony with nature" man could insure both his present and future happiness. I have not time to go into this now, ... but this much of Taoism must be understood by anyone who wishes to read Chinese poetry, for it is full of allusions to the Tao (Nature's Way). In the third and fourth centuries A.D. a great reaction against state service occurred. Many scholars felt that they would be happier living in poverty and retirement in the country than in submitting to the arduous round of official obligations. Of all these recluses, none is so famous as T'ao Ch'ien. Following the usual course for all men of education, T'ao Ch'ien became a magistrate. He held the post for eighty-three days. The truth is he was totally unfitted by temperament for any such position; his resignation took place on his objecting to receive a superior with the usual ceremonial, alleging that he "could not crook his back for five pecks of rice a day." Thereafter he retired into the country and occupied himself with poetry, and the cultivation of flowers, especially chrysanthemums. He was so fond of music that he declared he could hear the sounds of his table-lute by merely looking at it and imagining that he was playing on it, and he often carried a stringless instrument about with him over which he moved his hands. His philosophy is stated in a poem, "Substance, Shadow, and Spirit," which Mr. Waley has translated in his *One Hundred and Seventy Chinese Poems*, but it is too long to quote this afternoon. His love of nature, however, is shown in this little piece which I give in Mrs. Ayscough's and my translation: (Quote: "Once More Fields and Gardens," *Fir-Flower Tablets*, p. 132.)

The great period in the history of Chinese poetry is the T'ang, which lasted from A.D. 618 to 906. The initial efflorescence which leads to experimentation was over; the poets of the T'ang Dynasty were engaged in perfecting an instrument which they had inherited. A modern Chinese critic has said, "Poetry came into being with the 'Odes,' developed with the '*Li Sao*,' burst forth and reached perfection under the T'angs." As a matter of fact, this very perfection, like all perfections, had its drawbacks. Poets who are content to polish their predecessors' forms seldom have the vigour and originality of these same predecessors. During the T'ang period, this weakness of the original element is shown chiefly in the choice of subjects. Poetry had a tendency to become, as it has so often done with us, a habit of looking backwards. Battle-poems dealt with campaigns of the Han Dynasty, rather than with contemporary happenings. There were numbers of poems inspired by old ruins and vanished towns. Stock subjects were good enough to elaborate upon, and these were used unblushingly. Classical allusions were delighted in, and classical allusion, as Mr. Waley says in one of his prefaces, has always been the vice of Chinese poetry. But all these properties of the poetic trade were so exquisitely furbished up, and presented, as to be things of beauty just because of the way they were done. And it was not yet too late for the original urge of poetry to leap up again.

The two great poets of the period were no slaves to *lü-shih*, and, particularly, Li T'ai-po insisted on every kind of freedom he desired. True, this great poet was not above the plagiarism of the time: he even went a step farther, he plagiarized himself. But his bounding originality would not be held in bond. It was in poems in the Old Style that his genius chiefly lay. Even Tu Fu, master of *lü-shih* though he was, found himself so stirred by the horror of the civil war he witnessed, a war in which China lost thirty million men, that the rigid regulations of formal verse were inadequate for the expression of his feelings; instead he let himself go in a series of poems in the Old Style which are among his best work.

Before, however, examining with any minuteness these three poets I have chosen, I must paint you a little picture of the kind of China in which they lived and worked.

China, as everyone knows, is a very large country of widely differing geographical and climatic conditions. On the South and East is seaboard, on the North and West mountains and an arid desert. It is intersected by two great rivers, the Yellow River and the Yangtze Kiang. These rivers have innumerable tributaries and are, even to-day, the main arteries of China. Up and down these rivers go the boats, from the heavy freight-barges to the slight and swift "foot-boats." The Yellow River runs peacefully through sandy loess, but the Yangtze has ground its bed out of sheer mountains. The Yangtze gorges are so steep and high that the river at their base is confined to a very narrow space through which it "rushes with incredible speed," as an old poem has it. In winter, the water is low, but in summer it is a boiling flood; and, as it is full of sharp rocks, navigation in its time of spate, when the rocks are concealed, is extremely dangerous. This danger is referred to again and again in Chinese poetry. The ascent of the upper Yangtze takes several months to perform, as the boats have to be pulled up by men walking on the banks. In spite of the steepness of the banks, many towns and villages are built upon them, and rise tier on tier up the mountain sides. Up and down these rivers went the poets, the officials, all who had occasion to travel. A farewell to someone leaving in a boat is a very common subject of Chinese poetry. As it nears the sea, the river makes a great sweep round Nanking and flows through what was once the State of Wu, now Kiangsu. This and the neighboring states of Yüeh and Ch'u (the modern Chêkiang and parts of Hunan, Kweichow, and Kiangsi) is the country painted in such lovely, peaceful pictures by Li T'ai-po and his brother-poets. It is an extremely fertile country; willows line the rivers and canals, plum-trees blossom before the snow is off the ground and are succeeded by peaches, etc., while fields of rape or beans stretch out on every side. So much for the centre of China. But on the North and West are the great mountain ranges, so difficult to pass, that, in spite of the marvellous engineering feat known as a "terraced road," travel upon them is a matter of grave peril. The "Two-Edged Sword Mountains" was crossed by such a road, and it is the only pass over the range. I shall read you a poem about it presently.

Beyond the great wall, the Desert of Gobi was the camping ground of the Tatar tribes who were always threatening a descent upon China. It was to help guard the Northern boundary that the Great Wall was built. The Jade Pass, which we meet so often in the poems, led into this desert, and far off to the northwest were the tall peaks of a range known as the "Heaven-High Hills." Over this terrible waste went the soldiers, and many there were who never came back. Besides the regions of reality, the superstition of the ancient Chinese had built up another, the "Western Paradise," in which dwelt the countless beings who had attained immortality.

The topography of Chinese poetry may be said to fall into three main divisions: The beautiful and varied country of the Eighteen Provinces, the desolate region beyond the Jade Pass, and the glorious "Western Paradise."

History, so often referred to in poetry, we shall have to take for granted this afternoon, but a slight sketch of the social fabric of those old days I must give or the poems become quite meaningless. The emperor of China was a supreme ruler. He was called the "Son of Heaven" and was supposed to derive his power directly from God. He ruled through officials of varying ranks who were chosen in what we should consider a very odd way. Examinations were held every so often, and these examinations were purely literary. To pass, one must know the classics by heart, be able to write essays with ease, and compose poetry. No one could hold an official post who had not successfully passed his examinations. The first of these examinations was merely a portal to the second; after passing the second, a man was eligible for offices of minor grade; the third led to positions of greater importance; while the fourth really conferred a dignity rather than a degree, for those who succeeded in it became members of the Imperial Academy, which meant a salary for life and the highest official posts in the empire. As office-holders were not allowed to hold positions in their native provinces, these officials were constantly being sent to distant places. Innumerable are the poems of longing for home written by these unhappy exiles.

The emperor had a large seraglio; the most beautiful girls in the empire were reserved for him. They were established at Court, but very often they never obtained an interview with the emperor. Occasionally these superfluous Palace Women were dispersed and married to officials; this practice is frequently referred to in poetry. There was only one empress, whose title was *Hou* and who had her own palace; next in rank were the imperial concubines, or secondary wives, called *fei;* usually there were two of them and each had her own palace and household; after them again came the *p'in,* "imperial concubines of first rank." These concubines, unlike the empress and the *fei,* all lived in one large palace and, once they had attained the rank of *p'in,* could not be dispersed. The Palace Women I have spoken of were of a lower grade still, but at any time one of these might captivate the emperor's fancy and be raised to the position of *fei,* to say nothing of *p'in. Fei* who no longer enjoy the love of the emperor, and who are banished from his presence, are frequently alluded to in poetry; often they are the *dramatis personae* of the poet; not infrequently also they did really write poetry. One of these unhappy ladies was the Plum-Blossom Concubine of the Ming Huang emperor. She was superseded by the beautiful, but unscrupulous, Yang Kuei-fei. After her banishment, the emperor, who still had a lingering regard for her, secretly sent her some pearls which had been received as tribute. Plum-Blossom returned them with this heart-rending little poem: (Quote: "A Letter of Thanks," *Fir-Flower Tablets,* p. 143.)

270

I am sorry to keep saying I cannot go into this or that, but we certainly cannot, to-day, speak of the symbolism of plants and animals which plays so engrossing a part in the composition of Chinese poems, nor of the supernatural beings who imposed themselves on life at every turn. A short list of these will be found in Mrs. Ayscough's introduction to *Fir-Flower Tablets*, and various books on China will provide longer ones. For this background, it is necessary only to add that the Chinese year begins a month later than ours, and that the day is divided into two-hour periods which are not duplicated in name for the whole twenty-four. The Chinese of the T'ang period told time by means of water-clocks, or evenly burning sticks of measured lengths.

Undoubtedly Li T'ai-po is the one poet of China whose name is in the least familiar to English readers. Writers on Chinese literature are constantly announcing that Li T'ai-po is China's greatest poet, but the Chinese themselves place him second to Tu Fu. We may consider Li T'ai-po as the poet of the many; Tu Fu as the poet of the few. Li T'ai-po is a great romantic; his energy is overflowing; his ease and abundance unsurpassed. But Tu Fu has a depth and seriousness which make us understand the preference accorded to him by the critics of his own country. No one can fail to delight in Li T'ai-po; no one can fail to admire—and stand a little in awe of—Tu Fu. Enough has been translated of both these poets to enable us to form an opinion about them for ourselves.

Li T'ai-po was born in A.D. 701, of well-to-do parents, in the Village of the Green Lotus in Szechuan. The family name was Li, but his mother, having dreamed that she had conceived him under the influence of the planet Venus, called him T'ai-po, or "Great Whiteness," which was a popular name for the planet. He was a precocious youngster and by the time he was ten years old could recite the formidable classics by heart. But book-learning was only a part of his make-up, he was both athletic and pugnacious, a combination which got him into so sore a scrape (no less indeed than the killing of several people in a fray) that he was obliged to run away from home and take service with an official to hide his identity. Here again his talents got him into trouble, for he undertook on more than one occasion to finish his master's verses when that gentleman was at a loss for a line. These indiscretions at length drove him out of his place. After this, he spent five years among the beautiful Min Mountains, reading, writing, and discussing literature with a scholar whose companion he had become. At twenty-five, he left this man, who had stood to him in the relation of teacher, and started out to see the world, namely China. During his wanderings, he married and for a time settled down, but after some years—he himself says three—his thirst for travel set him off journeying again.

Perhaps it was odd that he never presented himself for any examinations; perhaps it was not. Great original minds often prefer to follow their own instincts in the matter of getting on in life. That without pursuing the usual routine he could not hope for an official career, evidently did not trouble him in the least. He discovered for himself a far more congenial life by forming a sort of society with five other young men. This society was called by its members "The Six Idlers of the Bamboo Brook." These precious young geniuses retired to the Ch'u Lai Mountain and spent their time in writing poems and

271

reciting them, in fashioning beautiful characters, in playing on the table-lute, and in drinking. Li T'ai-po himself was an inveterate drinker, and his drinking poems are among his best work, but this propensity cost him his agreeable post at Court, nevertheless. As to this post at Court, it fell upon him like a gift from Heaven. Going to Ch'ang An, the capital, with a Taoist priest, Wu Yün, this man, who was his ardent admirer, took occasion to mention his friend's remarkable talents to the emperor, which led to an order for Li T'ai-po to present himself before his imperial majesty. The Ming Huang emperor was so pleased with his guest's poems and conversation that he promptly made him a member of the Academy and attached him to his person as a sort of secretary. There never was a more brilliant Court than that of Ming Huang, and Li T'ai-po found the life he led there absolutely to his taste. His duties were supposed to be secretarial—the writing of edicts, etc.—but his real duty was to write what he pleased, and when he pleased, and recite these poems to the emperor whenever that august personage required. It mattered not at all that Li was quite apt to be drunk when sent for, because he could improvise or recite quite as well when he was drunk as when he was sober. He had great influence over the emperor, but another favourite whom he had displaced became, as time went on, his bitter enemy. This man, the Chief Eunuch, Kao Li-shih, at last found his tool for revenge in the emperor's beloved concubine, Yang Kuei-fei. Persuading this lady that one of Li T'ai-po's poems concealed a veiled insult to her, Kao ranged her on his side. Whatever influence the poet had over the emperor, Yang Kuei-fei's was naturally much greater, and, although Ming Huang appears to have resisted her innuendos, she did twice succeed in preventing the emperor from giving Li T'ai-po official rank. At last matters came to such a pass that there was nothing for Li T'ai-po to do but ask to retire from Court. This was granted, and again, gathering a company about him, he went to live in the mountains. This new association called itself "The Eight Immortals of the Wine-Cup."

But courts are not easily foregone, and Li T'ai-po never ceased to mourn for Ming Huang's. He wrote poem after poem bewailing that the "Sun" (the emperor) is hidden from him. The emperor is always the Sun to a Chinese.

Meanwhile the civil war of which I have spoken burst out. Inadvertently, and by no fault of his, Li T'ai-po became involved in a losing cause. Against his advice, Li Ling, Prince of Yung, whose service he had entered, decided to make a nice little hay-stack for himself amid the general disorder, no less a hay-stack, indeed, than the proclaiming of himself Emperor South of the Yangtze. He and his troops were captured, and along with them the unfortunate Prince's adviser, whose advice had not been followed. Condemned to death, but reprieved by the intervention of a friend, Li T'ai-po found himself banished for life to some outermost part of the empire. He started for Kuei-chow, a desolate place consolingly supposed to be peopled by man-eating demons, but before he arrived there a general amnesty was declared, and he was permitted to return and live with a disciple in the Lu Mountains near Kiukiang. Here, at the age of sixty-one, he died, leaving all his papers to this disciple, Lu Yang-ping. The tale of his drowning, repeated by Giles in his *Chinese Literature*, is pure fable, as an authoritative statement by Lu Yang-ping proves.

In describing Li T'ai-po's work, I cannot do better than to quote a passage from Mrs. Ayscough's introduction to our book: (Quote p. lxxvii in *Fir-Flower Tablets* to p. lxxix, and again p. lxxx.)

(Read poems: "The Perils of the Shu Road," p. 6; "The Northern Flight," p. 22; "The Lonely Wife," p. 10; "The Cast-Off Palace Woman," p. 19; "Poignant Grief during a Sunny Spring," p. 32; "A Statement of Resolutions," p. 41; "Parrot Island," p. 61; "At the Yellow Crane Tower," p. 93. Compare with "Gone," Giles, p. 66. Compare "Farewell by the River," Giles, p. 65, with "The Nanking Wine-Shop," *Fir-Flower Tablets*, p. 20. [Read:] "Song of the Marches," p. 1; "The Battle to the South of the City," p. 5.)

Tu Fu's life was very different from Li T'ai-po's. He was born at Tu Ling in Shensi, A.D. 713. His family was extremely poor, but his natural talent was so pronounced that when he was seven years old he had begun to write poetry, and by the time he was fifteen his poems and essays were the admiration of his small circle. At twenty-four, he went up to Ch'ang An for his first examination—and was plucked, because, forsooth, the opinions expressed in his examination papers were so radical that the conservative old persons in charge could not stomach them. The degree was withheld, and Tu Fu, an extremely erudite and talented man, was not even on the first rung of the ladder of advancement. There was nothing to be done, and Tu Fu took to wandering about the country, observing and writing, always very poor and with no hope of ever being anything else. On one of his journeys, he met Li T'ai-po, and the two poets became from that moment intimate friends.

When Tu Fu was thirty-six, an examination extraordinary took place at Ch'ang An, and Tu Fu went to the capital to compete in it. He waited for four years; no position was offered him. At last it occurred to him to present three of his "fu" to the emperor. The move was successful and he was given a position in the Chih Hsien library. This he held for four years, and it was followed by another appointment at Fêng-hsien; but a year later, on the breaking-out of the rebellion of which I have spoken, he went to live with a relative at the Village of White Waters. While he was there, the Ming Huang emperor abdicated in favour of his son, and Tu Fu conceived the idea of asking a new appointment of the new Su Tsung emperor. He set out on foot to travel to Fêng Chiang and prefer his request but was captured by brigands and kept prisoner for more than a year. When he did finally reach Fêng Chiang, his clothes were in rags, his bones sticking up from his flesh, his whole appearance pitiful in the extreme. His request for a position was granted and he received the post of censor, but this did not last long. Giving unasked advice to an emperor is an impolitic thing for an official to do. He was promptly relieved of his office and given a minor position in Shensi. With a foolish and pathetic bravado, he went to Shensi, only to refuse to carry on his office, after which magnificent harlequinade, he joined his family in Kansu.

Nothing could prove more succinctly than the lives of Li T'ai-po and Tu Fu that geniuses are, as a rule, sublimely unfitted for the routine affairs of life. The better the poet, the less the official. Evidently the literary examinations did sift the intelligent from the unintelligent, and probably no better method for doing this has ever been devised in a period when the things to be learnt

273

are few. But, although in China every mayor of a town, every governor of a province, could write routine poetry, it is extremely doubtful whether many of them were really poets other than by training. At any rate, these two poets are a living example to dot the question.

We need not follow Tu Fu's adventures in officialdom much farther. He held two other posts. One he endured for a year and a half, the other for six months, but what he really longed for was quiet, study, and freedom to wander at will. Sorrow pursued him, several of his children died in a famine which swept the countryside; his poverty was always extreme. On one of his journeys, he was caught in a flood from which he took refuge in a ruined temple; here he nearly starved before help could reach him, and he survived his rescue less than an hour. His life had been one long strain of disappointment and suffering, and he was only fifty-five when he died.

Chinese writers are never done with comparing the styles of Li T'ai-po and Tu Fu. Yüan Chên, a poet of the T'ang period, a great friend of Po Chü-i's, has written: "The poems of Li T'ai-po are like Spring flowers; those of Tu Fu are like the pine-trees, they are eternal and fear neither snow nor cold." Shên Ming-chên says: "Li Po is like Spring grass, like Autumn waves, not a person but must love him. Tu Fu is like a great hill, a high peak, a long river, the broad sea, like fine grass and bright-coloured flowers, like a pine or an ancient fir, like morning wind and gentle waves, like heavy hoar-frost, like burning heat—not a quality is missing." But, to my mind, the finest criticism is that of Tao Kai-yu: "Tu Fu's poems are like pictures, like the branches of trees reflected in water—the branches of still trees. Like a large group of houses seen through clouds of mist, they appear and disappear."

(Quote from *Fir-Flower Tablets:* "The Thatched House," p. 104; "The Excursion," p. 107; The "Recruiting Officers," p. 109; "Crossing the Frontier, II," p. 112; "Thinking of Li Po," p. 114; "Moon Night," p. 118.)

Po Chü-i was not born until both his great predecessors were dead. Li T'ai-po died in 762, Tu Fu in 768. Po Chü-i was born in 772, at T'ai-yüan in Shansi. He passed his examinations in 800, and a year later settled in Ch'ang An. Doubtless he was accustomed to the thought of officialdom, as his father had been a second-class assistant department magistrate. Po Chü-i was a shy and rather stiff young man, apparently, and he found it hard to make friends in the bustling life of the capital. Like all Chinese men of the period, friendship was the air he breathed. One friend he did make, however, the poet Yüan Chên. Five years later he sent him this poem: (Quote Waley, I, 161.)

Other friends came in time, but death and the constant official departures broke up his circle. On Yüan Chên's banishment for a political misdemeanor, Po Chü-i wrote a pathetic poem to him: (Quote Waley, II, 163.) Po Chü-i himself incurred official dislike for two long memorials "On Stopping the War." His enemies fell upon these with avidity, and later when, on the occasion of the prime minister being murdered, he addressed a memorial to the throne on the necessity of allaying the prevailing discontent, it was made an occasion for a serious charge. With this was coupled another, ludicrous enough it seems to us. His mother had been drowned by falling into a well as she was leaning over it to look at some flowers. Po Chü-i had written two poems, one was called "In Praise of Flowers," the other bore the title "The

New Well." That he could write poems on such subjects was considered an act of filial impiety. As nothing, short of murder and hardly that, is worse in the eyes of a Chinese, Po Chü-i was banished to Hsün-yang with the rank of subprefect. Three years later, he was appointed governor of Chung-chow, a remote place in Szechuan.

But Chung-chow was noted for its beautiful flowers and exotic trees, and these were a great source of happiness to the exiled governor; besides, on the way thither, he had met Yüan Chên, and the two had spent a few days together exploring the rock caverns near I-ch'ang.

In 819, Po Chü-i was recalled to the capital as a second-class assistant secretary. But two years later a new emperor ascended the throne, and his mismanagement of affairs caused a fresh outbreak in the northwest. Again Po Chü-i felt called upon to write memorials, and again he was banished from the capital, this time to become governor of the important town of Hangchow. As his beloved Yüan Chên held a judicial post at Ningpo, the two friends could sometimes meet, which mitigated the severity of his exile. His governorship expiring in 824, he went to live at the village of Li-tao-li, near Loyang. Here he surrounded himself with a strange assemblage of birds and ladies, taking into his house two singing girls, and bringing two cranes and a famous "Indian Rock" from Hangchow. Two more governorships, those of Soochow and the province of Honan, together with various posts at the capital, fell to his lot.

Yüan Chên died in 831, and in 832 Po Chü-i rebuilt a part of the Hsiang-shan Monastery at Lung-mên, a few miles south of Loyang. Here he lived for the rest of his life, calling himself the "Hermit of Hsiang-shan." In 839 he had a paralytic stroke, but survived for seven years longer, dying in 846 at the age of seventy-four. He left strict orders that his funeral should be conducted with the utmost simplicity, and that his remains should be buried beside those of a favourite monk in the Hsiang-shan Monastery.

Po Chü-i was curiously didactic in his conviction that poetry should always point a moral. He cared more for the subject of a poem than for its artistry, but he was far too much of a poet to follow his own rules. Poems of moral intent, he certainly did write; but, to his disgust, people greatly preferred his lyrics, pieces in which the poet has run away with the moralist. It is an odd fact that his moral poems, "Satires," he calls them, are in Old Style, while his lighter poems are in strict *lü-shih* form. The popularity of his work during his lifetime was enormous. His poems were inscribed on the walls of schools, temples, even in ship's cabins; in short, everywhere. They were repeated by everyone, from the emperor and his concubines to grooms and porters. A dancing-girl is said to have put up the price of her favours because she could repeat by heart his poem "The Everlasting Wrong."

Po Chü-i is, in many ways, the most modern poet of medieval times. A number of his poems remind us sharply of much of the work that is being written to-day. He eschewed allusions and wrote simply of everyday events. This simplicity is probably one of the reasons for his immense contemporary popularity. His poetry knows no such rushing flights as Li T'ai-po's; it has no such depth or tenderness as Tu Fu's. There is nothing reflective about him; he ridiculed Taoism, and his poems have neither the lovely calm, nor the deep feeling for nature, of the followers of that sect. He seems the apotheosis of the ordinary man of his time. His poems are what they seem to be; we are not conscious of unplumbed distances below his pleasant surfaces. But for pure, straightforward, natural humanity, he has rarely been equalled. He tangles his pictures of the life he saw about him with no disconcerting digressions of the imagination; he is the recorder, pure and simple, and, for us, most valuable on that account. These poems are from Mr. Waley's translations in his two books of Chinese poetry: (Quote: "An Early Levée," Waley, I, 171. Compare with "An Imperial Audience," *Fir-Flower Tablets*, p. 122. [Quote:] "The Dragon of the Black Pool," Waley, I, 180; "The Old Harp," Waley, I, 185; "The Flower Market," Waley, I, 187; "Remembering Golden Bells," Waley, I, 178; "Hearing the Early Oriole," *Fir-Flower Tablets*, p. 119.)

I think we need follow the poetry of China no farther. Under the dynasties which succeeded the T'ang, it became ever more imitative and allusive, more inelastic and conventional. Good poems were written, of course, but on the whole Chinese poetry reached its climax and crisis with the T'ang. If ever a poetry was killed by its rules, Chinese poetry was. The result has been what many modern Chinese admit, namely, that they care more for the form and sound of a poem than they do for its substance. As one educated Chinese said to me, "You see, we learnt to repeat the older poems by heart before we knew what they meant. It was the sound which made an impression." But a new movement has sprung up in China within the last few years. Its aim is to produce a poetry written in the vernacular, and not in the literary and poetic speech in which it has been written for centuries. These poems of the T'ang period are written in a language far more unlike modern Chinese than Chaucer's English is unlike our English. Now that the old system of examinations has been abolished, it stands to reason that the great works of the past will be less and less read. China, who stood still for centuries, is breaking with her traditions and taking a great leap toward the ideals of the new world. To us, she appears to be losing more than she is gaining; to herself, she seems awaking from a long sleep. But her value to us lies in her literary and artistic past, and what she is willing to discard so blithely we shall do well to gather up and treasure.

Appendix V

LETTER FROM J. MIDDLETON MURRY

The Old Coastguard Station, Abbotsbury, Dorset, 5th April, 1926

Dear Mrs. Ayscough,

I am very sorry indeed that I cannot be present at your meeting. Had I been in London I should have counted it my bounden duty to add my tribute to the magnificent work upon Keats done by your dear friend, Miss Amy Lowell—a duty the more obligatory because I feel that it has received but a grudging acknowledgment from English criticism.

The reason of this grudging acknowledgment, I am afraid, is the reason only too often lurking behind halfhearted praise and timid criticism—ignorance. No one who has not made a patient study of Keats' life and work can possibly know what Miss Lowell has done in her *magnum opus*. (Neither can they know what she has not done: but that matters less, for what she has done immensely outweighs what she did not do.) I, who hold a very different view of Keats from Miss Lowell's, should like to put on record my conviction that she has written the final biography of Keats. Subsequent generations will, I think, alter and amend her critical views; but the substance of all future attempts to recreate Keats in his habit as he lived will be the work of Miss Amy Lowell.

I had not the honour of knowing Miss Lowell; but I occasionally corresponded with her. And I think I am right in saying that, of all her literary work, her labours on Keats came to be nearest her heart—and that an assured and undying remembrance of these would compensate her for any diffidence posterity may feel towards her more personal work. Such, at least, was the sentiment she expressed to me in a letter written scarcely a month before her sudden death. She has had her chief desire, for I have no doubt at all that the gratitude of posterity is secure to her for a work in which imagination, sympathy, passion, and self-effacement are so remarkably combined as in her Life of John Keats.

Believe me, my dear Mrs. Ayscough,

Yours very sincerely,

[*Signed*] J. Middleton Murry

Appendix VI

NOTES FOR MEMORIAL ADDRESS, APRIL 15, 1925 AT KEATS MEMORIAL HOUSE

Florence Ayscough

Mr. Chairman, Ladies and Gentlemen:

It is a great pleasure and privilege to speak at the Keats Memorial House about my dear friend Amy Lowell, who was so deeply interested in its preservation.

This afternoon I do not mean to refer specifically to her work; that exists—in nine volumes of poetry and three of prose for all to read who are interested in literature. I shall not attempt to analyze the movement in America of which she was an acknowledged leader, nor shall I speak of her gifts as a lecturer; for one thing I have never happened to be in America when she spoke in public and swayed great audiences by the power of her diction—but I have heard, and read, a great deal about these occasions and regret very much that English audiences have been denied the opportunity of hearing her. No, this afternoon I wish to speak of her personality and surroundings—and a little of our collaboration in the rendering of Chinese poems, as I do not think the remarkable piece of work she did in connection with the Far East is fully realized.

And firstly as to her surroundings. "Sevenels," the house where she was born and where she died, stands in Brookline, a little township on the outskirts of Boston. . . . .

Soon after Miss Lowell's death, I went to "Sevenels" and took a number of photographs, which, combined with a few other pictures already existing, form the series of slides which I will now show. In describing the place, I shall quote at times from a charming article which Miss Lowell wrote some years ago. . . . .[1]

She loved the garden dearly and describes its arrangement in a charming little poem, "Planning the Garden":

> "Winged sweet-peas shall flutter next to pansies
> All down the sunny centre—
> Foxglove spears,
> Thrust back against the swaying lilac leaves,
> Will bloom and fade before the China asters
> Smear their crude colours over Autumn hazes."

[1] See Appendix I for quotations here omitted from the address.

She loved her animals too: horses the finest and swiftest to be found, and old English sheep dogs. For a number of years she had a great many dogs, but the kennels had to be given up during the war on account of the rationing, and she never started them again. The horses too, were given up then, and her affections, as far as animals were concerned, centered on Winky—Winky, of whom she wrote:

> "In the night, I hear you crying,
> But if I try to find you
> There are only the shadows of rhododendron leaves
> Brushing the ground.
> When you come in out of the rain,
> All wet and with your tail full of burrs,
> You fawn upon me in coils and subtleties;
> But once you are dry
> You leave me with a gesture of inconceivable
>   impudence,
> Conveyed by the vanishing quirk of your tail
> As you slide through the open door."

To return to her own account of the place: . . . .

"But, after all, a library is the heart of a house. Mine is walled with English oak. It contains—books; it also contains flowers, even all Winter long from my very little greenhouse. . . . ."

If the heart of the house be its library, then the heart of that library is its fireplace, and nowhere did Amy Lowell show her real self more fully than when she walked up and down before the blazing logs on that wide hearth. The drying of the long thin sticks of wood destined for use in the house was almost a cult, and when, after a process which took three or four years to perfect, they reached the fireplace, the glittering blaze with its handsful of sparks was wonderful to behold. It always seemed to me to affect her—and her talk sparkled as the flames sparkled. She was witty, intensely amusing, enthusiastic and impetuous—but there was nothing superficial about what she said, because her knowledge was deeply rooted, and she never, *never* made any pretense. In fact, if I were asked to single out the pre-eminent characteristic in her very complex make-up, I should say without one moment's hesitation, "complete, whole-hearted sincerity"; and to any lack of this quality in other people she was absolutely intolerant. Pose, affectation, pretense—these met with but short shrift at her hands.

I would like to quote a few lines from Professor John Livingston Lowes' fine critique of Miss Lowell's last book *What's O'Clock* in the *Saturday Review of Literature:*

"She has been for years enlarging our boundaries through her own keen, clear perceptions of beauty that most of us have missed, and through her fearlessness in saying precisely what she saw. No poet writing to-day, I think, save Thomas Hardy, saw and heard with more acute perception, or saw and heard and felt so many shades and tones and shapes of things—brilliant and subtle and fugitive and firm. And joined with this quick sensitiveness to physical impressions was an intellectual honesty as sensitive—a passion for truth

279

which never knowingly falsified the report of what was seen. And that alert and vivid sense of beauty, restless with a poet's craving for expression, yet in expression lucidly exact, has schooled us, skeptical and reluctant scholars, to a quickened vision of strange loveliness in familiar things. . . . . And more than any recent poet Amy Lowell sought and missed and won triumphantly experience and expression of those flashes of sudden beauty which pass before most of us can say: 'Lo! there!'—which pass before many of us even know they are."

The passion of her life was, of course, literature, and long before she herself had begun to publish she collected books, and especially "association books," also manuscripts. Many firsts of Robert Browning; the presentation copy to Frederick Locker of *Pauline* with the correction made in London for the edition of 1868. A wealth of Lord Nelson and Lady Hamilton material—the inspiration for "Sea Blue and Blood Red" in the volume called *Can Grande's Castle*—and so on and so forth. The Keats material is *very* fine.

And now I come to her work in connection with the Far East.[1]

In late November some ten years ago I arrived from China and went to stay at "Sevenels." I had with me some examples of "written pictures"—that is, a Chinese poem, written in beautiful characters and mounted ready to hang on the wall. . . . .

(Talk about Chinese translation. Read extracts from some of her letters. Our life while we were arranging *Fir-Flower Tablets* for publication. Read passage from her letter on yellow paper. Show upstairs rooms. Speak of her preparations for coming to England—of her sudden illness and death.)

I had not seen her since the December preceding—five months before. She was then just finishing the manuscript of her book on Keats and was very tired indeed.

[1] See above, pp. 20–32, "Amy Lowell and the Far East."

Appendix VII

CH'IN CHIA AND HIS WIFE HSÜ SHU

Under the Han Dynasty (at about the time of Christ), there lived a very learned man named Ch'in Chia, who for a long time did not obtain high office. He finally was ordered to the Capital, in Shensi, as a minor official. His very beautiful wife, Hsü Shu, suffered from an illness of long-standing. Unable to go with him, she lived at her own family home in western Kansu. Wearying without her, Ch'in Chia sent a travelling cart and retinue to bring her to him. She was too ill to go—the cart returned empty. He wrote the poem No. I. She replied with No. II. At that time she and the famous Pan Chieh-yu were the only two women who could write five-character "lu" (poems).

After Ch'in Chia's death, which occurred while she was still young and very lovely, she was beset with offers of marriage. Finally, that her suitors might no longer trouble her, she destroyed her beauty by scratching her face so badly that she was permanently disfigured!

CH'IN CHIA TO HSÜ SHU. NO. I

1. Man's life is like the early, the morning dew. (At the moment when the moon disappears, and the sun rises.)
2. While he lives in this world many troubles come;
3. Sorrows, difficulties recur often, and come quickly;
4. Happy meetings, already experienced, recur seldom and come slowly. (The idea of the two lines is that sorrows, etc., pounce upon one quickly, whereas happiness seems as if it would never come.)
5. I think of you—the time has arrived when I must go away on the Emperor's business.
6. From you each day moves me further and further.
7. I sent a chariot to receive you—to bring you to me.
8. Empty it went—empty it has returned whence it started.
9. In my thoughtful hours my love makes me sorrowful and sick at heart.
10. Looking down at my food, I cannot eat;
11. I sit alone within my empty house.
12. Who is able to encourage me, to rouse me to action?
13. Through the endless night, I cannot sleep;
14. Lying on my pillow alone, I turn over and over;
15. Sorrow which has come upon me surrounds me as an unbroken circle;
16. It cannot be rolled up and put away as is my sleeping mat.

1. Body of your unworthy servant, Hsi-i-i-i, is valueless.
2. Old illness envelops me, Hsi-i-i-i-i—so I have returned to my old home.
3. Sunk down like a stone, I am restrained, Hsi-i-i, at the door of my home.
4. Time passes, Hsi-i-i-i-i, there is no alteration (no improvement in her illness);
5. Desolate, useless, Hsi-i-i-i-i, I cannot wait upon my Lord;
6. My love, my devotion, Hsi-i-i-i, I am separated, far from him.
7. My Lord now, Hsi-i-i-i, must attend to his Imperial duties;
8. Far off he goes, Hsi-i-i-i, to the great Capital—
9. Far, far, Hsi-i-i-i, he is separated from me.
10. There is no means, Hsi-i-i, of discussing that which is treasured in our hearts;
11. I feel as though I must stand on tip-toe and strain my eyes gazing at the distance, Hsi-i-i-i; I stamp my feet with grief—
12. I stand still, waiting, Hsi-i-i-i-i; I walk backwards and forwards irresolute,
13. Thinking of my Lord, Hsi-i-i-i, my emotions are like knotted silk cords;
14. In dreams I reflect, Hsi-i-i-i, on the brightness of your face (i.e., the light on your face).
15. My Lord must go forth, Hsi-i-i-i, he must proceed far upon his journey
16. From me, Hsi-i-i-i, daily separated farther.
17. How I *hate* that I am unable, Hsi-i-i, to have wings and fly—
18. To fly high, Hsi-i-i-i, and follow you that we may be together.
19. Long moans, Hsi-i-i-i, long-continued are my sighs,
20. Tears fall, Hsi-i-i-i, and drench my clothes.

ANALYSIS I

1. Jen	Man	An upright being who, unlike animals, has rites	
	Sheng	Life	Plants coming more and more out of the earth
	Pi	Like, compared	Words; a figure, meaning words of authority
	Chao	Early morning	2 old forms: (1) sunrise, a sea mist seen from a boat; (2) moment sun rises and moon sets
	Lu	Dew	
2. Chu	Live		
	Shih	This world	
	To	Many	
	T'un	Hard, laborious	Germination underground, a plant struggling to pierce the soil
	Chien	Trouble, difficulty	

282

3. Yu	Sorrow	
Chien	Distress	
Chang	Often	
Tsao	Early	The sun at the height of a helmeted man
Chih	Arrive	A bird dropping to earth, wings folded; it has *arrived*
4. Huan	Happy	
Hui	Meeting	Words one says at the door in meeting, a salute
Ch'ang	Formerly	
Jo	If	
Wan	Late, slowly	
5. Nien	To think, reflect	Make the thoughts actually present at the moment to the heart; heart; now
Tang	Ought	
Feng	Imperial duties	
Shih	Time	Time defined as the period when vegetation wakes under sun's influence
Ju	Serve	
6. Chu	Go from, leave	
Erh	You	
Jih	Daily	The sun
Yao	Move	
Yuan	Far	
7. Chien	Send, appoint to a post	
Che	Carriage, cart	
Ying	Receive, go out to welcome	
Tzu	(No need to translate)	
Huan	Return	
8. Kung	Empty	An excavation in a rock, or in the earth, made by labour
Wang	To go	
Fu	Return to where you have been before	
Kung	Empty	
Fan	Come back	
9. Hsing	Time one is awake	
Shih	Time	Vegetation springing under influence of sun
Ching	Love	Heart; the colour of Nature
Chi	Alas	Heart; the figure for wife
Tsang	Sorrows	Heart; things stored therein

283

10. Ling	Look down on	A prostrate official, listening to orders of a superior
Shih	Food	Cooked grain; figure for union—that is, grains united, collected
Pu	Not	
Neng	Able	
Fan	Eat	Figure for "food" (see above) and to turn over
11. Tu	Alone	
Tso	Sit	Two men sitting on the ground
Kung	Empty	Line 8, char. 1
Fang	House	A doorway; a square (which is the phonetic)
Chung	Centre	
12. Shui	Who	
Yu	Associate	
Hsiang	Together, mutually	
Ch'uan	Encourage, soothe	Strength; figure for happiness
Mien	Make an effort	Strength; figure for a man making an effort
13. Chang	Long	
Yeh	Night	
Pu	Not	
Neng	Able	
Mien	Sleep	
14. Fu	Lying on	
Chen	Pillow	
Tu	Alone	
Chan	Unroll }	These two characters mean restlessly turn over and over
Chuan	Turn over }	
15. Yu	Sorrow, grief	Sorrows in the head and heart which last a long time
Lai	Come	
Ju	Like	
Hsun	Follow, proceed in order	A step; a round shield
Huan	Bracelet, circlet	Jade; and the phonetic. The two characters *Hsun* and *Huan* mean a complete, never-ending circle
16. Fei	Not	
Hsi	Sleeping-mat	
Pu	Not	
Ko	Can	
Ch'uan	Roll up	Two hands working over things

REPLY TO CH'IN CHIA BY HSÜ SHU

	Chi	Sent (by)	
	Hsü	Gentle, dignified	} The wife's name
	Shu	Clear, Virtuous	
	T'a	Reply (to)	
	Ch'in	A kind of rice	Name of a State, also a surname
	Chia	Approve, admire, excellent, good	
1.	Chieh	Unworthy, humble, concubine	A term often used by wives
	Shen	Body	
	Hsi-i-i-i-i		Alas! Ah!, or any sound you like simply to prolong cadence
	Pu	Not	Pu Ling means worthless or useless—a polite form of speech
	Ling	Command	
2.	Ying	Surround	A woman; a necklace of precious cowrie shells
	Tsi	Illness, which has lasted a long time	Illness; an arrow
	Hsi-i-i-i		
	Lai	Comes	
	Kuei	Returns	
3.	Chen	Sink like a stone	
	Chih	Restrained, impeded	
	Hsi-i-i		
	Chia	Home	A roof; a pig!!!
	Mên	Door, gate	
4.	Li	Pass through, calculate	
	Shih	Time	Vegetation springing under influence of the sun
	Hsi-i-i		
	Pu	Not	
	Cha	Alter	
5.	Kuang	Desolate, dreary	The sun shining on a vast place with yellow clay
	Fei	Useless, abandoned	
	Hsi-i-i-i-i-i		
	Shih	Wait upon, serve	
	Ching	See a superior	
6.	Hsing	Love, passion, heart	The colour of nature
	Ching	Reverence	
	Hsi-i-i-i		
	Yu	Have	
	Wei	Separated, disobey	

7. Chun	My Lord		
Chin	Now		
Hsi-i-i-i-i			
Feng	Salute, serve	The two hands receiving with respect the seal of office	
Ming	Decree, order	An order; a mouth. *Feng* and *Ming* together mean Imperial duties, or orders	
8. Yuan	Far		
Ti	Escort, change, substitute		
Hsi-i-i-i-i			
Ching	Capital City	Idea of elevation, the Capital, pivot of Empire	
Shih	Capital City, also means army, host	A commander of the first legion which is the one posted at the Capital. She means that his Imperial duties will take him far off to the Capital, but you might make it more vivid by referring to the army. *Shih*, analysed, is the commander of the first legion	
9. Yo	Distant, far-reaching	Heart; a man crossing a river and sounding the depth with a stick	
Yo	Distant, far-reaching		
Hsi-i-i			
Li	Separate		
Pieh	Divide	A knife cutting things apart	
10. Wu	Without		
Yin	Means of		
Hsi-i-i-i			
Hsu	Speak		
Huai	Heart's affairs	Heart; something treasured between the clothes and the breast	
11. Chan	Look at, regard	Eyes; a man standing on a high cliff looking	
Wang	Gaze		
Hsi-i-i-i			
Yung	Stamp feet with grief	A foot; the figure for "brave"	
Yu	Jump	A foot; a bird; wings	
12. Chu	Stand still		
Li	Stand erect		
Hsi-i-i-i			
P'ei }	Walking backwards	A step; figure for back to back	
Huai }	and forwards, irresolute	A step; figure for to revolve	

13. Ssu	Think of	Head; heart. When one thinks, vital spirit goes from heart to head
Chun	My Lord	
Hsi-i-i		
Kan	Emotions	Heart; to wound
Chieh	Tie in a knot	
14. Meng	Dreams	Eyes looking in different directions, or things seen confusedly at night
Hsiang	Reflect, think	
Hsi-i-i-i		
Jung	Appearance	
Hui	Bright	The sun; corps of soldiers with their chariot
15. Chun	My Lord	
Fa	Goes	
Hsi-i-i-i		
Ying	Draw out	
Mai	Proceed upon a journey	
16. Chu	From, go from	
Wo	Me	
Hsi-i-i-i		
Jih	Daily	
Kuai	Separate	A division between the horns of an ox. A different word to any used so far for divide
17. Hen	Hate	
Wu	Without, not	
Hsi-i-i-i		
Yu	Feathers	
I	Wings	
18. Kao	High, an eminence	
Fei	Fly	
Hsi-i-i-i		
Hsiang	Together	
Chui	Follow	A legion on the march
19. Chang	Long	
Yin	Moans	
Hsi-i-i-i		
Yung	Endless, eternal	
T'an	Sighs	

287

20.	Lei	Tears
	Hsia	Down
	Hsi-i-i-i	
	Chan	Wet, moisten
	I	Clothing, garments

I did not know when I translated it that Waley [*op. cit.*, pp. 53–54] had done Ch'in Chia's Wife's Reply—in fact only came across it yesterday. I am sorry, in a way, that we have done the same thing. . . . . He chose a different poem of Chin Chia's to the one the teacher, Mr. Nung, gave me, which he chose because he considered it the best, and deepest. As we have not the text of the one that Waley has done, I cannot say anything about that, except that the connotation at the beginning is to me not right. I mean, the picture it brings before one's eyes it not at all an old Chinese picture.

Waley says, p. 53: "Solemn, Solemn, the coachman gets ready to go": Now, since Chin Ch'ia was an official of low rank he would probably have travelled in an ox cart. In any case, the driver does not sit up on a box, as the word "coachman" suggests, but walks beside the conveyance with the reins in his hand. The pace is never fast unless the travellers are hurrying to make a resting place, before dark—or something like that—since, in a springless cart, it nearly *kills* one to go rapidly. When they do go out of a rather fast walk, the driver hops up and sits sideways on the shaft, as if he were riding on a side saddle. I use the present tense as the custom is the same to-day. I remember that when we were going to Confucius' tomb we had to hurry because of the dark, and I wish you could have seen the condition in which we arrived at our sleeping place. My hair was streaming down my back—and I anxiously felt in my mouth to see if my teeth were all there! So I think "coachman" conveys a wrong idea.

"Ch'in Chia's Wife's Reply" reads, in part, as follows:

1. "My poor body is alas unworthy."
   (Chieh, meaning unworthy, is the word we have used so often—which a wife uses in speaking of herself. It means, "*My* body is of no use." I have given you "The body of your unworthy servant is valueless." Waley *could* get "unworthy" out of "pu ling"—but, then, *where* does he get his "poor"?)

2. "I was ill when first you brought me home."
   (This is not the meaning. The old illness, which she had suffered from before, still clung to her, so she "lai kuei." That "kuei" is used of a woman's going to her old home. The *Tzu Yuan* is *most definite* about it. Strangely enough, Waley says she was ("staying with her parents" in his note to the first poem, "Ch'in Chia.")

3. "Limp and weary in the house"
   (Don't see how Waley gets that; Chen, Giles 649; I have given you "sink like a stone," one of Giles's translations. It seems to me the most expressive. It means severe in regard to illness.)

4. "Time passed and I got no better."

288

5. "We could hardly ever see each other:"
   (Where that comes from, unless it is out of his head, I don't know.)

6. "I could not serve you as I ought."
   (The "serving" is there, all right, but he leaves out her feeling of desolation and uselessness, the "Kuang, fei." I just see where he gets, I *think*, line 5, but he makes a very "free" translation; it is line 6, in my version, that he gives thus.)

The rest of it is not so far off—though I can't make out where he gets his line 12: "Interminably gazing at the road that had taken you." The worst "howler" is the one in regard to the "home," and, also, his misreading of the first line. The "kuei" would certainly convey to a Chinese reader the fact that she had gone to her "old home."

⟦ PRINTED IN U·S·A ⟧